DAILY WISDOM FOR
WHY DOES HE DO THAT?

DAILY WISDOM FOR
WHY DOES HE DO THAT?

Encouragement for Women Involved
with Angry and Controlling Men

LUNDY BANCROFT

BERKLEY BOOKS, NEW YORK

THE BERKLEY PUBLISHING GROUP
Published by the Penguin Group
Penguin Group (USA) LLC
375 Hudson Street, New York, New York 10014

USA • Canada • UK • Ireland • Australia • New Zealand • India • South Africa • China

penguin.com

A Penguin Random House Company

This book is an original publication of The Berkley Publishing Group.

DAILY WISDOM FOR WHY DOES HE DO THAT?

Berkley trade paperback ISBN: 978-0-425-26510-9

An application to register this book for cataloging has been submitted to the Library of Congress.

PUBLISHING HISTORY
Berkley trade paperback edition / April 2015

PRINTED IN THE UNITED STATES OF AMERICA

10 9 8 7 6 5 4 3 2 1

Interior text design by Kristin del Rosario.

INTRODUCTION

Living with an angry, controlling, or unfaithful partner is like being wrapped up in a tangle of about a dozen different strands of rope. Each time that you feel like you've finally worked out the knots, you discover that you've actually only pulled off one piece and plenty of rope remains. Naturally, it's easy to feel overwhelmed and as though you're never going to be able to get it all straight.

And, sometimes, in the process of untangling certain strands, you find that you are actually creating new knots. That's how dealing with a badly tangled rope goes; it often gets worse before it gets better. But if you keep at it, you will gradually sort it all out.

The pages ahead will help you to achieve clarity, strength, faith in yourself, and deeper connections to people other than your partner (including your children). If you approach the readings one day at a time, allowing the principles to sink in, you will find yourself in a different and much-improved life by the time you get to the end of this book. Where this growth will take you, and what that will mean for your current relationship, is a mystery that will unfold; there's no need to know the answer now.

A controlling partner causes profound tension and stress. For this reason, I have created a book of short daily readings, each of which you can digest in about ten minutes. This format makes it unnecessary for you to figure out how to carve out a long period of time to sit and read, which can be especially hard to do if you have young kids. If your partner's behavior makes it hard for you to focus or concentrate, you will be relieved to find that you'll just be working on taking in *one* concept at a time, allowing it to circulate around inside of you for twenty-four hours or so. You can do this, no matter how great the challenges you face right now.

Use this book in the way that works best for you. Some people will want to read the pieces in order, one per day. The advantage of proceeding this way is that the readings build on each other, progressing from concepts that are easier to take in to ones that can take a little more work to integrate. But you may find that it works better for you to skim around looking for parts that speak directly to the upsetting or confusing dynamics that you are currently struggling with. Or you may even want to let your spirit guide you, choosing pages at random as if you were holding the *I Ching* (the Chinese book of wisdom), and see if unseen forces lead you to the insights that will most hit the day's nail on the head.

I believe that the way to best ensure that you will gain from the readings is to write down your thoughts and feelings as you absorb them. Journal writing has proven to be one of the single most powerful paths to healing and empowerment, especially for people who have been targets of mistreatment. I ask you at various points in the pages ahead to try specific writing exercises, but I hope that you write your thoughts at many other times as well.

The writings in this book address the key question: *How valuable are you?* This question is aimed at women whose partners, over and over again, make them feel like they aren't worth much. Men who mistreat women in this manner employ a range of styles: the man may be distant, cold, and silent; another type will give lots of attention to other women and flirt with them, or outright cheat on his partner; a third type will verbally attack his partner and periodically shove or hit her. Ultimately, there is a common thread: the men in all of these examples are devaluing the women they are with, failing to see their humanity and their worth. You may be involved with a man who behaves in one of the aforementioned ways, and the truth is:

You deserve to be seen and treasured for who you are.

In the great majority of destructive relationships that women experience, the man's behavior is inconsistent. For days, weeks, or perhaps even months at a time, your partner may treat you with kindness and affection, and during these periods he may be sexy and romantic. Each time this happens you hope and feel that he has finally turned a corner and that this time he is finally going to settle into being a loving partner. But the wheel just keeps turning. Nothing you can come up with seems to solve his behavioral problems or convince him that you are worth treating with respect and commitment; after a while, he's back to his hurtful behaviors. Unfortunately, this pattern can draw you into an exhausting loop.

If what I am describing feels familiar to you, this book will speak to your situation, whether or not you think of your partner as angry or controlling. The reality is that when a man devalues his partner, his behavior always ends up having the effect of controlling her, even if control isn't his main goal. You can mentally substitute the word "devaluing" whenever I write "controlling" or "abusive," and most of what you find in these pages will still make perfect sense.

The readings in this book follow seven themes, one for each day of the week:

CLARITY These readings help you to recognize and understand your partner's unhealthy behaviors, and help keep him from confusing you or blaming you for his actions.

SURVIVING TO THRIVE These readings focus on helping you to manage the challenges of day-to-day living in your current circumstances. The philosophy behind these pieces is that you need to stay well today in order to build that great future tomorrow.

HEALING These readings are about approaches to healing your spirit from the wounds you have received as a result of your partner's mistreatment of you, and perhaps other wounds from previous life experiences.

YOUR OWN BEST FRIEND These readings are about improving your relationship with yourself. The goal here is to help you be kind and patient with yourself, to steer you away from self-blame, and to strengthen your belief in your own goodness and competence.

STAYING CONNECTED These readings are about breaking out of isolation, and improving your relationships with people other than your partner, such as your friends and relatives. One of the greatest challenges for a woman in a destructive relationship is figuring out how to stay connected to the world.

GUIDING CHILDREN These readings are about how to value yourself as a mother, how to help your children have the highest possible quality of life, and how to increase your enjoyment of the time you spend with your kids. If you don't have kids, you can skip these, but you may find them interesting to read nonetheless.

EACH NEW DAY These readings focus on bringing you strength and inspiration. They often include ideas for more satisfying ways to approach daily life, without necessarily being specifically connected to the challenges of dealing with a controlling or abusive partner.

Each reading ends with a sentence or two set apart from the rest of the text. These words capture what I most hope you will take inside of yourself from the ideas I have just covered. I encourage you to repeat these sentences to yourself several times, either aloud or in your mind, for the next twenty-four hours after reading them. If you have ever meditated, you might think of these bold sections as mantras to use for one day. If you allow yourself to absorb each key concept, you will get far more benefit in the long run.

Some pieces continue over the course of two, three, or even four weeks. So if, for example, you are reading a piece that's in the "Surviving to Thrive" category, and it says, "This is Part I," then seven days later, when the next "Surviving to Thrive" piece comes along, you'll find the continuation.

Finally, I want to be clear that this is not a book about how to get out of your relationship, though it can help lead you in that direction if you wish. Nor is it about how to save your relationship and make it work. Only you can decide whether it makes sense to keep working on making things better with your current partner or whether it's time to move on. My goal is to help you toward clarity, power, and faith in yourself, and I know you will succeed in moving in those directions. Where you go with your new power is up to you, and I respect the choices you make.

As you read on ahead, you will find occasional references to other books of mine, including *Why Does He Do That?*, *When Dad Hurts Mom*, and *Should I Stay or Should I Go?*

Why Does He Do That? explains what the controlling, angry, or abusive partner is up to. It was recently described to me as the "controlling partner's playbook," meaning that it reveals the tricks of your partner's behavior and the thinking that is behind them. It has become the most-read book in the United States on abusive relationships. If you frequently feel confused by your partner's behavior, *Why Does He Do That?* could play a role in helping you make sense out of it all. However, you do not have to have read that in order to use this book of daily wisdom; each concept is explained adequately here, and I don't assume any prior knowledge on your part. At the same time, some of these readings may draw your attention to certain issues that you'd like to know more about, such as verbal abuse, manipulation, or the role that sex plays in a destructive relationship, which are addressed in much more detail in *Why Does He Do That?*

In *When Dad Hurts Mom*, I explain how your children are affected when your partner is mean, devaluing, or intimidating to you. It takes you step-by-step through how to help them heal from emotional wounds they may carry from the mistreatment they have heard and seen. And, most important, it guides you in how to keep your relationships with them as strong and close as possible.

Finally *Should I Stay or Should I Go?* (coauthored with JAC Patrissi) explains how to figure out whether your current relationship can be saved, and what steps to take to get it back on course. I took two chapters from that book and adapted them so that they speak directly to the controlling partner who is serious about working on changing. If your partner says he's ready to actually look at himself, you can print those chapters out for him free at LundyBancroft.com, under "Articles." (And whether he chooses to actually do the steps in those chapters seriously will tell you how sincere he is when he claims he's going to deal with his issues.)

I also wrote a book for professionals and students called *The Batterer as Parent* (with Jay Silverman and Daniel Ritchie). That title is quite a bit more expensive, and it doesn't offer much guidance or advice for the abused woman herself. The times you might find it most valuable are if you are struggling with child protective services being involved with your family or if you have separated from your partner and he is fighting you over custody or visitation.

As with those other books, the one you're now reading is intended to help you gain perspective and insight, with the hope that you'll find that a better life is possible and is what you deserve. The readings ahead, if you take them a day at a time and digest each one carefully, will lead you to free your mind and your spirit. This is the path to reclaiming your true worth.

Finally, a few of the pieces in this book first appeared, in somewhat different form, on my blog, "Healing and Hope," which you can find at LundyBancroft.blogspot.com.

DEFINITION OF
"CONTROLLING OR ABUSIVE PARTNER"

For the purposes of this book, when I refer to a "controlling partner" or an "abusive man," I mean one who repeatedly makes you feel devalued. He may do this through verbal abuse and mental cruelty; through pressuring, hurting, or humiliating you sexually; through controlling the money; through cheating on you or giving lots of flirtatious attention to other women so that you feel like less; by focusing only on his own needs and ignoring yours (emotionally, sexually, financially, or in other ways); by using coldness and withdrawal when he doesn't get his way; by turning you into a servant; by chronically ignoring his responsibilities so that you are stuck taking care of things; or through violence and threats. Devaluation and domination take many different forms.

A man who uses these behaviors is usually out to control the woman he's involved with; but even when that's not his intention, it still has that effect. So rather than trying to puzzle out whether he *means* to control you or not, I encourage you to focus on whether his behavior ends up having a controlling *effect* on you. As I discuss later, your partner is responsible for the effects of his actions, not just his intentions. A woman can come out feeling as devalued by a partner who pays no attention to her as by a partner who monitors every move she makes and criticizes her relentlessly.

Much of what I discuss in this book can apply to your situation even if your partner happens to also be a woman; there are certainly women who control other women. I refer to the controller as "he" and his partner as "she" because my professional life has been almost entirely about situations where the destructive partner was a male in relationship with a female.

Some Simplicity in All the Confusion

Abusive and controlling men specialize in causing confusion. One of the ways that many of these men mess up a woman's mind is by turning all her grievances back on her. If you say that he is controlling, he may say that *you* control *him*. If you complain that he demeans and humiliates you, he may turn the tables and say that actually you are the one who talks down to him. He may even call you abusive.

Trying to argue about these points will go on endlessly, because he twists every point you make around so that it always ends up being about what's wrong with *you*.

The outcome of the way he argues is that he escapes ever accepting responsibility for what he does. To his unethical way of thinking, you are the cause of everything he does.

Here's a way out:

Make a decision inside of yourself—a deep decision—that you are 100 percent responsible for your actions, and he is 100 percent responsible for his actions. You have zero responsibility for what he does, and he has zero responsibility for what you do.

The only exception to this rule is if he actually orders you to do something; when one partner forces or threatens the other, that's different. But outside of this one exception, the rule holds.

The advantage of making this decision is that from then on when he calls you irrational, hysterical, abusive, or whatever other labels he likes to hurl at you, you are able to say to yourself, "It doesn't matter if what he is saying is true or not, because either way it's no excuse for how he's behaving." For example, if he says you yell at him, that doesn't make it okay for him to yell at you. *He is entirely responsible for his own actions. His behavior is his choice.*

If you can remind yourself of this point every day, you will be on the road to freeing yourself from his control.

"I don't make him do the things he does.
When men blame women for their own behavior,
that's one of the benchmarks of abuse."

Is This All Just Your Imagination?

Holding on to your sense of what is real is hard when someone else attacks it.

A controlling man tends especially to go on the offensive when his partner calls him on mistreating her; these are the moments when he becomes most determined to convince her that there is something wrong with *her*, and that she is just imagining that his behavior is mean or destructive.

He may even say that the very fact that she thinks something's wrong with what he's doing is the greatest proof of how messed up she is.

He can become particularly crazy-making when he tells you that important events never took place. I have heard hundreds of stories from women in which the abusive man has claimed to her face that he never made some of his most horrible statements, or that he didn't hit her, or that she was the one who did the things that he actually did. And most women I talk to tell me that they end up going through some times of wondering if he's right; it's hard not to find yourself thinking that maybe something is really wrong with you that's causing you to imagine big incidents that didn't really happen.

You aren't imagining things. Abusive men commonly deny their worst actions. They know that they're lying, but they feel justified in doing so. There are tremendous numbers of women who are struggling to keep their sanity while their destructive partners lie to them about events when the woman knows perfectly well what happened.

Trust your memory. Trust your best thinking. Trust your sense of what is real.

"He's trying to convince me that I'm delusional.
But I know I'm fine. He really did those things."

Coming to Terms with How Two-Sided He Is

Does your partner swing between powerful extremes? Are there times when he is the sweetest, most loving person a partner could be, perhaps fun and humorous as well, and then times when he is so mean to you that it seems like he hates you? Take a minute today to reflect on the ways in which his extremes wrench you around emotionally. You are being carried to high highs and low lows by his cycles. And the typical pattern with a destructive partner is that the good periods get shorter and more infrequent, and the hurtful ones take over more and more. Over time, you can come to feel exhausted from being swung around this way.

It can be challenging to find people who can understand both ends of your partner's swings. Some friends may understand how bad he gets when he's bad, and others will get his good side. But what would be the most helpful to you would be someone who can grasp how strong your feelings are about both sides of his pattern. Keep trying to find a person who can take this in and see all he is capable of.

Trust that your feelings are all okay. You deserve support and understanding about your love for him *and* about your resentments and fears regarding him.

"My feelings about him are a jumble,
and I need people in my life who can let me
feel all the different emotions I have."

I Admire You

No one is a worse source of information about a woman than a man who is bullying her. Out of a hundred people, your partner is the one whom you should *least* believe about who you are and what you are capable of becoming. He may sound incredibly certain when he speaks, but he doesn't know what he's talking about.

You have important strengths. You don't give up easily. You've been knocked down many times in life, but you keep getting up again, dusting yourself off, and reaching for a good life. You are profoundly strong despite how weak you may feel some days. You are bright; reaching for a book and working your way through it shows intelligence, openness of mind, and active thinking. You want a better life for yourself (and your children), Some deep place inside you believes that you can rise, and that you deserve to. You have an ability to recognize lies and distortions, and he has never succeeded completely in sucking you into his toxic mentality, as hard as he has tried. And you are open to receiving assistance if someone earns your trust. Look at how many important points I just listed. There is so much to admire and respect about you!

And I do admire you, just as I have admired every abused woman whom I have gotten to know. Anyone who really hears your story, anyone who takes in the mistreatment you have faced and gets how hard you have fought to keep your soul alive, can't help but be moved and inspired by your journey. Yes, I understand that there may still be a long road in front of you; but look at what you have already gotten through, look at how much you have survived, look at how far you've come.

When you have so many abilities and so much resilience, I don't think you can be stopped.

"I'm still here; I'm still on my feet. I will keep moving
until I find the freedom and peace I deserve."

He Sees How Your Family "Isn't Good for You"—Part 1

Is your partner critical of the family you come from? And is he saying that the reason he speaks badly about them is that he's concerned with what's best for *you*? If so, be cautious about where he's going with his "concern."

Here are some examples of common approaches that abusive men take when talking about the woman's relatives:

- "They are way too much in your business. I would never tolerate my family being all over me like that. They just want to control you."
- "You are so different when you're around them; you become like them. You are so much healthier when you aren't with them."
- "They can't stand to see you happy. They're jealous of you, so they look to find things wrong with your life. That's why they are trying to come between us."
- "They never have anything nice to say. They should appreciate you."
- "Your family is so materialistic." (This one can go in many different directions: that they are "so right-wing," or that they are "overly religious," that they are "alcoholic," or all kinds of other faults that he may find.)

Watch out! A partner who has your best interests at heart does not push you to reduce or cut contact with your family. He might support you in doing so if that's what *you* choose, but he wouldn't try to manipulate or pressure you toward that decision. And he wouldn't keep bringing up how bad they are.

If your partner is trying to drive a wedge between you and your family, then he is at least as toxic as they are. Try your best not to let his desires keep you from making your own choices.

✦

> "I'm going to be on guard when he says
> he's trashing my family to 'help' me."

You Are Their Mother

The title of today's entry may seem odd to you. If you have children, you're probably thinking, "Of course I'm their mother. What's up with that?"

In the rush of daily responsibilities and challenges—especially when you are in a relationship with someone whose behavior is a huge problem some days—it's possible to forget just how important you are to your children.

Biology is not the issue here; in fact, some of you are raising children you didn't give birth to. Motherhood is about so much more than giving birth or breastfeeding, as powerful and profound as those are. As your children's mother, you are their protector, their moral compass and teacher, their key source of love and affection and nurturing, their refuge, their source of faith.

You might ask, "Isn't their father supposed to be these things too?" Yes, although even the best father can't be exactly what a mother is. But if your partner is struggling with addiction, is deeply selfish, or is abusive to you, he can't even begin to be what the children need him to be. So your role as a mother grows even bigger.

The bitter irony here is that many destructive men attack a woman's sense of her value as a mother. Your partner may say that he knows better than you do what the right way is to raise children. He may even try to convince you that there is something toxic about you that your children are in danger of catching, and use that as an excuse to take away your parenting decisions and rights.

So when you say to yourself, "I am the children's mother," you are making a profound statement that is not about being their biological or legal parent. You are stating how absolutely critical your *role* is in who they are and who they will become, and how inalienable your right is to guide them and love them. Your children are looking to you.

"My children and I are a team. We belong together."

A Fresh Start

Whether you are picking this book up in the spring, summer, fall, or winter, today is the first day of a new year in your life. You are beginning a twelve-month journey into emotional wellness, centeredness, and freedom. Consider today your personal New Year's Day even if it's eighty degrees outside with thunder and lightning.

The beginning of a new year has always symbolized hope and change to people all over the world. We make New Year's resolutions as a way of saying to ourselves, "I can do it. I can make my life work better. I've been gathering my strength and now I'm ready. Here we go."

There's no need to wait for January 1. The time to begin the new period in life, to build the new you, is now.

Here are my thoughts for the year ahead for you:

I want you to be well. I want you to be treated in the way you deserve by everyone in your life: your friends, your coworkers, your relatives. Your partner, the person you are choosing to make the centerpiece of your life, has the greatest responsibility of them all. It is in your primary relationship that you should be able to feel the most sure of receiving kindness and support, of being carefully listened to, of being seen and understood.

Imagine the year that now stretches out before you, long and full of possibility. Begin to hold a picture in your mind of freedom and lightness, the weight lifted from around your shoulders. Take in the thought with each breath that this is the year when you are going to find a way to live in the kind of love that you deserve. Perhaps you will be able to transform the relationship you are in, or you may decide that it's time to bring it to a close and move on. Or love that rocks your life may come from an unexpected source; perhaps it won't be a lover or a partner this year, but instead a great new friend, or a mentor, or an elder.

Open yourself to the transformation that the next solar cycle can bring to your life.

"I am ready to have the upcoming
year bring me new life."

When Everything Turns into Its Opposite

Life with a destructive man can be like stepping into a mirror world, where everything is backwards. Does your head spin with confusion some days about contradictions in what your partner says and does? See if any of the following items fit your experience:

- When he rudely puts you down, he calls it "constructive criticism" or "just trying to get you to face reality," yet when you try to bring up a grievance about him, he says that you are "belittling him" or "putting him down."

- When he attacks you (verbally or physically), he says that he is defending himself, yet when you defend yourself he says you are attacking him.
- When he is openly flirtatious with women, he tells you it shouldn't bother you and calls you "insecure," yet when you try to have a non-flirtatious friendship with a male, or when another guy just asks you to dance, he is all over you with accusations.
- When you ask him to be less self-centered, he calls you a "demanding bitch" or says that you don't care about his needs, but if you ever need the slightest thing for yourself, he calls you "selfish."

These are crazy-making contradictions that can leave you wondering whether something is wrong with you. But you aren't crazy; his behavior and his justifications are crazy. Train yourself to notice the way he flips everything around in the wrong direction, and you'll have an easier time keeping your own head clear.

"He's a master at twisting everything around.
He's trying to make me cross-eyed, but I'm not
going to let it happen."

SURVIVING TO THRIVE

No Excuse for Verbal Abuse

Verbal abuse is usually followed by more verbal abuse. The pattern runs like this:

1. He verbally abuses you.
2. You show your outrage in some way about what he just said to you.
3. He verbally abuses you more to justify what he already said.

Here's a common kind of example:

HE: "You're a fat, lazy bitch."
YOU: "I can't believe you're saying that to me!"
HE: "The truth hurts, doesn't it! You just sit on your butt all day and
don't do a fucking thing!"

So here is a point to reflect on and digest deeply:
There is no justification for name-calling, using gross language, making fun of you, humiliating you, or putting you down. No reason is good enough. Period.
When I talk to women about the kinds of slurs that they've been exposed to, and I call the man's behavior out as abusive, they tend to reply with sentences that begin "Yes, but . . ." such as the following:
"Yes, but he's right that I haven't been getting much done lately."
"Yes, but it's true that I've been gaining weight."
"Yes, but he's frustrated because I haven't been in the mood for sex lately."
"Yes, but I say the same kinds of things to him."
Don't say "Yes, but" about your partner's behavior. *He has choices.* If he's upset or hurt or angry—including if he feels that you are the one mistreating him—there are always non-abusive options open to him to deal with that. Don't let his excuse-making habits creep inside you so that you start to make his excuses for him.

"I deserve to be spoken to with respect.
Always. No matter what."

Healing Starts Now

In the depths of darkness—the kind of darkness that you can be cast into if you have a partner who tears you to pieces—it seems as though the light will never come again. But it is, truly, possible to scramble your way back to freedom and dignity, and to smile again. You can get there.

The human heart has an almost unlimited ability to bounce back from spiritually destructive experiences. Some deep part of us, the soul, fights not only for life, but for a good life, and a just one.

Your healing can begin even if the mistreatment hasn't ended. Some important steps toward healing often happen for women while they are still mired in dealing with an abusive partner. Certainly, you can heal faster if you can make the abuse stop, whether by calling on the police and the court system if they are helpful where you live; or involving your friends and relatives; or by threatening to leave the relationship (if you can do that safely); or by going through with ending the relationship (if you can do that safely).

But healing can start right away, before you have figured out how to get yourself out of harm's way. For today, focus on being kind and supportive to yourself, and try to feel the place deep down inside you where healing comes from.

"As torn down as I feel, I am still a fully intact human being, ready to rise again."

"I Owe Him a Chance"

Commitment is important in relationships. Once you've developed intimacy with a partner, you have a responsibility to make an effort to make the relationship work, and not just bail out at the drop of a hat. You owe your partner an effort to work out your differences, to see where fears or old patterns are getting in the way, to communicate clearly about how you are feeling.

But certain behaviors on either person's part are *deal breakers*. These include:

- Cheating sexually
- Scaring or assaulting the other person, including threats or physical intimidation
- Forcing or pressuring sex
- Significant lies
- Repeated efforts to tear the other person down or control her life

Once your partner uses any of these deal-breaking behaviors, your obligation to him is over. From that moment on, any effort you put into the relationship is a *gift* from you to him, not something you owe him.

The controlling man often creates confusion on these points by saying that you owe him another chance. He may give reasons such as, "because I apologized," or "because I was drunk when I did those things," or "because you've done some bad things too and I still stayed here." But none of these confers any responsibility on you at all. Given how he has treated you, you don't owe him another minute of your life. He should feel lucky that you put any time or effort into staying with him.

> "If I decide to spend more time working
> on this relationship, that's a gift to him
> that is my choice, not my debt."

He Sees How Your Family "Isn't Good for You"—Part 2

We all tend to have complex relationships with our kin. We love them on a deep level, but in some ways they may drive us a little crazy. We get tired of certain dynamics, but we also feel the benefits of having family in our lives, and we feel what a big loss it would be to pull away from them. Sometimes we do need to take a little space, but we don't usually want to distance ourselves for very long. (Granted, people who come from particularly destructive families occasionally have to cut contact off altogether, but they take this step with great reluctance.)

In short, making choices about how much to involve our relatives in our lives is a highly personal and, at times, painful balancing act. *And that means that your partner has no business badgering you about those choices.*

Your partner may tap into frustrations that you have about your relatives. If he says, for example, that they are too much in your business, you may find yourself thinking, "It's true, my family is invasive. He's probably right that I should shake free of them." Notice if this is happening and don't let him sway you against them.

If your partner wants to gently and supportively raise his concerns about how your family treats you, the way a friend might, that's different. But he should be able to see the good in those relationships at the same time; he should never pressure you to cut contact, and he should not be bringing it up over and over again.

"My family relationships are hard in some ways, but they're important to me. If he wants what's best for me, he'll support me to stay connected to them if that's what I want."

Those Days When You Feel Like a Lousy Mom

Everybody has been there. You're tearing your hair out, and you can't believe that you are becoming the kind of parent you swore you'd never be. You're screaming at the kids, you called one of them a "little brat," you slammed a door, you've "lost it."

Deep breath. Let's take this one step at a time.

First, let's work on getting your partner's voice out of your head. You are not a terrible mother. You are not a hysterical woman. You are not out of control. He may have repeated these things to you so many times that they have become his mantra, but that doesn't make them so. Every parent in the modern world has days that he or she doesn't handle well. If he was looking after the kids for a significant amount of time each day—really looking after them, not just playing video games with them—he'd be losing it too, and much worse than you.

Next, no irreparable harm has been done. Apologize to your children. Tell them that they are great kids despite what you said earlier, and remind them that even when you are mad at them you still love them very much. Forgive yourself for today, and then resolve to make tomorrow go better. In the pages ahead, you will find guidance for improving your relationship with your children. For today, focus on how much you are already doing well, and on how much they love you.

Besides, your partner is no authority on how people should treat each other, or he'd be a lot better to you.

"I'm a good mother. Everybody has bad days."

Mindful Living

Take a moment to look around the place you are currently in, whether it's a room in your home, or a library, or a café, or an outdoor spot. Look to your far left and choose an object that looks nice or interesting to you, and allow your eyes to rest on it for a few moments. Take two or three breaths. Then turn your head slightly to the right, focusing now on a new spot. Work your way to your far right, choosing five or six items in total to gaze at briefly as you go. At each stop, take in the shapes and the colors you are seeing, and notice any feelings you have about the object.

Next, see how many different sounds you can identify around you. You might hear the wind, or a humming refrigerator, or birds chirping, or the music your children are listening to. Focus your ears and mind briefly on each sound. You are likely to find that your ears can pick up more sounds than you had noticed before you started listening.

Finally, run your awareness up and down your body, seeing how many physical sensations you can find. Feel your clothing against your body. Find any warm or cold spots, or any joints or muscles that feel uncomfortable. Feel what is going on in the more sensitive parts of your body, such as your tongue, your wrists, the bottoms of your feet, your sexual places. Move your focus all around your body, not staying too long in any one place.

When you are finished, make some notes in a journal about how this exercise was for you.

Getting ourselves rooted in our sensory awareness is a powerful path to overcoming stress, to healing from trauma, and to regaining power. For the rest of today try to notice frequently—every hour, let's say—what you are seeing, hearing, and feeling in your body. Make sure especially to do this anytime someone upsets you or gets you stressed.

※

"My senses are my gateways to myself."

Recognizing Crazy-Making Behavior

There are two destructive goals that abusive men succeed at more than any others. One is to make the woman believe that the abuse is her own fault; the other is to make her feel that there is something wrong with her mentally. Today we're going to focus on the second one of these.

Reflect on whether your partner uses any of the following tactics to make you feel like your mind isn't working right:

- *He denies things that are extremely obvious.* For example, he yells furiously at you but denies that he's angry; he stinks of alcohol but denies that he's been drinking; he has a lot of secret phone calls but denies that anything is going on; he assaults you physically or sexually and then later says it didn't happen.
- *He acts out dramatically in ways that reverse reality.* For example, one of my clients would be scary and intimidating to his partner, then would lock himself in a room and barricade the door with furniture, saying that he was scared of *her*. I've had other clients who would burst into tears and tell their partner how mean *she* was being after he said or did terrible things to her.
- *He tries to convince you that you are the only person who believes what you believe.* He may laugh at statements of yours or insist that "everyone knows that's not true."
- *He messes things up for you, then tells you that you messed them up yourself.* For example, he hides bills and then says you forgot to pay them; he doesn't give you messages, so you miss important dates, then he swears he told you; he damages objects around the house and says that you are the one who did it.

Crazy-making behavior can make you feel crazy; that's what it's all about. Learn to recognize these tactics and you'll have an easier time keeping your sanity.

"I can see what he's doing, and
I'm not going to let him make me nuts."

Resisting Brainwashing

We all have a natural ability to recognize falsehoods and distortions. But if a claim gets repeated with enough frequency for a long enough time, we start to feel that it must be at least partly true, especially if the person speaks with authority and certainty. And the brainwashing is even more powerful if the person insults or demeans anyone who dares disagree with him.

Does your partner keep telling you things like: "You're fat," "Your friends are losers," "You don't know what you're talking about," "You're messing up these kids," "I don't have a problem [with drinking, with abusiveness, with womanizing, etc.]"?

If so, part of you is naturally going to start to doubt yourself and think that maybe he's right.

The impact of his indoctrination will deepen if he's making it hard for you to spend time with other people. Brainwashing people while they are isolated works. So how do you hold on to your knowledge about what is real?

First, have a daily ritual where you repeat several times, "My mind works fine, my mind works fine." Do this in front of a mirror, or while you are holding an object that is precious and grounding for you, such as a favorite rock, candle, or photograph.

Second, start a journal, to help you keep your thoughts clear and to give you a record to check your memory against when he tells you that you are remembering things wrong.

Third, build relationships with friends or relatives who are operating in reality and can confirm for you that you aren't crazy.

Finally, notice the untruths that he repeats a lot, and write them down for yourself. One of your best defenses against brainwashing is to notice when it's being used and record it.

"When he repeats something a thousand times,
that doesn't make it so. I know what's real."

Journal Writing

If you don't have a journal, get one. If you do have one, pull it out, dust it off, and put it into regular use. If you are afraid that someone will read what you write, figure out a hiding place in a basement or in a crack in the wall. There is no single greater contribution you can make to your own healing than to write often—daily if you can—about your life, your thoughts, and your feelings.

Consider your journal a special type of best friend. This is a friend who asks nothing from you except the plain truth about what is going on inside you. Tell your journal the things you aren't telling anyone else. Tell it what you fantasize about, what you are reaching for, what terrifies you. (You can burn it in a couple of years if you don't want your grandchildren to discover these things about you when they go through your basement in the year 2075.)

Writing is often misunderstood as being a medium for expressing thoughts, but actually it is a *way* of thinking. We have a different internal process when we write than when we speak. Our feelings move through new channels, and ideas emerge that hadn't been born yet, including solutions to problems that seemed unsolvable.

And an entire additional set of ruminations and changes will occur inside of you when you go back weeks or months or years from now and read what you wrote today. Your journal reflects yourself back to you in ways that help you see more clearly. Spend a few minutes writing today.

>꒳₰

"My journal is my confidant, my creative channel,
my inspiration, and my reality check."

Stop Putting Yourself Down

A destructive man's behavior has a way of creeping inside your head, so that you start to do his unhealthy work for him. When he isn't around to examine and exaggerate all of your shortcomings, you may find that your own brain takes over and sends you those messages itself.

Don't let it. Start noticing how often the voice in your head is actually his voice, not yours. Listen for put-downs like "What's the matter with you?" and "Why can't you do anything right?" Observe how many times a day you are saying to yourself, "You idiot" or "You fool." And each time you catch yourself mistreating yourself in these ways, *stop it.* One critical step toward freedom is to stop enslaving yourself.

Your partner's abusive behavior teaches you to do on the inside the same things that he does on the outside. So it's time to start *unlearning* what he has taught you to do. When you catch yourself in self-abuse mode, say to yourself in a kind voice, "Oops, there I go again, falling into his trap. Time to climb out!" Then gently shift your mental focus to something positive, including supportive thoughts about yourself, and carry on with your day.

"I'm going to break the habit of speaking badly to
myself, and treat myself with respect."

He Sees How Your Family "Isn't Good for You"—Part 3

Over the last couple of weeks, we've looked at some of the ways in which your partner may drive wedges between you and your relatives. I pointed out how he may highlight some of the less healthy aspects of those relationships to pressure you to distance yourself from them. But here's another issue: Many times, the real reason a destructive man is criticizing a woman's relatives is because of the *strengths* and the *wellness* in her family, not its problems. He's claiming that her family affects her negatively, but in fact they support her, increase her self-confidence, and make her less dependent on her partner.

In short, while your partner says that your family wants to control you, what's really bothering him may be that they're making it harder for *him* to control you.

In so many cases a man persuades or bullies a woman to drive her family away, and that clears the path for him to be a much worse bully to her than he had been before. He ends up being more damaging to her than her family had ever been, even in their worst moments.

And if he succeeds in damaging your important connections in this way, it can be a long road for you to repair them, especially if it looks to your relatives like you made your own decision to cut them off.

If your relatives—and the same goes for your friends—are any source of strength to you, fight like hell to protect those relationships.

"What really bothers him about my connections
is that they keep me strong."

What Do Your Kids Most Need from You?

All parents have times of worrying about how their children are going to turn out. Are they going to grow up rude and demanding? Will they ever do anything with their lives? Will they be smart enough to succeed? Will they be good citizens?

The atmosphere that an abusive man brings to the house can intensify these worries. He focuses so much on people's faults, sending the message that you and the children need to be rescued from turning out hopelessly flawed. He wants to remodel all of you into something that he considers good enough.

You will be more help to your children if you can avoid getting caught up in this "disaster prevention" kind of thinking. They need to see that *you* have faith that they will be okay, especially if their father obviously doesn't. *You have to be the counter to the negativity, criticism, and intimidation that he brings to the home.* Help them believe in their self-worth. Give them the experience of receiving patience and forgiveness. Let them see you being fair with them and their siblings. Allow their voices to be heard and take their opinions seriously, so that they can feel what that's like. Help them learn how to stand up for themselves. Don't let them get away with behaving badly, but at the same time keep reminding them how loved they are. *These are the things that will really matter to how they turn out.*

The rest is small stuff, so don't sweat it; the great grades, the athletic achievements, the perfectly clean room, the right impression for the neighborhood. Let these things go.

<hr>

"What will most influence how my children
turn out is my love, patience, and respect."

<hr>

EACH NEW DAY

Putting Full Value on Unpaid (and Underpaid) Labor

When two people live together as a couple, the work that they each do to contribute to the household has equal value, hour for hour. This is true regardless of whether some of that work is unpaid (such as household and child-rearing work), and regardless of whether one partner earns a lot more at work than the other.

This is a critically important concept for the rights of women, because on average women do far more unpaid work at home than men do—often ten or twenty times as much in cases where the man is controlling or abusive. And when women do work outside the home—as the great majority do nowadays—they get paid an average of 70 cents on the dollar compared to what men make.

Spend a moment doing the following simple math: Think through a typical week, including the weekend, and add up all of the hours you work. Include your paid work if you have a job, but also include every single thing that you do for your household: cleaning, food shopping and other purchases, preparing meals, washing dishes, spending time with your children, making their lunches, making phone calls related to your children's needs, taking the car to the mechanic, working in the yard, *everything.*

Next, I'd like you to do the same for your partner. Add up his work hours, his time spent with the kids (which does *not* include time he was watching television or staring at his computer while he was "looking after" them), his work around the house or in the yard, and any other work contributions he makes.

Compare your total hours worked per seven-day week with his.

Unless his number of hours comes up far larger than yours, *then by all rights all of the money coming into the household belongs to both of you.* Any other definition is exploitative of the woman.

So when he says, "I pay for this, I pay for that; if it weren't for my money you wouldn't have anything. I bought you that car, you went to school on my money," and so on, he's using what is called "financial abuse" or "economic abuse." You earned that money just as much as he did. So when he "takes the family out for dinner," you're actually taking the family out just as much as he is. The kids should be thanking both of you equally. And half of the money he "bought you that car with" was your own money.

"My work is just as valuable as his, hour for hour."

"Why Does He Get *So* Angry?"

Does your partner sometimes seem like he's insane with rage, perhaps over some tiny thing? Maybe his face turns red, he screams and waves his arms around, he makes accusations—in a word, he goes kind of berserk. His reactions are extreme and out of proportion to whatever the issue is.

You can find yourself wondering, "How did he get so bitter toward me? How did his outlook on me turn so *ugly*? How did I turn so horrible in his eyes?" It can almost feel like he hates you.

The problem is in him, not you. Even if you had been the most perfect partner in the world, he still would have come to the same place he's in now. So what's going on? Why is he so messed up emotionally?

Well, actually, he isn't. The problem isn't in his emotions, it's in his *attitudes*. The man who has explosive, unreasonable rages toward his partner has a deep belief that the woman exists to meet his needs. She is supposed to cater to his every whim, and be a magical servant who can fix everything. In other words he wants a genie in a bottle, not a real-life woman.

You had no way of knowing, back in the wonderful early days of your relationship, that he had these unfair and unrealistic expectations. As his real attitudes started to emerge, you naturally found his changes quite shocking. Try not to let his toxicity creep inside of you; keep reminding yourself that you did not cause this transformation in him; these problems already existed hidden inside him.

⁓⁓

"I can't solve his problems, and it's not
my fault that he thinks I should."

Will He Settle Down Once We Have a Child?

Babies are not the answer to the problems in a relationship. They can bring great satisfaction and joy to the lives of the parents, but they will not help the dynamics *between* the parents. In fact, it takes a strong relationship to be able to hold together through the profound challenges that parenting a newborn brings. If your relationship is not going well, adding a new young life to the mix will just make conditions get worse, and perhaps a lot worse.

For women who have angry or controlling partners, this reality is even more true. The man who chronically mistreats his partner is an individual who chronically puts his own needs first, including doing so at the worst possible times, and gets bent out of shape when he has to make significant sacrifices. He doesn't respect his partner's opinions if they differ strongly from his, and in fact he lacks respect for her overall. These characteristics are *opposite* to the ones that a man has to have in order to be a safe, loving parent to a baby and a kind, supportive co-parent with his partner. These problems are not going to go away because a baby has arrived; in fact, they will be sharpened.

Notice if you are having any of these thoughts about having a baby:

"He'll finally realize I'm not trying to cheat on him—I mean, I'm obviously not looking at other guys if I'm home with our baby."

"He'll finally get it that it's time to grow up and be responsible, so he'll stop drinking and he'll get serious about finding steady work."

"He'll be a lot happier, because he wants to have a family, so then he won't be so grouchy and mean to me."

It never works. His problems go so much deeper than that. You have to solve relationship problems first, *then* bring a baby into the picture.

And believe me, the last thing you want is to end up in a custody battle with an abusive man.

><?>*

"He has to prove to me that he's ready to
be a responsible parent and a kind partner
before we can start a family."

HEALING

How Do I Know When It All Has Become Too Much?

You are a stronger person than you give yourself credit for. Take pride in your ability to struggle through hard situations. But at the same time, it's important to recognize when a challenge you are facing in life—such as the highly stressful relationship you are in—has become too much to handle. How can you tell when "managing it" is no longer manageable? What are the signs that you are getting overwhelmed, and that it's time to start reaching out for support and assistance? When is your life telling you that the way you are living may have to change?

Here are some markers that women have shared with me.

- Notice when you start to see behaviors coming into your own parenting that are upsetting to you, and you are no longer being the kind of mother you want to be.
- Notice, too, if you are losing your friendships and connections with your relatives.
- Changes in your health can tip you off, such as if you are gaining a lot of weight, or if you are not eating or sleeping.
- Your stability may be slipping, so that you find yourself "losing it," screaming and storming around the house or feeling on the edge psychologically.

If you are starting to see any or all of these indications in yourself, don't fall into the trap of seeing them as signs of *defeat*. Instead, view them as *warnings*, as messages to you from your inner self. These signs are telling you that you are human, and that you only have human powers. They are telling you that you have done everything you can, and that you don't have anything left to give in this direction. It's time, in other words, to start looking in a new direction. The first step is to start reaching out to trustworthy people, and to other resources, such as programs for abused women and supportive websites.

"I need to listen to the messages I'm getting about
what's too much for me. I'm human."

Doing Things for Yourself

One way of summing up what an abusive man is all about is to say this: He wants a relationship where he can take *way* more than he gives. When you are living with this style of partner, your days become more and more twisted in the direction of trying to figure out how to keep your partner happy, so that you don't get much time to think about how to make your own life work for you.

Let's work on stepping out of that sweeping current. Get a piece of paper or grab your journal, and make a list of everything you can think of that you need to do for yourself. The list may begin with mundane aspects of daily life, such as "I need to do my laundry. I need to get my hair done." Next, take the list up a level, looking at taking care of your well-being; you might write down items such as "I need to get exercise. I need to eat more healthful food." Think of ways to be good to yourself. Finally, go up one more level, to things that you might not get to until weeks or months from now, but that you know you need to do to be happy in your life. This list could include things like "I need to get a different job," or "I've got to plan a nice vacation for myself."

Next, start getting in the habit of making the *first* thing you do each day something you do *for yourself*. Before you think of your partner's needs, or your children's needs, consider what you need. And make a step, even if it's a small one, toward getting it done.

It's great to be a loving parent and a caring partner. But your own needs have to stop disappearing. And since your partner keeps brushing your needs aside, you are going to have to work extra hard to keep putting them back at the center of your life. So today, and every day, keep asking yourself, "What do *I* need?" Then plan at least one step you'll take toward giving it to yourself.

*"My needs can't keep getting pushed
to the bottom of the list."*

How to Be a Good Friend—Part 1

One of the ways to have successful relationships is to make a difference in people's lives. When people feel your positive impact they are going to value you and want to spend time with you.

The reality is that you have a lot to give. You may not feel that way right now; your partner may have torn down your self-opinion a lot, and the stress of your relationship may leave you feeling wrung out and needy. *But don't get caught in this trap*; if you don't believe you have much to offer your loved ones, pretty soon you really won't.

So don't hold back from people. Your friends and relatives want you to be connected to them. You can matter in their lives in many ways. Begin by *being a really good listener*. If you work at it, you will find that you can lay your own distress aside for substantial periods of time and really focus on other people's lives and concerns.

Part of being a good listener is to be aware of not talking on too long about yourself. Try to share talking time equally with your loved ones. When you are in pain or confusion, it's tempting to talk on and on about your relationship (or some other issue), but reel yourself in. A good friend keeps the time balanced even when things are hard. I don't mean that you should hold back regarding going to friends for support;

go ahead and spill your heart. Just pay attention to giving back, and try to make good listening part of each interaction.

⟡

"I can be a great friend, even when
times are hard for me."

Are You the Children's Friend or Their Parent?

Raising children seems like it might best be done by gymnasts because it involves so many balancing acts. We have to be deeply caring and present, yet not make them feel like we're always meddling and advising. We have to instill discipline, but at the same time not teach kids mindless obedience to authority. We want to raise kids who have good food and exercise habits, but we don't want them to get obsessed about food or about their body image.

One of these many balancing acts is trying to walk the line between being overly authoritative and overly palsy-walsy. We have to develop an intuitive feel for when our kids need a parent and when they need a friend.

HERE ARE TIMES TO BE A PARENT:

When children need to be looked after

When danger is chasing our children or when our children are chasing danger

When children can't stand up for themselves or haven't learned how

When children are behaving selfishly or irresponsibly and need firm guidance and limits, and need consequences when the limits fail

When there are crucial things they need to learn (but only a few per day—don't teach all the time)

When you are having a hard time emotionally (in other words, try to hide your difficulties from your children and focus on being the grown-up to the fullest extent you can).

HERE ARE TIMES TO BE A FRIEND:

When you are telling your children what you appreciate about them (Friends speak in a tone of appreciation while parents tend to speak in a tone of approval, and appreciation is a better tone.)

When your kids are sad, afraid, or in other forms of emotional distress (Children at these times need more support and understanding, and a lot less advice, than they typically get from their parents.)

When you're doing something fun together, playing or cooking or laughing or listening to music

When you are cuddling with them

When everything is going well

Parents help their kids the most when they don't act like a friend when it's time to be a parent, and don't act like a parent when it's time to be a friend. You can train yourself to feel the difference. By doing so you will also help yourself, because you will enjoy your time with your children more by being clear on when it's time to play which role.

"I am both a parent and a friend to my kids.
Each role has its time."

Good Intentions Aren't Enough

I was sitting in a little breakfast joint with friends a few weeks ago. Well, three of them were friends, and the fourth guy was someone they knew but I didn't. And guy number four was unbearable. He took over the conversation so no one else could get a word in, he made "jokes" that weren't funny at all, and then he capped it off by making a crack about how little the rest of us were saying!

I said I had things to take care of and got up and left.

When I talked it over with my friends later, they laughed it off, saying, "Oh, that's just the way Kelly is. He doesn't mean any harm; that's just his way of being friendly." But that doesn't mean it's my obligation to let him walk all over me. Kelly is responsible for the *effects of his actions, not just his intentions.*

I'm telling this story because this theme plays out in the lives of women with destructive partners. Other people tell her, "I'm sure he didn't really mean to hurt you," and he himself is forever saying, "You take things the wrong way, I wasn't trying to do anything bad at all." The repeated message is "Don't pay any attention to how you are actually being affected by what he's doing; just focus on the fact that he isn't evil."

When you are badly affected by your partner's behavior, *that's what matters*. No one has the right to tell you to ignore the actual *impact* of what he does.

✘ ⏀ ⏀

"His good intentions don't help me;
I need to be treated well."

Looking at His Anger Problem

When a man chronically mistreats his partner, his anger is often his most obvious quality. The result is his partner is likely to believe that his anger is the problem, and therapists or other professionals who get involved tend to jump to the same conclusion. Many judges order abusive men to attend "anger management" programs, which won't help. Why not? Because his rage has little to do with how he behaves.

His problem isn't that he's angry; it's that he's *abusive*. Let's look at the difference. Angry behaviors are things like speaking loudly in a resentful tone of voice, waving his arms around, pacing back and forth, or storming out of the room. Abusive behaviors are things like calling you names, twisting your words around, throwing things or punching walls, treating you like you're beneath him, not letting you say your side of the argument, or cheating on you.

Compare these lists with respect to your own relationship. Are your partner's angry behaviors the main reason why you are feeling bad?

Doesn't the problem actually have much more to do with his *abusive* behaviors? A partner who is too angry can cause you stress, but abusive behaviors are far more destructive. Almost every time a woman complains about her partner's anger, it's really his abusiveness that is harming her.

This is why "anger management" doesn't do any good for an abusive man. If he learns techniques to lower his anger level, he simply shifts to being abusive in a more calm or calculated way—in other words, his abusiveness continues, it just gets less angry. What good does that do?

An abusive man can't change by dealing with his anger, his drinking, his childhood, or any other issue in his life. He can only change by facing up to his abusiveness, and dealing with that problem head-on.

⊱⊰

> "When I look carefully at his behaviors
> and his attitudes, I can see that his
> anger isn't really the issue."

SURVIVING TO THRIVE

Looking to Your Partner for a Better Morning

Today let's look at the challenge of having a partner who can be rude, cold, or critical first thing in the day. Starting your day with an interaction that feels like a slap in the face can send you spiraling downward in an emotional descent that is hard to break.

It's natural that you would hope for a hug and a kind word from him when you get up—that's certainly what you deserve—but looking for it just sets you up to feel hurt and deflated. You don't want the quality of your day to depend on him, given how changeable he is. So tell yourself, "I have to stop looking to him for what I need in the morning, and instead get it from sources I can count on." Those sources can include yourself, your faith or philosophy, your children, and any close friends or relatives you have. See also if you can have less contact with him in the mornings; perhaps get out for a jog, or go to an early yoga class, or make some other excuse to avoid being around him so much.

On those days when his nasty or rejecting side comes out first thing, tell yourself, "His coldness is his problem, not mine. He's the one who's missing out. I'm not going to let him ruin my day."

> "I am going to set the tone for my own day.
> I'm not letting him determine it for me."

Understanding Your Rights

When the subject of human rights comes up, most people think of the public sphere of life. We associate these rights with issues like being free from unwarranted searches by police, being able to criticize the government, or having the right to a trial by jury. But what does the concept of "rights" have to do with wishing your relationship would go differently? Aren't relationships part of the private sphere?

Actually, your rights go with you all the time, in public or in private, with a huge crowd or alone with your partner. No one has the right to take them away from you. And many of your most important rights are specified in international treaties. These rights are "inalienable," meaning that your partner never has a good enough reason to take them from you, no matter what he says. They include:

- The right to free speech. He has no right to punish you for what you say or to silence you.
- The right to "freedom of cultural expression," which in daily life particularly means your right to wear what you want to wear. That's right, he can't control your clothing.
- The right to pursue economic well-being and independence. This means he can't interfere with your right to work or go to school, and he can't take your money, even if you are married.
- The right to safety and integrity in your body. He can't touch you when you don't want to be touched, he can't badger you into having sex with him, he can't expose you to sexual infections by cheating on you.
- The right to freedom of association. You have the right to choose which friends and relatives you want in your life and how much time you spend with them. He doesn't get to decide which ones are good influences or bad influences.

I realize that if you showed him this list, it wouldn't help. But it is important for your spiritual well-being to at least remember *inside yourself* that when he controls you he is violating your internationally recognized rights. The fact that he's doing this inside of a relationship doesn't make it any less serious or less wrong.

✹

"I am going to grow stronger inside by developing
an awareness of when my rights are being violated."

Your Mind Still Works

Your sense of your own intelligence and clarity are getting messed with. The techniques your partner uses to undermine your intellectual self-confidence may be obvious or they may be well hidden. Perhaps he's right out there with his contempt for your ideas, calling you "stupid" and "ridiculous" and "crazy." Or he might come on an almost opposite tack, smiling at you with condescension, feeling sorry for you because you can't see as clearly as he does, gently (or so it seems) correcting and improving your errors of thinking. Either way, you come to doubt your own intelligence and clarity.

Of the two examples above the second one can actually be just as bad, or worse. The woman who lives with a man who acts calmly superior comes out feeling like an ignorant and helpless little child, and it's hard for her to put her finger on what is eroding her self-confidence. Either way, you can get to a point where you feel, "It's very hard to get my thoughts straight. My mind just doesn't work right anymore."

There's nothing wrong with you. You are having trouble thinking clearly because your partner is pouring glue into the workings of your mind. It's a problem that he's creating.

Find ways to create space for your own thoughts, apart from him. Take deep breaths and let your mind flow while you're in the shower, or write in a journal, or take a quiet walk. If you carve out time to get back in touch with yourself and your own beliefs and opinions, the glue he is pouring will start to clear out.

"I am a smart, clear-thinking woman. I'm not going to let him throw my mind off course."

How to Be a Good Friend—Part 2

Last week we looked at how you can be a good friend to people at the same time as you lean on them for support in a hard time. Here are some additional gifts that you can give people that will make them value having you in their lives and keep them from perceiving you as a burden. In fact, these are great habits to practice even at easier times in your life:

Remember the themes in people's lives. We all have certain key aspects of life that fill up our minds. A few examples include our work, our relationships, our teams or clubs, our children, our elderly parents, our health. If you can keep track of the main themes in a loved one's life and check in about them, your support and thoughtfulness will be appreciated.

Give a little advice, but not a lot. People like to get suggestions and ideas for how to handle challenges or opportunities in their lives, but they prefer them in small doses. If you give too much advice, people end up feeling like you don't really want to listen to what they are telling you.

Remember to have fun. We need a balance between seriousness and play. A good friend isn't afraid to go into heavy subjects—it doesn't work to only want to deal with the easy stuff—but also knows when it's time to laugh, or go to a movie, play Ping-Pong, or watch the sunset. Build happy memories with your loved ones, and they will associate you with those memories.

"Being a good friend is a skill that takes practice,
like any other. And I can do it well."

Finding Balance When Kids Misbehave

Modern parenting styles seem to be drifting toward two opposing ends of the spectrum. At one end are moms and dads who sit passively while their children behave rudely or aggressively toward other people or even right to their parents. At the other end are parents who come down on their kids like a ton of bricks, scolding them with harsh disapproval—which stings kids much more than we realize—for misbehaviors that are just plain normal childhood development.

Both of these extremes are causes for concern. It's healthier for children when we strike a middle course with them, calling them on unacceptable behavior but leaving them with some dignity, and avoid sending them the message that they are bad. (If you succeed in convincing a child that he or she is profoundly bad, you'll have a chronically Bad Kid on your hands; that's where that path leads.)

Getting angry at kids once in a while is fine—in fact it's good for children to learn that anger is a normal part of life, and that it can be expressed appropriately and nonviolently. But save it for when it really matters. If you're too frequently angry at them, they will become increasingly resistant to guidance. And if your anger toward then comes out in demeaning or shaming ways, it will cause even more problems in the long run.

At the same time, don't cater to kids who are using a rude tone with you. If your child barks at you, in a demanding and imperious voice, "Where is my orange juice?!" it's best not to respond with "Just a minute, I'll get it, I'll get it." I recommend instead that you say, "Now I'm going to make you wait extra long for your juice, because you are absolutely not going to talk to me that way!" Make sure that rude behavior is not rewarded.

"My children need to receive my respect, and they need to be required to show me respect in return."

Jealousy Is Not Love

Jealousy and love actually have nothing to do with each other. At one time in life you might have a guy head-over-heels in love with you who shows no signs of jealousy, acting relaxed regarding your interactions with other men. He just trusts you, and he doesn't take the attitude that he owns you. In another relationship, the guy you're with might be crazy jealous over you while in other ways showing that he doesn't care that much; for example, he might frequently verbally abuse you, which is certainly not a sign of love. He might even cheat on you while he accuses you of cheating on him, a remarkably common behavior pattern among controlling and abusive men.

So love and jealousy are as separate as they can be.

It's common to believe that the more jealous and possessive a man is, the more he loves you. You might find yourself telling a friend, "My partner just goes ballistic if I even talk to another guy. I've never had a man so crazy about me." But the fact that he goes ballistic just shows that he views you as a personal possession. And possessiveness leads to a huge collection of problems. So stop believing that his jealousy says anything about how strong his healthy feelings are for you. See it instead as a glaring indicator of his unhealthy attitudes.

- 42 -

"Jealousy is in no way a sign of love."

When He Tries to Make You Jealous— But He Denies It

Men who like to control women aren't always obvious about it. Some controllers don't yell or call names or threaten, but instead they keep women insecure and fighting with each other.

Here's how this style of guy tends to operate. First, he talks about other women and interacts with them in a way that throws you off-balance. He may say, "I just appreciate beauty; there's no reason why that should bother you." Another common line is, "If you were secure in yourself, it wouldn't make you jealous when I talk to a woman." He may also throw in occasional comparisons, making you feel a little less sexy, or thin, or beautiful than other women he's examining.

He's trying to convince you that you are an overly jealous woman, but your gut instinct is telling you different. Whether or not he actually cheats on you, he's got a routine going to keep subtly (or not so subtly) making you feel like you're less desirable than other women, and that you have lots of competition.

His behavior is not only making you feel insecure (which he then blames on you), but you also end up wondering how committed he is. You say to yourself, "Is he really 100 percent *in* this relationship with me?"

You have every right to be bothered if he checks women out or compares women to each other or to you. Ditto if his interactions with women have a romantic or sexual tone to them. If he behaves in those ways, don't let him convince you that the issue is your jealousy.

꒰ ? ꒱

"I deserve to be made to feel attractive and desirable, and not be compared to other women."

His Brilliant Thinking

Let's take a look today at the messages your partner is sending you about your intelligence, and about his. These messages may be obvious—taking the form of overt insults, for example—or they may be subtle. I have worked with abusive men who are good at pretending to support a woman's thinking when they are actually undermining her; for example, I had a client who would frequently say to his partner, "That's a good point you just made, but here's a key idea that you're missing . . ."—so his supposed compliment was actually a criticism in disguise.

Consider whether your partner is telling you, in his words, his tone, or his facial expressions:

- That he thinks clearly and you think sloppily.
- That you have a lot you need to learn from him and that he is your teacher.
- That he understands a lot of things that most other people don't.
- That everyone knows that you are wrong.

- That your opinions aren't even worth taking seriously.
- That he understands what people are really up to, while you are naïve.

The underlying message is that his mind is full of brilliant insights and opinions, and that you need to empty your own thoughts out of your head so that he can fill you up with his.

But you don't need him to manage your mind for you. Each person's thoughts and perspectives are important. Your mind was working better before he started messing with it.

"I can think very well for myself.
His supposed 'improvements' of my
thinking are just getting in the way."

Recording Your Partner's Patterns

When you have a partner who intermittently turns irrational or mean, you naturally find it hard to make sense of how kind or fun or loving he can be at other times. You wish so badly that he could just be in "nice mode" all the time. So part of what your mind does during the good periods is block from memory what his ugly behaviors look like; his selfish or demeaning acts start to seem far away and not so big, and some of them you forget about altogether. Sound familiar?

This forgetting process can help you to enjoy those loving periods that you crave so much, but it is a trap. The next time he's being awful to you, you find yourself thinking, "I can't believe I'm back in one of these horrible situations with him again. I'd forgotten what a nightmare he turns into." And this process can continue for dozens of cycles: blocking it all from memory and then feeling shocked when it comes around again.

The solution is to start keeping a record in your journal of every time his behavior gets nasty or rejecting. Begin over the next few days by writing down every incident you can remember when he has hurt you, verbally, physically, or sexually. You will be amazed by how many there are once you start to write them down. Then from here on record each new one as soon as possible after it happens.

Maintaining this kind of inventory will do wonders to keep you sane. And it will lead to you having much greater clarity about the choices you have to make regarding your relationship.

"I need to keep a record of his behavior patterns;
otherwise I lose track of them, and then I keep
being surprised."

Creating a Good Reflection of Yourself

You are a good person. You are smart and capable, and you know how to treat people well. You have good intentions and are trying to do your best.

But an abusive man's behavior can creep inside of you. You may find yourself yelling at him, swearing, making accusations, and using put-downs. Some days you may even use these behaviors in front of your children. And after each of these incidents you feel bad about yourself, thinking, "I'm becoming just like my partner. I'm no better than he is."

You can step out of this pattern. To do so, you have to avoid two extremes. One extreme is to decide that you are a bad person. The more you believe badly about yourself, the worse you are likely to behave, because you won't expect any better from yourself.

The other extreme is to justify your own behavior problems by blaming them on your partner. It's a mistake, for example, to tell yourself, "I can't help how I'm acting, because he drives me to it," or to think, "He behaves this way, so why can't I? I'll give him a taste of his own medicine." These are unhealthy thought patterns; in fact, they are *his* thought patterns, and you don't want them.

The solution is to steer a middle course. Yes, his mistreatment is causing you stress and emotional injury, but no, that does not take away your responsibility for your actions. You are continuing to make choices. And you need to hold yourself to a higher standard than he applies to himself. Don't sink to his level.

Why not? Why should you have to behave well while he is behaving badly? *Because you have to keep your faith in yourself alive.* The more you act like him, the more you will dislike yourself; it will make you weaker, not stronger. Taking on his behaviors gives him more power over you, not less.

I'm not asking you to be perfect. But fight with all the strength you can muster to hold on to the person you want to be. Don't let him drag you into his way of doing things. Keeping your integrity is crucial in order to move toward getting your life back.

～◯₣

"I'm not going to let him turn me into what he is."

Putting a High Value on Your Women Friends

Our society swirls with messages that encourage women to devalue their relationships with each other. Music videos, movies, popular songs, and advertising speak with an almost unified voice, shouting, "Your relationships with men are the ones that really count! A relationship with a man is what makes you whole. Once you have a man, you shouldn't need anyone else. Make your whole life revolve around him!"

The regrettable outcome is that women often feel that they shouldn't spend too much time with their women friends once they are with a man, and that the relationship with him should always come first.

Have you ever been on the other end of this deal, when a good friend of yours suddenly has no time for you because she's with a guy? And when you do see her, all she can talk about is him? If so, you know how second-class that can make you feel.

So don't be the one to do it to your friends. Make time with them a priority, and when you are with them don't make your man the focus of all your conversation. And don't cancel plans with them because he suddenly wants to spend time with you. Above all, value your women friends in your thoughts. Keep them central in your mind; treasure the love and support they give you, and never take them for granted. Your good friends are the most precious aspects of life.

※◯⟋

"I'm not going to let anything get between
me and my women friends."

Helping Kids with Their Anger—Part 1

At some point, your children are going to struggle with questions about anger—their own and other people's. These struggles are likely to be potent for your kids because they are trying to digest your partner's behavior and figure out what it means for their lives. It will be important to their development for them to resolve their issues regarding anger in a constructive way, and you can help them do that.

Here are some ways to talk to them about their confusion:

Am I a bad person for being so angry? No, it's completely natural that you would have a lot of anger in you about the kinds of things that have happened in this house. In fact in many ways it's a healthy sign; you *should* be angry when people are treating you, or each other, badly.

Is my anger going to cause me to hurt people? No, you always have the choice not to hurt anyone, no matter how enraged you feel. You don't have to be afraid of your anger.

Can my fantasies of hurting someone cause actual harm to that person? No. It's common for kids who witness abuse or violence to fantasize about hurting the abusive person. Those thoughts do not have magical effects, even though it seems like they could.

Am I going to turn out like my dad? Not if you don't want to. His problem isn't that he's angry; it's that he's disrespectful and he makes excuses. As long as you respect women and children, and you realize that you can make better choices, you won't be like him.

When I'm angry, does that give me special rights about how I behave? No. You can't justify mean behavior by blaming it on how angry you were. I know that [Dad, your stepdad] uses his anger as an excuse, but it isn't okay when he does it either.

"My kids need me to have very direct conversations
with them about their anger."

Distinguishing Between Feelings and Reality

Your negative feelings about yourself do not reflect reality. Emotions are just emotions; they are very important to you, and you should pay careful attention to them, but they do not tell you what is *real*. Your mind and your wisdom have the job of sorting out what is accurate and real.

In other words, when you are feeling that you aren't very smart, or that no one would want you for a friend, or that you are unattractive, those are just feelings; they are not the truth about you.

Our emotions come from a range of sources. Yes, to some extent they are connected to what is happening right now. But they also spring from painful experiences we had in the past, and from lies and misinformation we've been exposed to along the way.

Let's say, for example, that you are feeling incompetent today. Part of that feeling may come from a mistake you just made. But it's also growing from times when you were put down by other people when you were a kid (we've all had lots of those). Another big contributor is the ways in which your partner devalues you. These all add up to create a situation where your feelings contain a lot of messages that aren't accurate about you.

You have a deep wisdom inside that knows the truth about you, and about other aspects of life. Feel your feelings—it's important not to push them away—but don't be guided by them. Think through issues carefully, and then tap into your well of wisdom. That is the place you want your beliefs about yourself, and the direction of your life, to come from.

※ ☜

"My negative feelings about myself are
just feelings, including a lot of old stuff.
The reality is that I'm a good person."

He Wants Sex at the Wrong Times

Verbal abuse is not sexy. Intimidation is not sexy. Public humiliation is not sexy. Ruining the day is not sexy. So why does he think that a short period of time—say a couple of hours—after he's been treating you terribly could somehow be a good time for sex? He really thinks that this is when you are going to be in the mood?

Not exactly. The problem is that he isn't thinking about you at all; he's thinking only about himself. He wants sex to reassure himself that he hasn't driven you away, and that he still has access to your body. He thinks that if he can get you to have sex, that also means he has erased from history the destructive acts he did earlier. And he wants to have sex because in some twisted way his ugly behavior made him feel close to you, even though it made you feel anything but.

Because of the ways he's been tearing you down, it can get hard for you to say no to sex that you don't want; you may end up feeling like giving him what he wants is the only way to settle him down so that he doesn't launch into more abuse, or even violence.

He is the one whose reactions are unhealthy, not yours. The feelings you are going through are completely natural for a woman who has been demeaned and bullied. When he has sex with you following one of his incidents, that is a form of sexual abuse, even if you don't—or can't—fight him on it. Keep reminding yourself that the sickness is in him, not in you.

"Sex after abuse is additional abuse."

The Relationship Dead Zone—Part 1

Sometimes a relationship feels like it has broken up while you're still together. You are still living in the same place and going about your daily routines, but you might as well be strangers; you are barely speaking to each other, you're avoiding each other's eyes, you don't touch each other in bed. The tension is thick but mostly unspoken, and the squabbles you do have are mostly about small stuff, not about the real issues.

This is what I call the Relationship Dead Zone.

The first question to ask yourself is whether this is an "us" problem or a "him" problem. Sometimes when a woman says, "We aren't speaking to each other," she really means, "He's not speaking to me." Trace this silent period back to its roots; did it begin when you stood up to him about something? Did you call him out on a bad way he was treating you? Did you refuse to do something that he was dictatorially ordering you to do?

In short, are you being punished for resisting his control?

A destructive man holds tightly to the belief that he has the *right* to control you. So when you refuse to be pushed around by him, he feels entitled to get you back for that. He is locked into highly distorted thinking.

If you conclude that this Dead Zone is indeed a form of retaliation by him, stop thinking of it as something that is happening *between* you and reframe it more accurately as something that he is *doing*. Clarifying for yourself what is happening will help you figure out how best to handle it.

"I don't have to live like we're strangers
in the same house. Something has to change."

"But I Owe Him a Lot"

Many women have spoken to me about their sense of indebtedness to their partners. Here are just a few of the many stories I've heard:

- "I was a drunk when we met and he helped me get sober."
- "I was broke and he took me in and let me live at his place."
- "I've learned so much from him, and he has helped me a ton."
- "He has really been there for me through some hard times in life."

It's great that he made these kinds of contributions to your life. But acts of generosity and assistance by a partner can cause confusion when they come mixed with periods of treating you badly. Here are key points to keep in mind so that you stay clear about all this:

1. People give to each other in relationships; that's normal. In other words, the fact that he at times has been supportive or come through for you does not make him unusually generous. In a healthy relationship, partners make sacrifices and do each other big favors. Your partner may make it sound as though what he has done is so special that you owe him endless gratitude and devotion, but you don't.

2. He's gotten a lot from you. You have given him love, affection, support, companionship. And you have shown him much more consistent kindness than he has shown you. He may make it sound as though the giving in your relationship has been a one-way street, but he wouldn't have stuck around unless he was getting a lot out of it himself.

3. You never owe it to anyone to put up with mistreatment. And you never owe anyone your life. If your partner did big things for you, then you owe him appreciation for what he did—which I'm sure you've already given him lots of. That's all. His moments of generosity or assistance do not give him any license to control you, insult you, act selfishly, or frighten you.

In fact, at this point the debt is the other way around; because of his destructive behaviors toward you, he now owes *you*. And what he owes you above all is to respect whatever you decide about whether you want to keep pursuing a relationship with him or not, and on what terms.

"I receive, and I give back. I don't owe him another minute of my life; from here on whatever I choose to give him is my choice."

"I Feel Like I'm Losing My Mind"

Maybe he's telling you you're crazy. Or maybe he's making you crazy. Either way, you can sort it all out. You're going to be okay. You're not crazy.

Insanity is not about being overemotional; it is a powerful set of dangerous and destructive behaviors combined with delusions about reality. So if you end up crying or screaming or pacing wildly around the house after your partner has messed with your mind with his twisted tactics, that has nothing to do with being crazy. He will of course label you overemotional, but in the first place he's wrong; your reactions are completely understandable given what he's pulling. And even if you were overemotional, that doesn't at all equal "crazy."

He also may say that the fact that you think he's abusive shows that you are delusional. Well, viewing someone as abusive is an opinion; you can't be delusional for having an opinion of him that he doesn't like. (Delusional would be if, for example, you keep thinking that he's the Queen of England.) Or he may say that you are delusional because you suspect him of cheating on you; but his behavior would make most women suspicious, wouldn't it? Or he may say that you're delusional because you think your friends and relatives care about you. But he's lying; they do care about you, and he knows it. Your partner wants you to believe that you're crazy so that he can have complete power over you, and so that he won't have to look at himself. The alternative would be for him to face the fact that he is treating you terribly, and that he's the one whose thinking is twisted.

A final thought: If you have gotten in worse and worse shape emotionally and mentally the longer you've been with him, that isn't proof that you have deep problems; if anything, it's proof that he's not good for you.

*"There's nothing wrong with my mind.
If anyone here is crazy, it's him."*

Fighting Fair with People You Love

Whoever said "Love means never having to say you're sorry" could not have been more wrong. The people we feel closest to are the ones we should treat the very best. Conflict is inevitable, but dirty fighting is not. So what does fair fighting look like?

The key point is to think about what the overall goal is of the conflict. Let's say you are in an argument with a good friend of yours. Is the goal to see which of you can say the most hurtful things to the other? No. That's not fair fighting, that's war. Instead, you want to:

- Express feelings
- Have each person hear and understand the other person's side
- Make amends, such as apologies, or changes, such as agreements to do things differently

Certain behaviors will always get in the way of these goals. On this "off-limits" list are name-calling, put-downs, telling the other person what she is "really" saying or meaning, telling her what she is feeling, and not letting her do her share of the talking. That's all dirty stuff.

In addition, avoid accusing the other person of having bad intentions and confronting her in front of other people (which will embarrass her and increase the tension between you—this applies to kids too).

If you are upset with your friend, tell her what she did that you didn't like, without insulting her. Tell her what you need her to do to set it right, such as apologizing or fixing a problem she created, and state what you would like her to do differently in the future.

Finally, show her that you still care about her even though you're upset with her. Love should be unconditional.

You'll notice that I have been talking about a conflict with a friend (or a relative, or your child). That's where these principles can help you. They won't help much, or at all, with your abusive partner, so don't pour energy in that direction.

⁂

"When I fight fair, I make a huge difference
in the success of my close relationships."

GUIDING CHILDREN

Helping Kids with Their Anger—Part 2

A week ago we looked at ways of talking to kids about some of the internal struggles they have about their anger. There's one more key question they wonder about, and it's a little trickier than the others to answer:

What should I do about this anger that is burning inside of me?

The first point to tell them is that no matter how angry they are they can always choose not to behave destructively. They need to hear this principle over and over again, because they may have absorbed the false message for years—from your partner—that anger causes people to "lose control."

But kids also need to know how to keep their anger from eating them up emotionally and causing long-term harm. What are positive ways that they can deal with it?

Talk to you about it. Tell them that they can always bring their anger to you, and you'll hear them out. For this to work, though, you need to not talk them out of their anger or try to fix it for them; it's important to just listen and say supportive things like "I really understand how you feel. I can see why you'd be so angry."

Write about it. Encourage your kids to write in a journal, or to write poems or short stories, about their rage. Making art or playing music can also be a good channel.

Get moving. They can relieve some of their bitterness by going running, playing a sport, taking a dance class, or engaging in other vigorous physical activity. Help them think about how they could do this when their anger is getting to them.

Listen to music. They may have favorite songs that express angry feelings and can be cathartic for them. Encourage them, though, to also listen to music that soothes them, so that they can learn to settle themselves back down after experiencing anger.

Support them to cry. Talk to your kids about what an important role crying plays in relieving stored up anger. And when you see them crying, be supportive to them and don't pressure them to stop.

≻⊙≺

"My kids can work through their anger just like any other feeling."

If You Ever Think About Ending It All

Women who are in abusive relationships make up a large percentage of the people who call hotlines or seek mental health care because they have sunk into deep despair. If you have had days when you feel that there is simply no way out, you are not alone. During one of these periods, death can start to look like a tempting escape. But you don't need to take that path; there are other avenues to freedom.

The first thing to remember is that your partner is the cause of this darkness. He has taken control of your life, while simultaneously convincing you that you are a useless person. Some abusers are effective at making a woman feel like she is repugnant, as if she were a fundamentally diseased person; and the result can be that she comes to hate *herself*. But you are worthy of love, and you can return to loving yourself.

You deserve to live. You have so much to give to the world. Most of what you are struggling with is *his* ugliness, *his* depravity, *his* internal corruption. Don't confuse yourself with him.

You can take your life back. Every day of the year, thousands of women free themselves from abusive relationships. Don't give up.

Even if your partner is a terrorist, the style of guy who says, "If you ever try to leave me, I will hunt you down and kill you," there are ways to escape. I have talked to dozens of women over the years who have managed to get away from truly terrifying men.

Make a call *today*—right now would be best—to an abused women's hotline, or a suicide hotline, or both. In the back of this book, you will find national hotline numbers that you can call for help right now. If you don't have access to a phone, you can find a way to make contact through your town library, through your computer, or by checking yourself into a hospital. Reach out for help. We want you to survive and thrive.

ᴪ

"I'm not going to let him
drive me out of my own life."

The Proof That He's Wrong

Men who are controlling or abusive sound so sure of themselves, so certain that they are right. But the truth is that they are almost completely wrong, at least when it comes to describing the women they are with.

How do I know this? Because the very fact that a man abuses his partner shows that he has profoundly distorted thinking. In order to bully, control, or demean a woman, a man has to create a mental image of her that takes away her humanity, erases her intelligence, and casts aside her creativity; how else could he justify to himself the terrible things he does to her?

When an abusive client of mine says to me, "You don't know my partner like I do," my response is, "Actually, you don't know your partner well at all. I don't care if you've been with her for twenty years. If you really saw her as a person, you couldn't subject her to this kind of cruelty."

So let's throw into the trash all the bad things he says about you, no matter how sure of himself he sounds while he says them. *No one is a worse source of information about a woman than a man who is bullying or devaluing her.* Out of a hundred people, he would be the one you would want to believe the *least* about who you are. He's the one who has the poorest understanding of what you are like now and what you are capable of becoming in the future.

> "He may understand certain things about me,
> but in the big picture, he doesn't get me at all."

The Relationship Dead Zone—Part 2

Last week we were looking at those periods when you're still living together, but you might as well be in different countries because no relationship is happening between you. You're not saying much to each other besides hello and good-bye and the occasional snarl about some detail of daily life. And it all feels pretty miserable.

We looked at whether the cause of the silence was that he was punishing you for standing up to him. Now let's suppose that you thought it over and decided that's not really it. In fact, it seems to you that the cold war is actually coming to a great extent from you.

In that case, I'll ask you to begin by reflecting on these two questions: What safe ways (if any) have you found to stand up for yourself in this relationship? And what ways (if any) of standing up for yourself have you found that actually work? These are two different questions; the first looks at whether he gets revenge against you for challenging him, while the second looks at whether he actually does anything to address the concerns or grievances you are raising.

For example, when you try to talk about problems, does it go absolutely nowhere? Does he find a way to twist everything around on you, so that your complaint ends up being evidence that something is wrong with you? When you try to have a voice in a conflict, do you keep getting silenced? Do you end up wishing you'd never brought your feelings up in the first place?

Maybe you have lapsed into silence and resentment because you know that there is no avenue open to you to get him to deal with what's not working for you. Maybe your experience with him has taught you that nothing will work, so you've just shut off. And maybe that's the best way you can protect yourself, given that he isn't willing to deal with issues in a fair and constructive way.

If what I'm describing fits, give yourself some time to digest this reality, and to start reflecting on what that means for the future.

"If I'm having to be so silent,
it's time to look at why."

Letting Go of Convincing Him

Throughout this book I describe concepts to make it harder for your partner to confuse you, and especially to help you recognize when he is trying to make his behavior your fault. He is 100 percent responsible for his own actions; you don't make him do things. We look at issues such as how you decide which partner is the abusive one; which behaviors are controlling and which aren't; how you tell the difference between protecting your own rights and trying to take someone else's rights away; and when jealousy is okay and when it's not.

Now here's a crucial point about these insights: *They are likely to mostly be useful inside of you, not between you and your partner.* Putting a lot of energy into using the concepts I lay out in order to "make him see" is likely to lead to great frustration for you. Use them instead as a way to keep your own head clear.

Abusive and controlling men tend to have an endless collection of strategies to avoid having to look at their behavior and change it. They are highly attached to an unequal, privileged position in their relationships with women, and as a result are simply not willing to operate respectfully, since that would mean operating as equals.

So when you confront him with a concept like "payback," for example, he will probably quickly turn the tables on you and say that you are the one who uses payback against him. If, for example, you pull away from him emotionally for a period of time because his abuse just won't stop, he'll say you're using withdrawal as revenge against him because *he* refuses to be controlled by *you*. What he is doing is turning the concept of payback around backwards, saying that your efforts to protect yourself are a way to be mean to him.

You will almost certainly not succeed in convincing him; his thinking is too distorted, and he is too invested in not looking at his own behavior.

You are much better off, then, focusing on maintaining your own clarity, and not letting him cause you to feel crazy or blame yourself. This clarity will gradually lead you toward solutions.

꒰ ꒱

"The truth is the truth whether he believes it or not.
I don't have to convince him."

Building Your Independence No Matter What

Women who are involved in a relationship that isn't working tend to tell themselves, "If I decide to leave this relationship, I'm going to need to take a lot of steps to build a life where I'm not dependent on my partner. When I feel ready to leave, I'll start working on those steps."

But the time to start building your independence is *now*. Knowing that you can rely on yourself, and that no one person controls your destiny, will make you a happier person even if you stay with your current partner for the rest of your life. Every adult woman needs to feel that she can take care of meeting her own needs.

Feeling more in charge of your life will also improve the decisions you make about your relationship. The more you feel you would be okay without your partner, the more you won't settle for less than respectful behavior from him.

So start immediately working in the following directions:

Move toward economic self-sufficiency. Have a separate bank account. Keep some money hidden away that your partner doesn't know about. Plan a job future for yourself, including taking a training or degree program. Learn about personal money management. (See "Resources" at LundyBancroft.com, under "Economic Empowerment.")

Move toward emotional self-sufficiency. Be kinder and more loving with yourself. Put less energy into your relationship with your partner, and more toward your connections with friends, relatives, and other people you care about. Widen your social connections; the more people you have supporting you, the less you depend on any one of those people.

There's no reason to wait for later to start getting stronger.

"I need to be more independent whether I stay with him or not."

Are There Any Good Men Out There?

The perfect man does not exist. Prince Charming is not going to arrive, sweeping you off your feet and making life heavenly. No man can fulfill you; no single person can take away your sadness and fears. It will ultimately be up to you to build a good life, with or without a partner.

But are there good men out there? Yes, there certainly are. There are men who are kind, generous, and respectful, and stay that way through decades of partnership. There are men who can struggle through conflicts without having to hurt their partner for standing up for herself or silence her for challenging their views. There are men who are excited by their partner's triumphs and accomplishments, and who support her to pursue her dreams. Some men consider their partner their best friend, and cherish her accordingly.

The man who is devaluing and bullying toward his partner wants her to believe that his style of treating her is as good as it gets. So he may say to her, "You're lucky to have me, I'm good to you," meaning that she should be grateful he isn't even worse. Or he may say, "You're fat, you've got three kids, you screw everything up, what other man would want to be with you?"

He doesn't want you to have any hope that life could be better, and that someone could love you and appreciate who you are.

Over the years, I have spoken with countless women who left abusive relationships and found a kind, loving partner. These women found a real person, who wasn't without imperfections. But even with his flaws, it was night and day compared to the life each of these women had known with a man who cared only about himself and didn't care about the pain he inflicted on others.

~

"I deserve to be with a man
who loves me the way I am."

Helping Kids with Their Anger—Part 3

The past two weeks we've looked at ways to help kids understand, express, and release their accumulated anger. Today we'll examine some of what goes on inside of them regarding *other people's* anger.

Here are some of their most common questions, with answers that you can share with them:

Am I in danger when someone is angry at me? Are they going to hit me? "Anger is just a feeling; it doesn't make people act violent or scary. So you don't have to be afraid of someone's anger unless you know it's someone who hurts people. I won't hit you, so you don't have to be afraid when I'm angry." (But after saying this to your child *you have to keep your word*, and that means no spanking either. If you want kids to learn not to be afraid of anger you have to make your own anger safe for them.)

Is Dad "that way" because he's so angry? "No, Dad uses his anger as an excuse. Dad's problem comes from the fact that he doesn't respect women and kids, and because he pretends he doesn't have a choice about how he acts. Anger is not the problem." (Kids *really* need to understand this point in order to have healthy responses to their own anger and other people's.)

If someone's angry at me, does that mean I've done something terrible? "No. You aren't a bad person just because you've upset someone else. Your job is to try to understand why they are mad, and to figure out whether you should apologize. Remember that sometimes someone will get angry at you when you actually didn't do anything wrong. And even if you have done something you shouldn't have, you're still a good person."

If a person is angry at me, is that an excuse for them to be mean or scary to me? "Absolutely not. No one has the right to try to hurt you, physically or emotionally, no matter what."

Helping your children explore these questions about anger is one of the most valuable contributions you can make to their future; clarity on these points will help them grow into emotionally healthy adults who treat other people well—and who insist on being treated properly themselves.

"I can help my kids learn how to handle anger—their own and other people's—in healthy ways."

"Everyone Needs to Look at Their Part"

Our society is replete with philosophies that say that when something bad happens between two people, they have each played a part in why the injurious interaction occurred. Many self-help books teach readers to assume that they have "co-created" any emotional wound that happens to them. Therapists are fond of saying, "Let's look at what you brought to that interaction," after a client describes an experience where he or she was mistreated. And you've undoubtedly heard the expression "It takes two to tango."

These philosophies do not apply when we're talking about human cruelty. In the vast majority of cases where people are subjected to cruel treatment, they have done absolutely nothing wrong. And in the few remaining cases where they have done something bad, it's still unacceptable to be cruel to them.

There are, of course, some times when two people are equally responsible for why a hurtful exchange took place. But sometimes the responsibility is 70–30. And plenty of times one person did nothing whatsoever to contribute to what went wrong; the whole problem was created by the other person. Where did people come up with the ridiculous idea that responsibility is always 50–50? The assumption that responsibility in a relationship is always equal ends up doing particular harm to women who have abusive or controlling partners. You have 0 percent of the responsibility for why he mistreats you. You are responsible for your actions, not his. Don't let anyone—including your partner—rope you into sharing the blame for his actions or his issues.

"There's nothing 50–50 about what goes on between my partner and me."

"He Says *I'm* Taking Away *His* Rights"

Because of your partner's behavior patterns, in many ways your life is dedicated to trying to recover the rights he has taken away from you. So it can make you feel severely frustrated, or even a little crazy, when he starts to snarl at you that *you* are the one taking away *his* rights. Let's shed some light on a few of the distortions in his accusations.

He says you are taking away his right to express himself. Remind yourself that you have the right, as everyone does, to set standards about how you are willing to be spoken to and how someone can treat you. You do not deny him freedom by setting limits and boundaries about how he can act toward you.

He says you are punishing him. It isn't punishment to insist that someone listen to, and understand, how his behavior has affected you; nor is it punishment to demand that the injurious behavior stop.

He says you are controlling him. Telling your partner to clean up his messes is not control. He's the one who is controlling you by treating you like a servant. You have the right to speak up about how you are affected by his irresponsible and selfish behavior.

He says that you are intimidating him. Self-defense is not intimidation. When you threaten to call the police, for example, or you seek a protective order, you are doing so because his past behavior has put you in danger, whether or not he's ever gone through with actually assaulting you.

You aren't going to be able to convince him on these points; his self-centered outlook will cause him to keep turning the tables back on you. But keeping clarity *inside yourself* is important to maintaining your sanity. Recognize the times when he is turning reality into its opposite.

"When I demand decent treatment from him, that doesn't take his freedom away."

He's Wrong Even If He's Right

Controlling men use different tactics when trying to prove a point, including calling names and trying to make the woman feel stupid. What follows is a typical exchange between a controlling man and his partner:

WOMAN: "I don't get paid for four more days, so I'm going to give a postdated check to the guy who fixed the roof, and I'll cover it on Friday."

MAN: "That's really irresponsible. He could deposit it anyway, and then we'll get all these overdraft fees."

WOMAN: "He can't deposit it before the date; that's the whole point of dating a check."

MAN: "Sorry, Little Miss Know-It-All, but a check is good from the time it's written, as you would know if you didn't have parents who do everything for you like you were a baby."

WOMAN: "I am so sick of being put down by you. I told you, I'm not living with this abuse anymore."

MAN: "Stop acting like an idiot. You're the one who doesn't know what you're talking about."

The man will go on insisting that he's right, and in one sense he is: In many places you can deposit a postdated check. *But that's completely beside the point!* Why? Because being "right" doesn't give him any justification to control his partner by calling her names, insulting her relatives and her relationships with them, and trying to make her feel stupid.

This is a key point, and the controller does not understand it. The destructive man, for example, will probably come back an hour later with proof about bank policies, and then throw that up in the woman's face as if it justifies his verbal abuse, which it doesn't. Once verbal abuse (including a demeaning tone of voice) begins, the original substance of the argument no longer matters; the new issue is the verbal abuse, and that's all that matters until it stops.

So when he's behaving this way, he's wrong even if he's right.

"I have every right to disagree with him,
even if it turns out I'm wrong. That doesn't
give him any right to abuse me."

HEALING

"If I Leave Him, Will I Just End Up with Another Guy Like Him?"

When you first got involved with your current partner, he seemed like a great guy. He was kind. He thought you were great. He was eager to spend time with you. He was attracted to you.

But now you feel shaken up because of how dramatically he has changed. You feel like any guy you get involved with in the future could turn out to be another destructive person, and you'd never know ahead of time, right?

Well, actually, next time you can recognize the danger signs. You've learned a lot about relationships, and about men. You've gained wisdom the hard way. If only you'd been taught the warning signs of an abusive partner back when you were a teenager; unfortunately, girls rarely receive that key information.

So what have you learned? Watch out for a guy who is controlling. Don't let him separate love from respect; in other words, if he doesn't think about you and treat you in respectful ways, that isn't love. Don't get with a guy who has a chip on his shoulder against females, including one who is holding on to his resentments toward past partners. Stay away from the man who makes a lot of excuses and avoids responsibility for his actions.

And, above all, steer clear of the guy who can't handle it when you stand up to him. A safe partner is one whom you can challenge when you disagree with him or when you don't like something he did. A safe partner gives you space to be angry with him. A safe partner values your willpower, rather than trying to knock it out of you.

Yes, abusive men can keep their dark side hidden, but the warning signs are there early. Now that you know what to look for, you'll see them. You can trust yourself to find a relationship where you will be respected. (You can find more about early warning signs in *Why Does He Do That?*)

"I don't have to fall into this trap again;
I know what it looks like now."

Taking Proper Care of Yourself—Part 1

Spend a moment picturing yourself in one of your best caretaking moments from the past few years. If you are a mother, this image might be of a time when you were looking after one of your children and being especially loving and tender. If you don't have kids, remember a time when a friend or a relative was sick or troubled, or when you were nurturing people by cooking for them or helping them with a challenge. In your mind's eye see your kindness, your gentleness, your generosity.

It's time to get in the habit of turning that level of caretaking inward, giving yourself the absolute best of what you have to give to others.

If you do have children, it may be especially difficult to carve out any space to care for yourself. And if your partner is highly demanding and self-centered, the challenge grows all the more. But keep looking for opportunities. You will find a few at first, and then you'll learn how to find more as the months go by.

⚶

"I will take care of myself the way a wonderful
mother or a best friend would."

Good People Abound

You may feel shaken up in your view of the human race. Any woman who suffers serious mistreatment from a partner she loved and trusted struggles with feelings of betrayal. And betrayal can knock you off your foundation at a core level, resulting in the following:

- The world starts to feel like an unsafe place.
- Everyone's motives start to be suspect.
- You start to question your sense of what is real.

If your partner were terrible all the time, it would actually be easier to deal with in many ways; you would tell yourself, "Well, he turned out to be a jerk." But when someone you love goes back and forth between kindness and cruelty, generosity and selfishness, tenderness and intimidation, loving you and cheating on you, you can come to feel that it's impossible to understand people. Your partner may further feed this insecurity by encouraging you to think badly of others. He may tell you that people are lying to you or taking advantage of you, that your friends have hidden motives, that you are naïve in your dealings with people, that "everyone is just out for themselves." (He's talking about himself, without realizing it.)

Sure, there are sharks out there. But the world is full of so many thoughtful, caring, honest individuals. Most people *don't* use other people, or trick them, or threaten them. In fact, most people are doing their best to live ethical lives and to be decent and responsible toward other people.

So don't let your partner distort your outlook. Look for the good in people, and notice their efforts to make a human connection. Don't harden your heart. You will find many gems in the human race.

❧

"I will stay open to people and give them a chance.
I'm keeping my heart alive."

GUIDING CHILDREN

Who Sets the Tone in the Home?

Your partner knows how to win. He knows how to yell louder, use more devastating put-downs, twist logic into a knot, and "prove" that everyone else in the world agrees with him and not with you.

That doesn't mean he's right. There's a bumper sticker that says, "War Doesn't Show Who's Right, Only Who's Left." You could say roughly the same about control and abuse; all his behavior proves is that he has the power to wind up with the upper hand.

Try your best to let him be gone when he's gone. What I mean by this is that when your partner is out of the house, his attitudes and style may live on in how people in the family treat one another, but you can work hard to keep this from happening. You don't have to become hypercritical of your kids, or super-restrictive, or sarcastic, just because he is. In fact, it will help your kids a lot if you can be everything the opposite of what he is.

Second, soft voices can sometimes be surprisingly powerful. The constructive messages you give your children while reading them bedtime stories, while cuddling with them before they go to sleep, or while sharing a meal with them when your partner isn't home, can carry more weight than you might imagine. The secret is to be warm, keep your messages consistent, and speak in a tone that conveys that you deeply believe what you are saying.

You don't have to mention what your partner has said in order to contradict his negative messages; it's actually better if you don't. On a deeper level, your children will absorb over time the fact that you are teaching them a very different philosophy of life than he is.

"Without being obvious about it, I can shift our
family's culture in a healthy direction."

Drawing Strength from Animals

Human beings are awfully complicated, aren't they? Some days, it seems that figuring out how to get along with people, deciding whom to trust, and trying to put our experiences into words just all seems overwhelming. At those times, we need a connection with little or no conflict, powerful loyalty, and no need to talk about anything. Sounds like what is called for is an animal friend.

The healing power that animals have in human life has been gaining increasing recognition in recent years. Several programs across the continent now use horses in helping people to recover from trauma. Service dogs are being used not just for people who are blind or have other physical challenges, but also to assist with emotional challenges or breakdowns.

If you already have a pet, open your heart to the healing energy and love that can be transmitted to you by the animal. And if you don't, see if you can spend more time with animals that belong to friends, or visit a farm where there are horses or other animals that you can be around (and maybe you'd like to take horseback riding lessons). You also might volunteer to help look after animals at a shelter.

And speaking of shelters, there are always pets in need of a home. Unless your partner is cruel to animals, this might be a good time for you to have the companionship of a dog, cat, or rabbit. (Just be aware that if you are getting ready to leave your relationship, having a pet can be an additional complication when you take off.)

⚓

> "People aren't the only source of love
> and wisdom in the world; we have many
> cousins in the animal kingdom."

"Constructive Criticism"

There are countless tactics that an abusive guy uses to convince the woman that his bullying behaviors are her own fault. In one common example, the man says something along these lines to his partner: "I'm just trying to give you a little constructive criticism, and you can't take it. If you would be a little more open to what I'm telling you, you could better yourself. But, hey, if you want to just stay stuck in your problems, that's up to you."

Maybe he has a point, right?

Wrong. He is absolutely wrong.

How can I be so sure? The easiest way is to take a look at what truly constructive criticism looks like. When people are actually trying to give you useful feedback, their comments have the following qualities:

- They describe what bothers or upsets them about your *behavior*, they don't tell you what's wrong with you as a *person*.
- They speak to you in a respectful tone of voice, as an equal, not as a superior. They understand that feedback can be hard to hear.
- They explain what they wish you would do differently.
- They acknowledge that they have things that they need to work on too.

Does your partner's criticism of you meet the description from this list? I'm willing to bet it misses by a mile. And that means he's really just putting you down; he is calling it "constructive criticism" so that he can blame you for not liking the way he's talking to you.

It's good to be open to feedback from someone who is approaching you in a caring way and who does not make you feel belittled. But when the comments are disrespectful, try to internalize them as little as you possibly can.

$\times$ $\mathcal{D}$ 元

"I can tell the difference between someone
who is trying to support me and someone
who is tearing me down."

"Does Taking My Life Back Mean Leaving Him?"

You know what a good person your partner could be, because you've seen him at his best. You can't help thinking about the times when he's been fun and loving and romantic, and how delightfully crazy he has been about you, especially back in the early days of your relationship. Now you're realizing that the quality of your life is going downhill and that you need to take your power back. But you don't want to give up on the hope that he will learn how to stay away from his bad side. So you struggle with the question "Is breaking up with him really the only way I can reclaim my own life?"

Time will tell. I have met a few women who have stayed in an abusive relationship and found ways to get past the man's efforts to dominate her; but honestly, they are in the minority. Here are strategies you can try that occasionally work:

Use the police and prosecution. The next time he commits a crime against you, call the police, and follow through with the process *all the way*, until he pleads guilty or is convicted. (Nothing less will do any good; believe me, it's been tried endlessly.) Some men make real changes once they have a criminal record for domestic violence.

Leave him for an extended period of time, not less than three months. And you might have to do it a second time and a third time. Some men finally get serious about stopping their abuse if each new incident leads to at least three more months of being on their own. But this doesn't work unless you leave him *each* time he acts out again, *including verbal abuse.*

Separate yourself from him emotionally. Be polite, but stop having a lot of conversation, stop having sex with him, and don't look to him for support. Put all of your energy into your friends, relatives, and other connections. Don't reconnect with him until he makes meaningful changes, and pull away again as soon as he backslides. Don't take any of his promises seriously; actual action is the only thing that matters.

※

"I can't make him change; he'll only change
if he decides to do the work."

One Step Toward Healing

You are not your partner.

His issues are not your issues.

His behavior is not your behavior.

His destructiveness does not prove that anything is wrong with you. You are separate people.

A voice in your head may tell you, "Well, I chose him. And I'm choosing to stay with him." But, first of all, you *didn't* choose him the way he is now. You chose someone whom you thought was a really good guy. And you may have many reasons for staying with him, including your children, your financial situation, your caring for him, and your hopes that he'll change. You aren't looking for mistreatment, and you aren't "just like him."

Make this distinction between you and your partner even greater by paying close attention to how you treat people as you go through your day. Watch your interactions with friends, with cashiers, with strangers on the street, with your children. Focus on being kind, patient, and respectful in every interaction. Be honest and supportive. When you need to raise a grievance with someone, bring your complaint in a tone of caring and decency, not of hatred and rejection. When your kids are driving you crazy, express your anger or annoyance without putting them down or speaking in a demeaning tone to them.

The more you live each day this way, the better you will remind yourself that your partner's unhealthy patterns are not yours. And seeing yourself as separate from him will help you to heal from his mistreatment of you.

✂ ⊃

"I treat people well, and I'm going
to do it even better in the future."

YOUR OWN BEST FRIEND

Taking Proper Care of Yourself—Part 2

Last week we started examining some ways that you can become more nurturing and caretaking toward yourself. Save some of your best loving energy to pour in your own direction. You deserve and need it.

Think broadly about how to attend to your range of needs. Cook tasty, healthful food for yourself. Make yourself go outdoors, to see the sky and move around in spaciousness. Exercise, ideally in a form that you enjoy; remember, for example, that dance and yoga can be vigorous forms of exercise. Cater to the other needs of your body; relax in a bath, put lotion or oil on your skin, do some stretching, take care of sexual needs by yourself that your partner isn't meeting.

Emotional needs are as important as physical ones. Work to have a kind discussion with yourself in your mind, rather than having an inner dialogue of criticism and impatience. Search for ways to fit some human contact into each day with someone other than your partner; a few phone calls, a lunch with a friend, a walk after work, emailing with your sister. Pay careful attention to what is good for you emotionally and what isn't.

Pour as much love inward as you pour outward. You will enrich your life, and you will actually have more to give to others.

"I am one of the people that should
most receive my loving care."

He's Not an Expert on People

During the coming several days, I would like for you to look around at the people in your life, both the ones whom you see fairly often and those who live far away, and reflect on the following question: How has my partner shaped my view, positively or negatively, of these people?

The controlling man wants his partner to like the people that he likes, dislike the people he is bothered by, and trust only the ones that he has put his seal of approval on. And he may cast a lot of aspersions, especially about anyone you connect with. He might say about Friend #1, "She's using you," then tell you that Friend #2 "is just pretending he wants to be your friend but really he's after you," and that Relative #1 "is always running your life."

Here's a critical point: Over time, these negative ways that he characterizes people *will start to seem true to you*. A controlling partner colors your view over time, without you necessarily realizing it. He does so by sounding extremely certain of the pronouncements he makes. Depending on his style, he may also convince you that people are lying or sneaking around you, and try to make you feel unsafe to trust anyone; in this way he can make you more reliant on him.

So start taking a fresh look at *everyone*, including people you may have come to really dislike. It's time to reevaluate and form your own opinions about each person, based on your own experience and not on anything you've been told.

> "I don't need someone to tell me who is
> trustworthy and who isn't—I can figure
> it out for myself, and do it better."

GUIDING CHILDREN

"The Kids Don't Know What's Going On"

Yes, they do.

They may not know the details, but they know the dynamics.

Children have powerful radar for what is going on in their homes. When the atmosphere is tense between their parents, they pick up on it. If the fighting has been going on for weeks or months, they absorb the tension. If one parent is afraid of the other, they can sense it, and they start to feel less safe themselves. If their mother is getting torn down, they take it all in.

Parents often believe otherwise, saying, for example, "Oh, we wait until the kids are asleep to have our arguments." But children pick up far more than adults realize.

Haven't you had the experience of being surprised by something one of your children knew? Haven't you ever asked one of them, with considerable surprise, "How did you know that?" Well, just as their knowledge on other subjects catches you by surprise, so would their awareness about the dynamics of your relationship with your partner. They sense tone and notice facial expression. They hear more from their rooms than you think they do. They pretend to be asleep sometimes when they aren't. And siblings share a lot of information with each other.

Children often give their parents no inkling of how much they know. But they are digesting it all, and it is affecting them.

You can help your children deal with the tensions and dynamics in the home. But to do so, you have to stop pretending that everything is okay, which the kids already know isn't true. Trust yourself to find constructive ways to talk to them about what's happening; by opening the door to these unmentionable issues, you can build closeness with your kids and help them learn some of life's most valuable lessons.

"I don't have to pretend with
my children that this isn't happening."

EACH NEW DAY

A Man and His Best Friend

During the dark periods of an unhealthy relationship, you may be asking yourself, "Do relationships between a man and a woman ever get any better than this? Or is this just the way men are?"

The answer is that there is nothing genetically wrong with men. Your partner wants you to believe that you are the cause of his mean behavior. He sends you the message that he would value you if you were worth valuing. In short, he wants you to think that all men are like him, and that the fault is with you.

Not all men are like him. In fact, there are men who treasure their partners. There are men who consider their partners their best friend, or at least one of their best friends. I know men myself who speak fondly and respectfully about their partners after decades of being together. In my travels I talk to other men who are on work trips and just can't wait to get home to spend time with their wives.

There are men who love long, interesting conversations with their partners. There are men who consider their wives or girlfriends their favorite person to sit down with to watch TV, or to join for a walk in the park, or to meet for tennis.

Of course longtime couples aren't dizzy in love as if they just met. But I observe endless examples of pairs who have been together for years and years, and who have raised children together, who still enjoy each other's company, still have sexual energy between them, and still put much more focus on what they love about each other than on what bothers them. This is how it can be, and this is how it should be.

"I deserve to be valued and
treasured like a best friend."

Your Strengths Upset Him

You undoubtedly have to deal repeatedly with times when your partner's angry or upset behavior is baffling to you. Your mind starts to race as you ask yourself, "What on earth could have set him off? What is this all about?"

Sometimes the answer is that he can't tolerate the fact that you have personal strengths. He wants you to be like putty in his hands, without strong opinions or abilities; yet at the same time, he wants to criticize you for being a weak person. In other words, there's no way to win with him.

For example, he is likely to:

- Accuse you of using sloppy thinking or of being stupid at precisely those moments when you are being the clearest and making the most sense
- Accuse you of making poor decisions about what people to have close to you in your life precisely when your relationships are at a strong and healthy point
- Accuse you of wasting your time with respect to the work you're doing precisely when you are feeling the most progress at work or the most satisfaction in it
- Attack your spiritual or religious beliefs or practices precisely when they are giving you the greatest inspiration and guidance
- Call you a bad mother and say that you are messing up the children precisely when they are doing well and your relationships with them are strong

In many ways it's easier to notice when your partner tries to hurt you in your weak spots. Start to pay attention to how often he's attacking you exactly where you are feeling strong and doing well. That pattern reveals so much about his desire for power and control, and his unwillingness to enter into a true partnership with you. A healthy partner would be delighted by your strengths and successes.

"His criticisms are often
a sign of what's *right* with me."

SURVIVING TO THRIVE

Struggling with Whether to Have an Abortion

No woman wants to have an abortion. Facing the question of whether to terminate a pregnancy is an emotionally laden process. Questions arise that carry tremendous weight: "Am I emotionally ready to raise a child? Do I believe that abortion is a moral option? Can I afford a child financially? Is my partner going to be a good parent?"

These inner struggles can be intensified for women with destructive partners. The stress of raising a child while your partner mistreats you—or ignores his responsibilities—is huge.

It's tempting to believe that the arrival of a child will improve your partner's attitude and behavior, but the reality is that men who are controlling or abusive become an even more serious problem when children are involved. Some of them get a little nicer for a while during the pregnancy, but once the child is born the abuse goes full speed ahead.

If you are philosophically opposed to abortion, your values need to carry weight. But at the same time, you are understandably concerned that your partner's unhealthy behaviors could cause an unsafe atmosphere for your child. And it's reasonable to wonder whether you would be able to give the baby the best of yourself with him around.

At the same time, your partner has no right to pressure you to have an abortion if you don't believe in it; he's way out of line if he bullies your decision in either direction. Unfortunately, research shows that abusive men are much more likely than other men to try to force a woman to carry a baby to term against her will, *or* to force her to abort a pregnancy when she wants to have the child.

Reach out to people you can talk to about your decision, especially people who will support you to do what you believe is right. Be aware that even "pregnancy counseling" services sometimes have a hidden agenda. You might want to contact a respected service such as Planned Parenthood, whose mission it is to help you reflect on all of your options, including adoption, without pressure.

Whatever you decide, you are a good person. Someone who is not living with the complexities of your situation has no right to pass judgment on you. Connect with the deepest parts of yourself, listen to your inner guidance, and go with what you believe is best. Be kind to yourself.

꒰ ꒱

> "I am the one who would be raising this child, so I am the only one who can determine the path."

HEALING

Managing Your Own Rage

Injustice is infuriating. If you feel enraged a lot of the time, you are having a normal reaction to how unfair and mean your partner's behavior is. In fact, feeling angry in the face of mistreatment is a *healthy* reaction;

it proves that you have self-respect still surviving inside of you. When an abused woman stops feeling angry, that's when I start to really worry for her.

But feeling enraged is uncomfortable, and it can take a toll on you over time. It's important to find ways to manage and channel your anger so that it doesn't eat you up inside.

Begin by accepting your rage. Our society puts out a lot of sexist messages that say that women shouldn't be angry, and that if they show anger then they're bitches. Don't let yourself be ruled by those false beliefs.

Find people *other than him* you can talk to about how angry you are. Every time you take your anger to him you'll end up even angrier than you were before, because he turns your anger back on you and hurts you with it. Take it elsewhere.

Use physical activity to help your anger move through you. Running and other forms of exercise—dancing, Zumba classes, or even a vigorous walk—can help you keep anger from getting bottled up. If you have a place to be alone, then you can release your anger through yelling, punching pillows, or throwing clothing around the room. Vigorous, angry movement frees anger.

Write your angry thoughts and feelings in a journal. Getting rage down into words has been found to be one of the most successful ways for a woman to keep herself emotionally healthy.

And finally, take action. If you are angry over and over again, that's a sign that it's time to make some changes in your life. Spend some time reflecting on what those changes might be, and then start moving toward bringing them about.

"My anger is a healthy emotion, and
I can learn to handle it in healthy ways."

Who Is the Controlling One?

Has your partner ever said to you, "You're the controlling one! You are always trying to control *me*! You're a controlling bitch!"

These accusations can create confusion for a woman. So let's clarify a few points.

It *is not* control when you:

- Demand that your partner treat you properly, insisting that your rights be respected (including demanding that you be spoken to with respect).
- Challenge your partner about the work he or she is creating for you (such as by leaving messes around the house).
- Press your partner to meet responsibilities that he or she is avoiding (and if you have to keep asking your partner over and over again, that doesn't make you controlling, it makes your partner irresponsible).
- Challenge your partner about behaviors that have large implications for the two of you as a couple (and for the family if you have children), such as abusing alcohol, gambling, ignoring the children, or being mean to the children.
- Call the police because your partner is hurting you or threatening to hurt you.

It *is* control when you:

- Ridicule your partner, try to make him or her feel stupid, or use demeaning names, especially when you are doing so in order to silence your partner or force him or her to do something.
- Physically or sexually intimidate your partner.

- Get revenge on your partner for not following your orders or for standing up for his or her own opinions.
- Impose double standards (make different rules for yourself than for your partner).
- Pressure or manipulate your partner into sexual contact that he or she doesn't want.

I'm willing to bet that when your partner calls you controlling, he is referring to things you do from the first list, and that when you call him controlling, you're referring to things he does from the second list.

And a final concept: The abusive man will call you "controlling" for *resisting his control*. Noticing when this is happening will be a huge help to you.

✎

> "Standing up for decent treatment for
> myself is the opposite of control."

"He Doesn't Seem to Like It If the Kids and I Are Close"

One style of controlling man, and a fairly common one unfortunately, gets bent out of shape when he sees his partner cuddled up with the children, or laughing and having fun with them, or showing in other ways that she is delighting in being a parent and that the kids are delighting in her.

He never admits, though, that he has a hard time with their closeness. Instead he passes his reactions off as superior judgment, telling her that she's spoiling the children, that she's over-involved with them, or that she's acting like a child herself. He may use anti-female comments to specifically attack her closeness to her sons, saying that she's making them into "sissies" or "mama's boys."

It's his issue. Don't let him pull you away from your children if you can possibly help it.

Why is he reacting this way? It can be a few things. First, the controlling man tends to be possessive, so he wants you all to himself and wants you focused only on meeting *his* needs, not the children's. (In other words, he's kind of a spoiled child himself.) Second, he's jealous of the kind of relationship you have with the children. But he's also entitled and lazy, so he doesn't want to do the work of building that kind of closeness with them himself. Third, the love between you and the children is making you stronger, improving your faith in yourself, and showing you what a good person you are. So he perceives your connection with them as a threat to his domination.

Your emotional and physical closeness with your kids is a wonderful thing. He should be celebrating your love, your laughter, and your support for each other. It's a human triumph. The fact that he can make that into a negative shows how twisted his thinking is.

✦

"The love that my children and I have for each
other is a beautiful and magical thing."

GUIDING CHILDREN

"He Is Way Overly Strict with the Kids"

There is a range of concerns that women bring to me about their partners' parenting, and one of the common ones goes like this: "My partner is controlling and dictatorial toward our kids. They don't have any freedom at all. He won't let them see their friends; he won't let them go places. Everything is just rules, rules, rules, and he'll give them punishments that are way over the top for little things they do wrong. I feel bad for them."

Of course, when your partner is a bully, you aren't in a position to just insist that he change his rules. But you can find ways to make a difference to your kids. The first is to communicate with them through eye contact, hugs, and other nonverbal messages, that you feel bad for them and that you realize that he's being too strict. The kids need to know that you get this.

Second, discuss the issue with them once they are old enough to understand. Explain that you and your partner disagree sometimes about the rules and the punishments, and that he isn't willing to compromise the way parents should. At the same time, you'll have to help your kids understand that they can't just go confront your partner with the fact that you disagree with him, which would make things worse for everyone.

Third, look for below-the-radar ways to give them some extra freedom. In principle it's best for parents not to undermine each other; but when one parent is abusive, the nonabusive parents has to make some separate decisions; that's actually what's best for kids in those circumstances.

"I may have to pretend to back him up, to keep him from getting even worse; but I'll find a way to let my kids know that I get it that he's too strict."

You Were Drawn to the Best in Him

Do you find yourself struggling with questions such as "Why was I attracted to a guy who treats me so badly? Is there something wrong with me for the fact that I liked him?"

Take a moment to think back to the beginning of your relationship. You weren't looking for an abusive partner, were you? Of course not. If you'd known about the kinds of behavior patterns that he was carrying hidden inside, you would never have gotten involved with him.

What did you love about him in the early days? Maybe his warmth appealed to you, or his sense of humor. Perhaps you noticed that he was smart and interesting, and you enjoyed conversations with him. Maybe he was good-looking, and you liked the way it felt to hold him. And almost certainly you were attracted to the fact that he was attracted to you, and that he held a high opinion of you. That felt great, right?

In other words, it wasn't his destructive qualities that appealed to you; you didn't even realize they were there. You were drawn to the best in him. You were looking for kindness, affection, and good companionship, and you thought you had found them in him.

So stop criticizing yourself for choosing an abusive partner. You didn't. You chose what you thought was a really good guy, who turned out to have abusive patterns that he had kept covered up in the early days. The fact that you believe in people is not something to feel bad about; it's a quality to feel proud of.

*"I wish he could have remained
the person he seemed to be at first."*

The Mousetrap of His Good Periods

I'm going to talk about mice for a minute. Scientists have done many experiments over the years to study the behavior of laboratory mice. One of the famous ones involved training mice to push on a little metal bar in their cage by giving them a favorite morsel of food as a reward when they did it. With some of the mice they would give them the reward every time they pushed on the bar; but with others they would reward them sometimes when they pushed the bar and sometimes not, following no clear pattern. So the second group of mice never knew when pushing on the bar would work and when it wouldn't.

The researchers observed an important pattern: The mice who were rewarded unpredictably actually worked much harder at pushing the bar than the ones who received a morsel reliably each time they did it. Psychologists refer to this discovery as the principle of "intermittent reinforcement." And it turns out that human beings, too, will work harder for unpredictable rewards than for reliable ones.

If you apply this principle to your own life over the coming weeks, you will notice that your partner's hurtful behavior patterns are having similar effects on you. The occasional times when he is loving or kind or sexy keep you more thoroughly hooked on him than you would be if he were a consistently good partner to you.

Observing this dynamic will help you start to unhook yourself from his toxic patterns.

᙮

"I deserve a partner I can count
on to be good to me every day."

Caution!—Part 1

Have you ever felt afraid of your partner? If so, take those feelings seriously. Notice whether you tell yourself things like:

"I'm overreacting—he would never really hurt me."

"He gets extremely angry, but he won't hit me."

"Yes, he has harmed me in the past, but he swears he won't do it again."

"He pushed me into having sex when I didn't want it, but it isn't like he assaulted me or anything."

These are all danger signs. Women's intuitions about their partners are crucial. As Gavin de Becker explains in his book *The Gift of Fear*, those scary feelings are there to alert you to dangerous situations.

Women get subjected to a stream of societal messages saying that they're too sensitive, that they perceive problems where none lie, and that they have nothing to be afraid of. This cultural training tells you, "Don't trust yourself, go ahead and walk right into danger."

An intimate relationship is a place where you should never feel frightened, no matter how furious or hurt your partner feels. If he's telling you that your fear is coming from somewhere else—such as your childhood experiences, or your supposed hypersensitivity—don't buy it. Ditto for anyone else who tells you that your fear of him is your own issue.

Taking Time to Cry

We are designed, deep down in our genetic structure, to heal naturally from emotional injury, including trauma. Amidst all of the focus on modern invention and discovery, we are missing the oldest route to emotional wellness: deep crying. There is no more effective painkiller on the earth, and that's what it's there for.

Crying actually does much more than just make us feel better; it literally heals grief, and does so more deeply and powerfully than any other emotional healing approach we know about. Eighty percent of women and 70 percent of men say they feel better after a deep and pro-longed cry. Tears wash our grief away.

Look for safe places and times to have a good, deep, no-holds-barred cry. It is free therapy, and will do you more good than most paid ses-sions would.

"Crying deeply is a sign of strength, not of
weakness. I can give myself this gift."

You Are a Smart Person

Yes, you are. I don't care what those voices inside your head are spewing. You can think clearly, you can make good decisions, you can manage your life. You probably did so for years before you met your partner. But even if you didn't, even if he rescued you from homelessness and alcoholism or got you out of an abusive home that you grew up in, you still have those capacities. You have had to use them to get as far as you have in life in one piece.

The reality is that all people have the capacity to be intelligent. We are born smart. You don't have to make a child smart; children grow up that way naturally. But you *can* interfere with a person's intelligence. You can make a person have trouble thinking clearly, you can make her *seem* as though she isn't very bright, by:

- Insulting her intelligence, telling her she's stupid
- Making her feel like she's constantly making mistakes, criticizing her all the time
- Ignoring her, never giving her any attention, never validating her thinking, isolating her
- Putting her in fear
- Violating her sexual boundaries
- Getting her hooked on substances

Is your partner doing any of these things? Is he interfering with your thinking, then calling you stupid? In reality, there's nothing wrong with your mind; it would work fine if he would stop messing with it.

"There is nothing wrong with my mind;
I just need a chance to clear him out of it."

Prejudice Pulls People Apart

I want you to make as many human connections as possible each day of your life. These connections can happen on different levels, from a two-minute interaction in the grocery store checkout line to an hour walking with a friend. Every moment of eye contact, every little joke or shared laugh, every small bit of assistance a person offers to another—all of these touch points have bigger significance than we realize.

And their importance grows for a woman whose partner is angry and controlling. When you are dealing with a lack of kindness at home, then those smiles and hugs out in the world are even more necessary.

This is a good time to take a look at any prejudices or assumptions that could be keeping you away from people. Friends may come in packages that you aren't expecting. Are you open to connecting with someone who isn't of your race? Are you judging people because they are single mothers, or because they don't have much education, or because they don't go to church? Do you stay away from individuals that you suspect are gay, or who have different political opinions than you do, or that your partner has told you are bad people?

This is a great time to stop passing judgment on yourself, and on other people as well. The world is full of great people who are trying to struggle their way through every imaginable kind of challenge. Open yourself to human connection in places where you would have previously thought it impossible.

ᒚ⟶ᐁᕼ

"I am going to turn what is happening to me
into a positive learning experience."

GUIDING CHILDREN

The Burden of Secrecy for Children

When there's a man living in the home who bullies people, the children start to keep secrets. They usually don't tell their friends about his behavior because they are embarrassed about it, especially if he is their father. They don't tell other adults, such as their teachers, because they're afraid they'll get in trouble if the abusive man finds out they've been talking about it. They may not even tell you what they saw, or what they felt about an incident, because they don't want to burden you or because they think they're not supposed to mention it.

Your partner may have threatened the kids that they better not tell anyone "what happened," meaning they can't reveal what he did. He may even have hurt them directly sometimes and then required them to keep it secret.

The hiding of these painful secrets is bad for kids. The emotions and memories that they carry inside of them are too much to be left alone with. Having to keep it all secret makes them feel like there's something wrong with them, as if the man's behavior somehow means that the children are bad because they are associated with him. And if your children feel that your partner's abusiveness is something they must hide, then they will start to keep secrets about other bad things also, such as if a bully at school is hurting them.

So help your children learn not to keep secrets about your partner's behavior. Make it an issue that it's okay to talk about.

><)><

"I'm not going to let my children get stuck carrying a weight no kid should have to carry."

When You Are Working Harder and Harder

Do you wake up in the morning feeling like you have to work harder and move faster? Anticipate other people's desires better and need even less for yourself? Give more love and shut off your hurt feelings? Quiet the voice inside you that wants to scream?

This is life on a treadmill. The angry and controlling man makes the rules, sets the rewards (few) and the punishments (many), and appoints himself judge. The whips he uses may be obvious ones: threats, snarling, violence, humiliation. Or they may be subtle ones: manipulation, deception, making you feel stupid, making you feel unattractive.

But either way, he has you channeled into feeling that you are not good enough, that you keep messing things up, that you just can't seem to please him. So you work harder and harder to get it right, to elevate yourself in his eyes and win his praise.

It isn't going to work, because you aren't doing anything wrong. The problem is in *him*. He doesn't respect your efforts. He takes way more than he gives (yet he still calls you "selfish"). His sense of fairness is twisted. He thinks he has the right to control you. He lives by double standards.

And since the problem is in him, *you can't fix it*. You can slave to improve yourself and improve your relationship, and five years down the road things will be even worse than they are now.

So start unhooking yourself, a step at a time. Little by little you have to take your heart back from him and put it in a safe place.

"Nothing I do will ever make him happy for long. I'm doing enough already. I have to focus on making *myself* happy and *my children* happy."

The Sculptor

The controlling man wants to mold his partner into a person of his creation, as if he were a sculptor and she were the stone he was chipping away at. He doesn't want a real-life woman with her own opinions and ambitions and willpower; he views her identity and her self-definition as being in the way. His mind-set is "Let me design the woman I want you to be, and then transform you into her; you'll be a better person that way, and I'll have the partner I want."

And then the harder he works to change you, the more he doesn't like what you are becoming! And to his twisted thinking it's your fault if the changes come out wrong, even though he's the one imposing them. So the more he takes control over you, the more he criticizes you.

Unfortunately, he isn't capable of learning from his mistakes. He won't think to himself, "I guess I should stop trying to change and improve the women I'm involved with. Maybe it would work better to understand and respect who they are. Perhaps I should support them to be the people *they* want to be, instead of forcing them to be the people *I* want them to be."

"The more I try to please him, the more dissatisfied he is. So it must be something wrong with him, not with me."

Caution!—Part 2

A responsible man hates the thought of his partner being afraid of him. There is nothing he would want less in the world. If she looked scared during an interaction, or if she told him later that he had been intimidating, he would have the following reactions:

- He'd be upset to hear that she had been afraid, and would act understanding and concerned about her feelings.
- He'd ask to know what exactly frightened her, and what he would need to do differently next time to keep that from happening.
- If she found his anger scary, he would work with her on figuring out safer-feeling ways to show and express his anger.
- If there were experiences from her past being triggered for her, he would think of that as a reason to be *more* careful about his behavior, not as a reason to trivialize her concerns.

- He would make noticeable changes in how he did things in the future to keep her from feeling scared of him, even when—in fact *especially* when—he was very angry.

If your partner is not taking these steps, then the fact that he says, "But I didn't mean to frighten you," *makes no difference*. In fact, I can promise you that he will scare you again, even if he swears that he won't. The man who skips any of the above steps doesn't really want—down deep—to give up his intimidating behavior. And therefore it will be back.

><)><

"I deserve support, understanding, and patience when I feel afraid. It's not okay to scare me."

Love as a Healing Force

Love is the most powerful healing force on the planet. People find important healing energy in books that they read, in spiritual systems, in therapy, in nature, and in many other places. But the deeper driving force behind all healing is to feel cared about by other people.

Your partner, unfortunately, only chooses to be loving once in a while, and the rest of the time he's distant and rejecting or he's tearing you down. His love of course feels good to you during the periods when he's being kind, but it can't contribute to your healing because it's too conditional and too intermittent.

And one of the things you most need healing from is the harm that *he* has done. Don't look for healing love from the same person who has hurt you over and over again; it is a dead end. (The same is true, by the way, for people who have a deeply injurious parent yet they keep hoping that love from that parent will heal them.)

Look, then, for ways to open your heart to giving and receiving love from other people. Work daily to keep a loving channel between you and your friends, your relatives, and your children. Notice when other people in your day, even strangers, are sending loving energy your way; you'll be surprised how many people move through the world spreading caring and kindness. Try to take it in, and then reflect that love back out into the world. There is no better way to free yourself from the negativity your partner brings.

"Love really does heal; it isn't just a saying."

Losing It

Many women have told me that one of the worst feelings in the world for them is when they start to behave hysterically or abusively themselves. They end up thinking, "I'm turning just as bad as he is."

To make matters worse, your partner may seem *happy* that you got "out of control." He loves it when you lose it, because then he can point at you and say that you are the crazy one.

You don't have to lose it. There are ways to maintain your dignity.

This isn't about convincing your partner that you aren't crazy; he *wants* to believe that, so he's going to continue to do so. Instead, it's about helping you feel better about *yourself.* And it's about helping your children feel that they can trust you to hold it together.

Here are some techniques to use:

1. Tell yourself, "I have a choice about how I behave, no matter how emotional I get." Don't tell yourself, "I can't help what I do when I'm upset," because if you think that way it will come true.

2. Stop trying to win, and get away instead. The longer you stay engaged in a fight, trying to make your partner see how unreasonable he's being, the more he can drive you over the edge. Get out of the room. You "win" by getting away.

3. Move vigorously. Go for a quick walk around the block, taking slow, deep breaths. Don't spend the walk planning the great "zinger" you will say to him when you get back; spend it figuring out how to disengage. Slowing down your breathing is key to calming yourself.

4. Focus on knowing inside of yourself how wrong he is, not on convincing him of it. He's never going to be convinced; that's why he has the problems he does.

5. Pay attention to your senses. The more you can notice what you hear, see, and feel, the more control you will gain over your own behavior.

"My behavior is my choice.
I can maintain my self-respect."

A Cheerleading Squad

Your partner's unhealthy behavior patterns can erode your connection to the world over time. Are any of the following dynamics playing out?

- You are keeping secrets from other people about his issues (such as his drinking, or yelling, or infidelity) because you don't want other people to think badly of him.
- You've pulled back from friendships because he is jealous of people you see, or because he doesn't like to socialize, or because you don't like the way he acts around other people.
- You've started to have a lot more conflict in your relationships with friends or relatives than you did before you were involved with him, but you aren't sure why.
- You just don't have the kind of energy for other relationships that you used to have.
- You're finding it hard to trust people.

A healthy relationship does not replace your friends and relatives, nor does it chase them away. In fact, when relationship partners support each other properly, their connections to other people in their lives are actually *strengthened*. You deserve to live surrounded by loving friends and relatives, your personal cheerleading squad. Perhaps from the position you are in now this seems like an impossible dream, but you can start building this squad one person at a time. Having several close personal relationships is essential to a high quality of life.

Make it one of your resolutions for the year ahead to build and strengthen your social network. Make new friends. Reach out to friends from the past that you have drifted from or had rifts with. Make your relatives a higher priority (unless they are toxic to you). Strategize ways to keep your partner's patterns from holding you back. A team of supporters is waiting to rally around you.

✄⋙

> "When I'm close to people, that's
> good for me and good for the world."

Those Days When the Kids Are Always Fighting

Some days you may feel like you spend more time arbitrating fights between your children than doing anything else. As soon as you put out one fire, another one erupts. At some point you end up yelling at them, "Why can't you just play nicely?! Why can't you just get along?!"

While we have no magic to bring about conflict-free relationships between our children, there are several adjustments that parents can make to help the kids' conflicts be less hurtful, and to train them to find their own solutions.

The most important change is to cut way down on how often you solve their conflicts for them. Try to stop being the judge who rules on which child is right and which one is wrong; I realize that it's the quickest way to end a fight, but in the long run it creates greater problems than it solves.

So strive to help your kids decide *for themselves* what's fair by requiring each child in a conflict to listen carefully to the other's side of the argument and requiring them to speak respectfully to each other. Then work with them to come up with their own resolution to the conflict, rather than imposing yours.

Handling a fight this way takes more time and energy on your part at first, but it will save you uncountable hours down the road, as your kids will develop indispensable life skills. The results will be that they won't constantly be looking to you to solve things (good news for you) and their relationships will go better (good news for them). Plus, they will learn how to stand up for themselves, which is perhaps the greatest success of all.

"My kids can work it out themselves. I will help them communicate instead of stepping in as referee."

Remember Your Dreams

You were a girl once, your mind swirling with imagination as it does for all children. Can you remember what your fantasies were? Perhaps you pictured yourself as a movie actor, or an Olympic skater, or a ballerina. Or maybe you pictured a family life, a cozy and loving home with spirited children running around, with games and humor, family vacations, birthday parties. See if you can remember those important dreams from your childhood years.

Then look at yourself at another time in life, when you were a late teenager or in your early twenties. At this stage your dreams may have shifted toward ambitions that were more connected to who you really are, to your personality and temperament. You might have envisioned developing an independent business, or creating a charity, or studying to be a schoolteacher.

When you're involved with a destructive man, your plans for the future can slip away. You get so focused on trying to handle his moods and demands, and just trying to get through each day, that your wishes for yourself get lost. It can even become painful to think about the future, because you feel so far off course from what your hopes were.

Start rekindling your dreams, even if it hurts a little to do it; it will be worth it. Make some notes in your journal, first about the visions you had as a child, and then about the ones you had in the years leading up to when you met your partner. Then spend some time reflecting on what you have written.

Your spirit needs you to keep your dreams alive. Don't let them disappear.

"I was a dreamer once, and I will be again."

CLARITY

Is Verbal Abuse Really Abuse?

"I wouldn't really call what he does 'abuse.' I mean, it's not like he hits me or anything."

Have you ever found yourself saying something along these lines? Many people believe that "abuse" only refers to physical beatings, the kind where the man leaves the woman with bruises on her body and swollen eyes. And they are badly mistaken.

Verbal abuse takes a huge toll on a woman, especially when it is combined with other injurious behaviors, such as controlling her or cheating on her. The put-downs, the humiliation, the ridicule—all of these can attack a woman's soul deeply, sometimes more deeply than assaults do.

What are the key messages that verbal abuse sends you? His vicious words tell you that you are *beneath him.* He sends the message that you *have no value.* His insults and rejection work to convince you that you are *not worthy of love.* His verbal attacks teach you that *everything you do is wrong.* His arrogance and demeaning treatment make you feel *stupid and incompetent.*

Tearing apart a woman's identity in this fashion can be every bit as wounding as pounding her with fists.

There is good reason why you feel emotionally injured. The problem is not that you are "too sensitive." Verbal abuse is one of the most toxic forms of human mistreatment. There is no excuse for the way he talks to you.

"It's totally normal for me to feel
wounded by his verbal abuse."

Caution!—Part 3

Few things in life are as confusing as having a partner who gets intensely scary, but then acts sweet, loving, and perhaps even lost and hurt at other times. When he has his vulnerable face on, it may seem like no one in the world would be less likely to harm you. You look at that side of him and feel that your fears must be blown way out of proportion.

Unfortunately, they aren't. The sad truth is that his times of turning soft do not reduce his dangerousness a drop. If anything those shifts actually *increase* the risk, because they show how quickly he can switch in and out of highly twisted thinking. When he is in his bad phase, he can forget that you are a human being with feelings and make you into a demon in his mind. It's important for you to go over a dangerousness inventory as part of assessing how much danger you are in. (See "Resources" at LundyBancroft.com.)

I have spoken to quite a few women over the years who seemed to be *underestimating* the danger they were in, but I can't remember any woman who was *overestimating* the danger. Listen carefully to what your deep intuition is telling you.

I don't want you to live in fear. But I also don't want you to think that you are manufacturing his dangerousness in your mind. Feeling and digesting your fear could be the path to a better life for you, because it could stimulate you to make your own safety your top priority. I hope you will.

✒️

"If I'm feeling scared, I need to listen to
that and pay attention to my inner signals."

Finding Five Quiet Minutes

At some point during this day I would like you to find a way to take a quiet period for yourself. Dealing with a partner who is demanding and self-centered creates a life where your thoughts are always revolving around him, and much of the time those thoughts are about tension and pressure. You can nurture your well-being by bucking this trend for at least a few minutes. Find some quiet space by going for a walk or sitting by yourself in your car, ideally somewhere away from home. If you can't get out of the house, go into your room or even lock yourself in the bathroom if that's the only way to be alone.

Five quiet minutes is all you are looking for, at least to start. You can find five minutes.

Once you've found the time and the spot, focus on calming yourself. Walk in a relaxed, steady way, or find a pretty place to sit. If you're indoors, sit comfortably in a spot that feels cozy to you. Take slow, relaxing breaths. Close your eyes for a minute and feel your breathing and your heartbeat. Then open your eyes and focus your view on the trees or the sky, or a houseplant, or a piece of artwork, or a photograph. You might light a candle and gaze into it; candle flames are exceptional in their ability to promote calm and centeredness.

Try to find a moment like this every day. It may seem like a very small break, but you will see that these brief quiet periods with yourself have a greater impact than you expected.

"I can find five minutes a day
to be quietly with myself."

When Your Partner Rewrites History

Do you find yourself having to struggle with your partner about how different your memories are of what has happened between you? A destructive partner can get you to doubt your own memory and to question your sense of what is real. He will sound completely certain of his version of events and outraged that you could claim that something different happened. His fury, and his tone of contempt, can cause you to scramble internally for solid ground.

Through this maneuver, *you* may come out feeling as though you've done something bad to *him*.

What's going on here? The main issue is that *he doesn't want to have to look at his behavior and how it's affecting you*. He's mad because he knows he did wrong, and he doesn't want to be called on it. So he's just going to change the facts around and turn the tables on you so that you're the one who comes out looking bad.

When he's in this mode, you won't be able to get him to stop twisting reality, no matter how hard you try. But here's the crucial point: *Inside yourself you have to hold on to what is real*. Go write in a journal, call a friend, or take a short walk, *reminding yourself that you know what really happened*. Don't let him take over your mind. You know what really happened. And the longer he denies it, the more that tells you about how deep his problem is.

"I know what he's doing. I don't have to
let him get me confused."

If Your Partner Is an Abusive Woman

Many women who are involved with another woman don't feel ready to have the whole world know that. When you start to realize that your partner is destructive, the sense of secrecy about your relationship can add an additional layer of complication to your reactions. For example, if you already fear that people will judge you negatively for being with a woman, you are going to feel extra reluctant to expose the fact that she tears you down verbally or has scary explosions. Homophobic people might take the stance that the abuse you are suffering is proof that same-sex relationships are unhealthy. (This is an absurd view, given the rate of abuse of women by men in heterosexual relationships, but that doesn't stop some people from adopting it.)

It's crucial to your well-being, though, not to let other people's prejudices cause you to end up isolated. Women who are being abused need to have people they can talk to about what is happening in their relationship. You can call a hotline for abused women anonymously; whoever answers the hotline is supposed to be trained in talking to women who are suffering same-sex mistreatment. And you can find people who won't judge your sexuality and who will listen to what you are going through. Don't give up on finding ways to reach out; isolation is your worst enemy.

"I can find people to talk to confidentially about how she is treating me."

Bad Behavior in Kids Can Be a Distress Call

Children's inappropriate behavior is not a sign that they are "bad" kids. In fact, they often are acting up because they are in distress and are trying unconsciously to call out for help. For example, children who live with an abusive man tend to experiment with treating their mother the way her partner treats her. *This behavior can, ironically, be a sign of how deeply distressed they are by his behavior toward her!* In other words, kids will try to make a terrible thing okay by playing with what they have witnessed, trying to make sense out of it.

What they need from their mother at these moments is firm—but not nasty—interruption of the behavior. They need to hear, in no uncertain terms, that treating Mommy that way is not acceptable. But the next piece is just as important: They need you to talk with them (when your partner's not in earshot) about how they may have seen Daddy behave that way but that doesn't make it okay. Daddy shouldn't act like that, and it isn't okay for the kids to do so either.

Then—and this is equally critical—they need to talk about what it's like when they see you treated that way. Ask them what goes on in their feelings and in their bodies when they witness those interactions. Ask them if they feel bad when they see Mommy spoken to that way, and see if they'll talk about it or show their feelings at all.

Even if they insist that they weren't bothered at all—as children sometimes will do when a topic is very sensitive—they now know that you see that it upsets them. And you have thereby begun a crucial healing process for them.

*"I won't tolerate bad behavior, but I'm
also going to look at what it's telling me."*

Your Freedom Is Your Right

I would like to work on separating two questions that may get jumbled together in your head. The first is "Do I have the right to stand up to him?" The second is "How badly will he make me pay for it if I stand up to him?"

When these questions get interwoven—meaning that you try to think about both of them at the same time—it gets hard to think clearly. So let's work on pulling them apart.

The key point for today is this: You have every right to stand up for yourself, all the time. Your partner does not have any justification for taking that right away from you. He may not like certain decisions you make, but he doesn't get to punish you for not giving into him.

I will go even further and say this: *The more you have to worry that your partner will punish you for doing something that he doesn't want you to do, the greater indication that gives you that the thing you want to do is valuable, important, and right.*

An abusive man is at his most punishing when the woman moves toward health, independence, and social connection.

You may decide not to stand up for yourself sometimes because your partner does such nasty payback against you when you do. I get that.

But that doesn't change the fact of what your rights are. And every time you feel forced to hold back, that's an indication that your partner is creating an atmosphere that is not fair to you.

✕

"I have the right to do what I think is best,
and to trust my own thinking."

Which Kind of Controller Is He?

Almost everyone gets a little controlling sometimes. We all can get caught up in wanting things done in a particular way: here's how to fold a towel, here's when to shift the gears. We want to say, "What are you doing? Here, do it like this."

So when does controlling behavior become a problem? There are people whose control is a bad habit ("annoying controllers") and people whose control is a style they are committed to ("coercive controllers" or "bullies"). How do you know which category your partner fits into?

The key difference is that the annoying controller doesn't retaliate against you when you tell him to stop controlling you. The coercive controller, on the other hand, is angry when you resist his control, acts entitled about it, and gets you back for standing up to him. And if you continue to refuse to give in, he gets nastier and nastier about it, saying that your resistance shows all kinds of things that are wrong with you.

Some of the most common ways in which a coercive controller retaliates include:

- Putting you down for not wanting to do it his way (e.g., "That's ridiculous, that's stupid, you don't know what you're doing" and so forth)
- Being cold, distant, and irritable after you resist his control
- Blaming you later ("Well, if you'd done what I told you to do, this wouldn't have happened.")
- Turning mean or scary because you won't do what he tells you to do

In short: If you ask yourself, "I wonder whether I should just give in, because I know he's going to make the day hell for me if I don't," then you are involved with a coercive controller.

"My decisions belong to me. If that bothers him, that's his problem."

Caution!—Part 4

Being involved with a man who can be two very different people at different times can shake up your ability to trust in the future. How can you predict what will come with a partner who is unpredictable? And the challenge isn't just that he has two sides, but that one of the sides shows you love and the other shows you hatred.

In this shifting context, it is no wonder that you might worry about him doing something really terrible, such as beating you up or raping you. What an extreme twist, to have to worry whether the person who claims to love you could carry out the most hateful acts in the world!

The fact that you are having to struggle with these questions alerts you to an important reality about your partner: *He isn't a safe person.* For most women, the risk of severe violence from their partners never even enters their heads; they know that would never happen. Your partner has no right to be creating fear for you. Whether he's doing it on purpose or not makes no difference; his behavior is unacceptable.

Even if he never does carry out a serious assault, he is having a big negative impact on your life and your mental health by making you afraid. You deserve, and need, a home and a relationship that are safe places to be.

✂━⃝🔆

"I shouldn't have to even think about whether my
partner could do me serious harm."

HEALING

The Turning Point

Sometimes we hit a point in life where we just can't take it anymore. Regardless of what the unhealthy situation is—a toxic work environment, a living situation with aggravating housemates, a marriage to a destructive partner—we may have gone along tolerating our distress for years, but one morning we wake up and we simply cannot live with it any longer.

The source of this internal shift is a mystery. Why after three years, or ten years, or twenty years of tolerating pain and stress does there come a time when we simply have to take steps, even if they feel scary, toward a better life? And what happens that makes all of our previous fears of change no longer hold us back?

Changing any of the fundamental pillars of our lives—our job, our home, our primary relationship—comes with risks. The next situation might be even worse. We might end up feeling alone and lonely. Some people we care about might turn against us because of the upheaval we're causing. We might not have the money we need to live at the standard we're accustomed to.

But a day comes when none of that matters. The dangers are still there, but they seem more tolerable than staying in the life we're currently enduring. We suddenly have courage that we lacked before. From somewhere has surged faith in ourselves that had vanished before, and energy that had been zapped out of us. We rise.

If your day hasn't come yet, it will come soon. One morning you will awake and burst forth, like a caterpillar out of a chrysalis becoming a butterfly. And if your relationship continues to stand in your way, you will end it, because you won't be able to stand being held back another minute.

"I will know when the day comes
when it's time to go."

YOUR OWN BEST FRIEND

Telling the Truth About Who You Are

Today I want you to write some things down. Get your journal if you have one, or grab a piece of paper. If it's hard to get privacy, lock yourself in the bathroom.

Think of the most common ways in which your partner puts you down, but don't write those. Instead, think carefully about the truth of who you are—the opposite of what he says, in other words—and that's what should go on the paper.

IF HE SAYS: "You are so stupid."
WRITE THE TRUTH: I am a really smart woman.

IF HE SAYS: "You don't know what you're doing, you're messing everything up."
WRITE THE TRUTH: I know how to live my life far better than he does.

IF HE SAYS: "You are so fat and ugly."
WRITE THE TRUTH: I am fine the way I am and I am attractive. (He chose to be with me, didn't he?)

IF HE SAYS: "You don't care about me, all you think about is yourself."
WRITE THE TRUTH: I have been very giving and loving with him, and I deserve a lot better than this in return.

The lies and distortions he tells you about yourself can start to seem real over time, because he repeats them so many times and sounds so sure of himself. It's important for you to state forcefully to yourself the opposite of his messages.

After you write these accurate statements about yourself (and hide them if you need to), practice saying them aloud when he's not around. Don't believe what he's saying about you. Write down what the "real you" is like, and fight to hold on to that.

And remember, if you have changed in some ways that you don't like since getting involved with him, the "real you" is the way you were before.

Is It Okay for You to Have Male Friends?

The answer is yes. Jealousy is a natural feeling, but it doesn't have to run our lives. Good friends are hard to find, and we can't afford to erase entire genders from the realm of possibility. If your partner can't handle you having male friends, that's his issue to overcome. If he loves you as much as he says he does, he should want you to have close friendships because they will add so much to your happiness.

Which leads to the key question: When you really love someone, is your focus on wanting to own that person, or on wanting him or her to be happy? True love looks much more like the second than the first.

Your partner may say, "How do I know there isn't something going on between you and that guy you're hanging around with?" There are several responses you could give:

"If you really love me, then that needs to include believing that my word is good."

"Isn't it better for you to deal with your jealousy than to stifle my life?"

"Isn't there less risk from a guy that I'm openly friends with, who

I introduce you to and bring around, than from someone that you never get to meet?"

"If I were the type to cheat, wouldn't I do it whether I had male friends or not?"

Some couples agree voluntarily that neither partner is going to have opposite-sex friendships. But if the truth is that you want to be able to have male friends, that's your right. If your partner finds that a huge threat, then he's got control problems.

> "I am a trustworthy person, and I don't want anyone telling me whom I can be friends with."

Don't Go to Bed Mad at Your Kids

One of the first pieces of wisdom I ever heard about intimate relationships was "Don't go to bed mad." Tensions that are left unresolved fester and grow over time, allowing small sources of bad feeling to become great big ones. The things that don't get said can destroy a relationship as much as the things that do get said. And when we hold back from conflict, we also end up holding back from expressing love.

This wisdom applies just as much to parenting relationships. Bad feeling accumulates over time between parents and kids just as it does between adult partners. Putting issues off until tomorrow is risky business, because life is going to come rushing in and sweep the bad feelings under the rug. And then later they will be released in a torrent, either from you or from your children.

Women who have controlling partners have an additional reason to maintain really clear communication channels with their children: Whether he does it on purpose or not, your partner's behavior is likely to widen any cracks that exist between you and your kids. As I explained in *When Dad Hurts Mom*, having an abuser in the home sets people against each other in a number of ways. Your best defense is to focus on resolving conflicts with your children, just as you would with a close friend. Try not to leave weak spots in any of your relationships that your partner can turn to his own purposes.

"The best time to work out today's difficulties with my children is today."

EACH NEW DAY

Trying to Manage Him

No matter how hard you work, no matter how patient and attentive you are, no matter how much you keep putting your own needs aside to focus on his, you simply can't keep a controlling or abusive man happy. Sooner or later, he's going to blow.

His behavior patterns can give you the illusion that you can control his eruptions, and he wants you to believe in that illusion. He'll keep saying, "I wouldn't have called you those names if you had just done what I told you to do," or "I smashed that vase because I'm sick of you not listening to me," or whatever his latest way is of blaming his behavior on you. When he's nice to you for a few days, or a few weeks, you tell yourself, "See, I can keep him in his good side if I pour all my energy into pleasing him."

And then when he blows again, he makes it your fault again.

Your efforts don't stop his next explosion; they just postpone it. All you can do is buy a little time. If you completely sacrifice yourself, you can probably put off the mistreatment he would have done today, or this week, or maybe even this month, but that's as far as it will go. The day will come when no matter what you do, it's the wrong thing, and he is going to have another one of his episodes where he viciously takes pieces out of you verbally or physically. You simply can't manage an abusive man in the long term.

There are two key things, then, that I would like you to focus on:

1. The next time he gets abusive, remind yourself that whatever he's blaming it on is not the real cause. He was going to explode sooner or later, because he considers it your job to fix life for him. It's not your fault.

2. Managing him as well as possible can increase your chance of getting through the day today, but it can't keep you emotionally or physically safe in the long run. You will have to find strategies for recovering the quality of your life that don't involve managing him.

"I am not responsible for what he does, even
if I wish I were. I can't manage him."

Maintaining Your Spirituality—Part 1

Most people haven't even heard of spiritual abuse. Is it a real thing?

Yes it is, and it's a form of abuse that can hurt a woman in some of the most important parts of her being. Spiritual abuse includes behaviors such as:

- Not permitting you to practice your faith (because he doesn't approve of it, or because he can tell it gives you strength)
- Ridiculing your religious beliefs, deliberately blaspheming what is sacred to you
- Not letting you teach your beliefs to your children
- Not letting you go to services
- Turning your faith community against you (such as by attending the same community and spreading lies about you)
- Using his religious beliefs as justifications for abusing or dominating you
- Making you feel that you're not living up to your faith's beliefs or aren't following your religion—or his religion—closely enough
- Not permitting you to have doubts or disagreements about faith or scriptures (when you are in the same faith as he is or when he is bullying you into joining his)

The list above can be upsetting to read if you're finding behaviors of your partner's on it. This might be an important time to write in your journal, take a bath or shower, or go out for a walk to digest these thoughts.

Spirituality can be a powerful source of strength, direction, and clarity. And that means that if your spirituality is being abused, you can feel knocked off center, as if the rudder guiding your life has broken.

Recognizing how your partner has been interfering with your guiding light can help you work your way back to your spiritual core.

✄

"When he attacks my spirituality, that is as serious as any form of control he uses."

Why Drinking Is a Dead End

Drinking certainly will soften the pain of being involved with a man who wounds you. But where does it actually lead?

The unfortunate answer is that it causes a downward spiral. The more you drink, the more power your partner has over you. And the more power he has, the more he can injure you emotionally. And the more injured you feel, the more you will crave alcohol to numb the pain.

Drinking will make you more dependent on him, and you want to be working toward needing him less, not more. It gives him a weapon to use to convince people that he's the one who has it together and you're the one with problems; a destructive man loves whispering to the woman's friends and family about her drinking. In fact, when the time comes for you to split up, he can use your drinking against you in fighting for custody if you have children, and in the court's eyes it will count more than his abusiveness does.

And finally, if your partner gets scary or dangerous sometimes, being under the influence of alcohol will impair your ability to make the kind of fast, clear decisions that you depend on to keep yourself and your children safe. You can't afford that.

At the same time, you don't need another reason to feel bad about yourself. So rather than feeling ashamed of your drinking, take it as a sign that your partner's behavior patterns have become too destructive for you to handle, and reach out for support and assistance. (See "Resources" at LundyBancroft.com.) Now is a good time to find constructive, forward-moving ways to deal with your emotional pain.

*

"There is a healthful path toward peace for me."

Is Sex the Only Way to Feel Close to Him?

Are you hooked on looking forward to the next time you and your partner will make love? Many women share stories along the following lines: "When we're having sex is pretty much the only time he's really kind and loving with me. And afterward, he doesn't complain about anything for a while; it's like he's finally happy instead of always finding fault with me. I'm so hungry for some caring and affection from him, and that's pretty much the only time it comes. Unfortunately, those times are pretty few and far between."

If this account feels familiar to you, you may have the style of partner who uses sex as a way to keep his partner longing for him. He may be a good lover when he shows up for sex, but he keeps intimate episodes far apart, almost like he's dangling them in front of your face.

The different aspects of his behavior fit together. The reason he is so stingy sexually is connected to his overall selfishness, and to his desire for power. He knows that you are craving intimacy, and he knows that he is increasing his control over you by rationing sex out sparingly. In other words, his sexual style is coming from the same place that his other devaluing and insulting behaviors are coming from.

Reflect on the question of whether you spend a lot of time hoping for lovemaking with your partner. If so, start working on getting yourself unhooked from that pattern. Stop looking to him for love and affection—he's not a reliable source—and start exploring how you can orient your life toward people who are more consistently kind and loving.

"It's not healthy to spend my life looking forward
to something that hardly ever happens."

"But I Let Him Do It"

When people picture an abusive or controlling man, they imagine him yelling, threatening, or attacking with his fists. These images leave so much out. They particularly miss one of the most insidious forms of relationship poison, which is when the man relentlessly—but not necessarily loudly—badgers, criticizes, pressures, and guilt-trips the woman until she gives in. This kind of vise-grip approach, where he just keeps tightening up the pressure until she can't take it, is especially common regarding sex, but it comes out with lots of other issues too.

Why is this pressure so toxic? One reason is that the woman comes out blaming herself. Over and over again, women say to me, "Well, I let him get away with it," or "I was stupid to put up with it." But the decision wasn't voluntary at all. You are not making a free choice if it follows an unending barrage of verbal pushing and insults and manipulation. And there usually is an implied threat, because you know from past experience that he is going to be cold to you for days to come if he doesn't get his way. Or he may make it clear that he will cheat on you if don't give in to him sexually. Threats don't have to be overt to be powerful.

You are not a voluntary participant when you have been bullied into doing things that you didn't believe you should have to do. And when a man bullies you into sex, or into a particular sexual act, that's sexual assault, not lovemaking.

"The fact that I was too exhausted or
intimidated to stand up to him anymore
doesn't make what he did any less abusive."

STAYING CONNECTED

Choosing to Isolate Yourself

When you are feeling at your worst, it's tempting to shut the world out and crawl inside of yourself. You may stop returning texts or phone calls, avoid gatherings, stay at home. You may not come out of your room much. You go into a kind of cocoon. You aren't happy in there—in fact you're feeling pretty bad—but the thought of coming out seems even worse.

A period of drawing inward can sometimes be a good thing. There's something about curling up into a ball that can help torn pieces inside of you to grow back together. The input pouring in from outside can start to feel like too much, so you just need to turn it all off. Good energy can start to be hard to distinguish from bad energy, so that when your mother calls you to see how you're doing, you feel as overwhelmed by that as you do when your partner snarls put-downs at you. You just need to push the "pause" button on life.

But isolating yourself also has its risks. Are you pulling away because you hate yourself at the moment, so you assume everyone else will hate you too? Are you withdrawing because you know it's time to leave your relationship, but you don't want to admit to anyone that you can't bring yourself to do it yet? Are you going inside yourself because you've decided there's no one you can trust?

If you are choosing isolation for these reasons, then spending a lot of time alone may do more harm than good. Cutting yourself off for the wrong reasons can send you sinking down into depression, and can hurt your relationships with the people who care about you.

Take a look at whether cocooning is working for you or against you. Either way, know that you are a much better person than you feel like right now. There are people out here, some of whom you already know and some of whom you will meet, who will be eager to connect with you as soon as you are ready.

"I need to reconnect with the world
just as soon as I can."

Helping Children Have Successful Friendships

In the modern world, kids don't tend to spend nearly as much time around other kids as they used to. During much of the day they are likely to be interacting with adults or sitting alone with pieces of technology— usually staring into some kind of screen—rather than interacting with other children.

Kids need to spend as much of their childhoods as possible with other kids. We can't turn the clock back to another time in history, but we can do our best to create as many opportunities as possible for social engagement. And we can teach our children how to have friendships that work.

This teaching is extra important for your kids, because your partner's example can lead them to sabotage their relationships. They may behave with their friends the way he behaves toward you, or they may become very afraid of conflict because of how mean they have seen him get. As a result, they may:

- Get furious when their friends stand up to them
- Decide that any friend who has some difficult aspects is a "jerk" and not worth dealing with
- Drop friendships as soon as there is any conflict, because they have no sense of how to work through it
- Expect friends to always cater to their needs
- Use insulting and demeaning tones of voice with their friends, put them down a lot, or be very competitive
- Focus on controlling their friends

Criticizing your children about these tendencies won't lead to much improvement, though you do need to call them out on their rude behavior rather than letting it go by. But what is most valuable is to take on the role of teacher. Say to your child, "Having good friendships is one of the most important things in life, and I want your friendships to go well. Here is what I'd like to see you try in order to make things work better."

Then *train* them. Train them how to have interactions that are fun instead of controlling. Teach them, with examples, ways of talking through disagreements and finding solutions. Explain why an insulting tone will drive friends away from them. Guide them in how to be a good friend the same way you teach them any other life skills. It may be the greatest gift you give them.

> "Kids can learn how to be a good friend the same
> way they learn their other skills."

No, This Is Not Normal

Once you've lived long enough with hostility, accusations, and the silent treatment, it can be hard to believe that there is anyone who doesn't live this way. You can get the impression that relationships are about people being *against* each other—because that's how your partner acts—instead of *for* or *with* each other. The whole world, in fact, can start to feel like an aggressive, injurious environment.

But the treatment your partner is subjecting you to is not just "the way it is." There are couples who are patient and kind with each other, who take an interest in hearing about each other's day, who have each other's back. There are so many good people in this world, including decent, generous, thoughtful men. Don't let your partner convince you otherwise.

And there are kind, loving families. I realize that life isn't like a television show where everyone gets along perfectly. But there are, truly, families that enjoy the great majority of the time they spend together, that laugh and have fun at dinner every night, that go for hikes and picnics together, that cuddle together at night to read stories. Don't give up on the life you want and deserve. It may be hard right now to see a way there, but keep that fire alive inside you. You will find your way to an atmosphere—and a home—of kindness, of mutual appreciation, of tenderness. It's real.

>⌒)≭

"This is not the whole story of what life can be."

Maintaining Your Spirituality—Part 2

Last week we looked at a list of behaviors that your partner may have used to hurt you through spirituality or religion. Some of the tactics involve putting you down for holding the spiritual beliefs that you do. Others involve using his own beliefs to bully or shame you. Either way, he's using spirituality to control or dominate you, and that's a form of abuse.

You have absolute spiritual rights, just as you have rights in any other area of life, that no one has any justification for taking away from you. These include:

1. You have the right to pursue your own spirituality. This includes that you can attend whatever services you choose to, be active in

your faith community, and get together socially with people you meet through that community. And it includes any practices or symbols that you want to bring into your home.

2. No one has the right to force his beliefs on you. People can try to persuade you, but they have no business telling you that you must see it their way, that you're a bad person if you don't, or that you'll go to hell if you don't. And that goes for your partner as much as for anyone else.

3. No one has the right to use his beliefs—or yours—as weapons against you, and must respect your faith even if he doesn't agree with it. That means that your partner has no right to make fun of what you believe. He also has no right to use his own beliefs as an excuse to mistreat, abuse, or control you.

Taking away a person's spiritual freedom is no different from taking away their right to free speech, freedom of movement, or any of their other basic human rights. Your spirituality is a precious part of who you are.

"He has no right to ever attack my spiritual
beliefs or hurt me with his."

SURVIVING TO THRIVE

If Part (or All) of You Wants Out of This Relationship

Do you have days when you find yourself thinking seriously that it might be time to move on?

The decision to end a relationship comes with powerful emotions of excitement, fear, and sadness. You feel excitement about what shape your life could take without your partner dragging you down. You feel afraid of how he will react to being left, and afraid of how you will feel being on your own. And you feel sad to give up a future that you once had such high hopes for.

The first step in getting ready to leave is digesting the fact that you are going to have all of these emotions at different times. It doesn't work to wait until you feel entirely ready to leave; that day is not likely to ever come. Women who are waffling say to me, "But I still have some hope left," or "I still have feelings for him," or "I'm still conflicted inside." This will not change. You have to go when you know it's time to go, even though your emotions are still moving in many different directions. Listen to what your deeper wisdom is telling you.

> "I can't wait until I'm ready. I have to
> go by my best thinking."

When He's the One Who Fixes It

Many days you may feel that your emotional world is driven by crosscurrents. You love your partner, and you fear him. He seems to love you, and he seems to hate you. He is the source of the greatest damage in your life, and you couldn't live without him. He helped you become a stronger person, and he wants to destroy every ounce of strength that you have. He is messing up the kids, and you need him to help you care for them.

This is a dizzying—and sometimes scary—set of contradictions to live with, isn't it?

One of these crazy-making contradictions plays out when he is the person who takes on the role of comforting you from the harm *that he himself did*. Perhaps sometimes you end up crying about how bad you feel about yourself—because of how much he's been tearing you down—and he ends up with his arms around you, telling you that you're a good person. Or maybe you finally collapse into illness from all the stress he is creating, and then he takes care of you when you're sick. Or maybe he injures you by hitting you, and then he's the one who takes you to get medical attention for your injuries.

This is a toxic dynamic. Notice when you end up feeling grateful to him because he was kind to you after hurting you. Notice when you feel close to him in the calm after the storm, when he is acting as a caretaker toward you after abusing you. If you don't notice these strange contradictions as they happen, you will be at risk to slip into depression, self-hatred, and shame. But if, on the other hand, you can remain aware of this unhealthy dynamic, his twisted behavior will be much less of a threat to your mental health.

✦

"I need to notice it when I feel close to him, or grateful to him, in the wake of abuse."

When His Put-Downs Sound True

Some of the hardest put-downs to deal with are the ones that seem to have aspects of truth to them. Maybe he's snarling at you that you can't handle money, and it's true that your finances really are in a mess. Maybe he's calling you fat, and in reality you have put on some pounds. Maybe he's saying that everyone thinks you're a psycho, and the truth is that some important friends have indeed turned against you.

Does this mean that he's trying to help you face up to things? Are you wrong then to feel bad about the ways you are being verbally torn apart?

No.

The truth is that even when he seems to be right, he's still wrong. Why?

1. Because he's exaggerating your difficulties in order to hurt you.
2. Because he's telling you that everything that is difficult in your life is your own fault, and that it shows what a weak person you are underneath. And that's false.
3. Because he's ignoring how profoundly his mistreatment of you has contributed to these problems, or even created them entirely. When you live with a chronically insulting and undermining partner, your self-esteem suffers, your friendships suffer, your concentration suffers. He's certainly not helping—he's making everything worse.
4. Because people's difficulties don't—and shouldn't—define who they are.

A man who chronically mistreats you is a terrible source of information about who you are. His vision is too distorted, too self-centered, and too self-serving to have any useful clarity, especially when the subject is you. In short, it is impossible for a man to see a woman clearly while he is controlling her, abusing her, or cheating on her.

"I will listen carefully to my own inner voices, and to people who love me and treat me well. His harangues need to go in one ear and out the other."

Why Is He Making It So Hard for Me to See People?

The man who controls his partner tries to make her feel alone. He tends, for example, to work hard to cause distance in her relationships with friends and relatives. He criticizes her if she gives too much attention to other people—even her own children—saying that she should be focused on him. He may listen in on her phone calls and read her emails to keep tabs on her communications with the outside world.

Why does your controlling partner want to cut you off from others? One of the main reasons is that he is addicted to having power over you. A woman who is isolated is more dependent, more afraid to stand up to her partner, more vulnerable. If he can keep you away from contact with other people, he can make sure that his voice is the only voice you hear, and that makes him become the Last Word, the Voice of Truth.

To his mind, isolating you keeps you from getting information that might help you (or as he would say, "that would turn you against me"). The more you have contact with the world, the more you might learn about your legal rights; or you might talk to someone who would help you realize you don't deserve the way you are being treated; or you might find out that he's been lying to you about important things. If you spend more time with other people, you will feel stronger. You will believe in yourself more, and you might take steps to get your rights back. He wants to make sure this doesn't happen, so he tries to narrow your world.

⌒

"I have a right to human contact with whomever
I choose. My life belongs to me."

Let Kids Be Kids

Childhood is not a stage in life that's about getting ready to be an adult. It's about being a child.

Our society has lost perspective on this point. Nowadays we're supposed to choose toys for babies (yes, babies) that will teach them numbers or colors, or that in some other way will make them smart. Billboards encourage you to spend your time with your children teaching them math or reviewing the letters of the alphabet with them. Wealthier parents are now dealing with competitive admissions processes for *preschools* to help them "get ahead."

Why is life all about tomorrow? What happened to today?

Certainly it's good to teach your children things. Do it when it's fun, do it when they're interested, do it four or five times a day. But spend the bulk of your time with them laughing together, enjoying the outdoors, joining in their wild imaginations, getting down on the floor and playing with them.

Children can teach us just as much as we teach them. They can show us how to live in the present moment, instead of being stuck in the past or looking toward the future. They can remind us how to make up stories, how to invent roles for ourselves. They demonstrate lack of inhibition to us, how to stop caring so much about what other people think. Children can be our best guides for how to live.

Push into the background your thoughts about who your children will become. Instead, focus your attention on respecting and honoring kids for who they are now.

✐

"My children and I are discovering life together."

Rethinking Charm

Nowadays we like nothing better than charm. When we meet new people, we love it if they are smooth, funny, entertaining, and flattering. We are charmed when they seem immediately ready to jump into doing favors for us. We love confidence, lively storytelling, and a sharp personal appearance.

And it all can be bad news.

The attraction to charm is a hard pattern to overcome. We have been heavily taught by romantic stories, by television and movies, by popular songs—by our whole culture, really—to fall in love with charm, and the result is that we are addicted to it. We run after charm like children after the Pied Piper, thinking it will deeply meet our cravings. And it usually leads either nowhere—which is okay, but disappointing—or into harm.

Abusers tend to be charming. Sociopaths tend to be charming. People with personality disorders tend to be charming. Con artists tend to be charming. Users tend to be charming.

Is every charming person exploitative? No. But charm is not a good sign. Our current thinking is: *"Because you are so charming, I will need a mountain of bad experience to convince me that you are actually not a trustworthy person."* We should switch this to its opposite: *"Because you are so charming, I will need a mountain of good experience to conclude that you are okay."*

In other words, charm should count *against* the person in deciding whether to trust him, not *for* him. If we would practice this, we would often save ourselves from abusive partners, people who steal our money through investment schemes, business associates who turn out to be terrors, nightmarish housemates, and other dark holes.

～ ♋ ❦

> "I can train myself to focus on a person's substance more, and on his or her surface less. I'm not going to let charm keep me from seeing warning signs."

When Control Becomes Abuse

Many people—perhaps most—have some "control issues." Almost anytime you hear a woman talking about her partner, you are going to hear her describe times when he gets irritable if he doesn't get his way, where he insists that things be done in a specific way, or where he turns rigid and unreasonable.

So you are faced with the question of which parts of his behavior are symptoms of life's normal problems and which ones are signs that he is abusive. By exploring the following questions, you can sort out the difference:

When you tell him to stop controlling you, does his control grow even worse instead of lessening?

When you point out the problem, does he blame it on you instead of accepting that it's his issue? Does he say that your objection to his control shows that something is wrong with *you*?

Does he retaliate against you for complaining about his controlling behaviors?

Does he justify his controlling behaviors by saying that he *has* to control you because of your faults? For example, does he say that if he didn't tell you how to do things, you would mess everything up?

If you find yourself answering yes to any of these questions, your partner is crossing the line away from "control issues" and into abusive and domineering behavior. And that means that he won't change— except for maybe a few days or a few weeks at a time—until he accepts that the problem is his, not yours.

"I am not the cause of his controlling behaviors.
I do not need to be controlled, and
he has no right to control me."

Expecting the Tenth Time to Be Different

Take a few moments now to answer the following question: How many times has your partner promised you that things are going to get better? Count them up carefully. Include all the times he has promised not to yell insults, all the times he said he would make you a higher priority, all the times he said he would stop having "things" going on with other women, all the times he said he wouldn't hit you or scare you again. In other words, take inventory of every time he said his treatment of you was going to improve.

Then reflect on this second question: What is the longest time that any of those improvements lasted? A week? A month? A year? Have any of them actually been held to permanently?

And lastly reflect on this: Given your answers to the first two questions, does it really make sense to believe that his promises matter anymore?

I'm not saying that he is being insincere; he may believe what he says at the time. But hasn't experience taught you that, no matter how much he means those promises, he doesn't keep them?

You are headed for more and more heartbreak if you keep taking his promises seriously. Start the process today of accepting the sad fact that they don't go anywhere.

⚬

"I'm a smart woman, and I'm not going to keep
trusting in things when my experience has
taught me they don't come true."

Paths to Healing—Part 1

Nowadays when people talk about healing, the first thought is usually to go to a therapist. But actually there are many, many paths to healing, and what works well for one person may not work at all for another. Later on in this book I will talk about how to know if therapy is a good choice for you. But first I would like you to consider the range of avenues for healing that people have found transformative, and encourage you to explore various ones of them, not just one.

Here are the paths that I hear the most positive results from in the lives of women who have been emotionally wounded by a destructive partner:

Support groups, especially ones at a women's program

Working with an advocate at a women's program

Yoga and meditation

Spending time in nature/outdoors

Spirituality/religion

Love (from friends, relatives, a new partner)

Finding people who can really listen to you and validate you

Alternative/nontraditional therapies

Journal writing

There are a few principles that apply to getting benefit from any of these approaches. First, you need to make a commitment to including the healing activity in your life each week, and multiple times per week if possible. Second, you have to give it substantial time to work—at least several months of real effort. Third, no one of these avenues is going to work by itself; build additional ones into your life to support the approach that you are choosing as your main one. Fourth, the right approach, the one that really works for you, might not be the best one five years from now; paths can change over time.

I see a huge difference in quality of life between those people who have found a healing path that works for them—whatever that path might be—and those who have not. I encourage you to consider emotional healing a necessary part of life just like food, rest, or exercise; healing is a friend you will want with you for life.

"I can heal. My life will always include healing."

Staking Out Your Ground

Standing up for yourself can be very difficult when you have a domineering partner. He may make you pay such a high price for your attempts to have a voice that you find it just isn't worth it. Many women stand up to their destructive partners less and less as time goes by because they can't take the pain of the stream of insults he hurls, the hateful look on his face, and his scary eruptions. Part of what defines an abusive man is his underlying attitude that if you stand up to him he's going to get you back for it.

So a woman's resistance to her partner sometimes has to become invisible—and the invisible ways in which you stand up for yourself can be profoundly important.

Invisible resistance takes many forms, such as:

- Reading books or blogs that help you feel stronger (as I hope this book is doing)
- Refusing inside yourself to believe what he tells you, even if you have to pretend outwardly that you do
- Writing in a journal
- Refusing inside yourself to believe that you are responsible for the way he treats you, even if you are the one who ends up having to apologize
- Having contact with people that he doesn't like or that he has tried to keep you away from
- Doing things your own way when he's not around to see
- Believing in your own goodness and intelligence
- Keeping secrets from him, hiding money, planning an escape
- Stealthily doing things that he forbids you to do

Examine your own actions and look for ways in which you invisibly resist your partner's power and control. Take pride in that resistance.

※

"I *am* standing up for myself, even if it's
in ways that he can't see. And I'm going
to keep doing so, and do it more."

Feeling Resentful Toward Women Who Tempt Him

Have you ever felt furious at a woman that your partner was flirting with? When a partner has cheated on you, have you felt that you wanted to get your hands on the woman he'd been with and kill her? Do you get sick of women trying to take your man away from you?

Consider making a big shift in how you look at these interactions. Your partner is not helpless about how he deals with women. A woman can't flirt with him unless he plays along with it. A woman can't sleep with him unless he chooses to participate. No woman is a threat to your relationship; your partner's lack of commitment and honesty is the threat.

The controlling man is fond of claiming that he just can't help it. He'll use as many excuses for flirting or cheating as he uses for verbal abuse or violence: "I was too emotional. I was drunk. That woman seduced me." And it's tempting for you to go along with this and project your anger onto the other women in his life, because then you don't have to take in how hurt you feel by his actions. You can tell yourself, "He totally loves me; it's just those seductive bitches who are the problem."

The truth, though, is that the more he succeeds in getting you to blame or attack other women, the more he increases his control over you. It's a power trip.

Consider reversing the roles for a moment. Would your partner accept the excuse that you were helpless in the face of a man's seduction, or that you weren't aware or sober enough, or that your desires overwhelmed you? Not for a second. He would completely hold you responsible for your choices. But in his eyes those rules don't apply to him.

"He's responsible for his own actions and choices. I
won't blame other women for what he does."

Big Goals for Our Children

I hear parents express a long list of expectations when it comes to what
they hope their children will be, characteristics such as: smart, athletic,
religious, drug-free, sexually abstinent until marriage, loyal, heterosexual, wealthy, vegetarian, polite, attractive, fearless, victorious, admired,
successful, marrying someone of the same culture or race, and so many
more.

Watch out. The more qualities you let yourself get emotionally attached to, the more ways your kids will have to disappoint you. Some of
these goals your kids just won't be able to live up to, and others they
will consciously reject.

But what *really* matters most in who our kids become? I recommend
paring it all down to these five points:

- "I want them to be happy."
- "I want them to be kind, fair, and respectful in how they treat people."
- "I want them to stand up for themselves, for others, and for what's right."
- "I want them to remain emotionally close to their family."
- "I want them to be able to take care of themselves."

Isn't everything else secondary? In fact, shouldn't everything else be kept from ever interfering with these five central goals?

I watch parents sacrifice these goals in pursuit of things that are much less important. I know a woman who was kicked out of her family because she married someone of a different religion. Parents sometimes reject their kids for being gay or lesbian. There are parents who can't talk to their kids because of their sharp political differences. I've heard parents rain shame down on their children for having the "wrong" interests or choosing the "wrong" career.

Don't let these tragedies happen to you.

When bad feeling is creeping into your relationships with your children, ask yourself whether the tension involves one of the five key points. If it does, then it may be worth fighting about. But if it doesn't, consider just letting it go. Being close to your kids is so much more important than trying to "make sure they turn out right."

⁓⁘

"I'm going to put my love for my
children first. There's no better way to
make sure they turn out okay."

EACH NEW DAY

Notice the Peace When He's Away

I would like to encourage you to start noticing the calmer times you experience when your partner is not with you. These may be times when he goes out for the evening, or when you are at work, or when you get a chance to hang with friends or relatives.

Allow your attention to focus on the ways in which you feel different at these times. Check in with how your body feels, scanning through your neck, your center, and your legs, seeing if you are more relaxed than when you are with him. See if your breathing is more regular and deep. Are you less worried that you might say the wrong thing? Does it feel good not to have to worry about his out-of-the-blue mood swings? Is less of your energy going toward proving that you are okay? Are you less on guard, not feeling like at any moment you may have to start defending yourself or making excuses?

If you have children, notice how the tone of your time with them changes when he is not around. Do you get to enjoy them more? Do they feel freer to be themselves and to be kids—for example, a little loud, a little rambunctious, a little messy, as kids are meant to be?

Paying careful attention to how those hours feel is important to gaining clarity about what you need in the time ahead.

"I'm going to start observing how I feel
when he and I are apart."

CLARITY

Shifting Sands

Your partner has too many rules. There are all kinds of things that have to be done just so, in the way he considers correct, or he's going to have a fit. Everything has to be his way.

And as if that weren't stressful enough, the rules keep *changing*, so there's no way to even keep up with what he wants. One moment he'll get all bent out of shape because the house isn't absolutely spotless and perfectly organized, but then at another time he'll be complaining that you never relax. He'll accuse you of cheating on him if you want to get yourself dressed up, but then later he'll criticize you for never wearing anything sexy anymore. He'll criticize you after the two of you have been out with other people, saying you weren't making enough of an effort to be friendly with people, but the next time he'll say you were talking too much. He'll call you "fat" over and over again and harangue you about needing to lose weight, but then he'll say you're obsessed with counting calories and analyzing the fat content of what you're eating.

No wonder you can't get it right with him; there isn't any way to get it right. A guy who is constantly changing the rules like this *wants* to find fault with you, and he's going to find a way to do it.

Don't blame yourself for not being able to please him. He has created a set of impossible binds for you, and that's his issue, not yours.

"It's not my fault that he keeps
switching what he wants me to do."

Financial Abuse—Part 1

Are you in a better financial position, or in a worse one, compared to how you were doing when you met your partner? A controlling partner can sometimes manipulate or bully you regarding money, and this type of abuse is among the least commonly recognized. Here are some questions to consider:

- Is he driving you into debt? Is he running up debt in your name, such as on your credit cards?
- Is he borrowing money and promising he'll pay you back? Is he saying that he's expecting to come into a large chunk of money soon—from a legal settlement, or from an inheritance, or from someone who owes it to him—and that you'll get your money as soon as he gets his? (*Watch out!* I've seen dozens of cases where this money supposedly coming back from a partner never materializes.)
- Does he spend irresponsibly and then get nasty if you call him out on it?
- Is he refusing to work because he's supposedly got some great money-making scheme that he's pursuing? And in the meantime, you're having to bring in all the income?
- Is he keeping secrets about money from you? Does he keep telling you just to "trust him," or keep refusing to let you look at financial information?
- Does he try to convince you that you are stupid or uninformed about financial matters, and that you should leave them to him?

An abusive partner uses women to selfishly meet his own needs. Sometimes taking advantage of his partner economically is one of the forms that exploitative outlook takes. Perform a careful examination of your partner's financial behavior, and see if this is a realm where his controlling patterns may be playing out.

"I need to be prepared to protect
myself from him financially."

Paths to Healing—Part 2

Last week I listed some of the healing paths that women have described as being the most successful for them. There were many approaches on the list. So how do you figure out which one is right for you?

Draw upon what you already know about yourself. Do you like the company of other women, and benefit from sharing mutual experiences? Then a support group might be great for you. Do you crave peace and stillness, and a chance to be present with your thoughts? Then pursue meditation. Does a lot of your stress go into your body, creating stiffness or ill health? Get involved with yoga. Are you someone who likes to talk about feelings and analyze them? A professional therapist might be a good choice. Do you like the outdoors and physical activity? See if you can spend more time in nature, and tap into its healing power.

Some people will tell you to push yourself, to strive to choose a path that is outside of your comfort zone. That may be a good idea a couple of years from now, but I don't recommend that as a starting point. Right now look for an environment where you feel as comfortable as possible, where you feel safe, and where you feel like the activity fits you. This is a time to be self-loving and to be patient with yourself. Seek an environment that feels like a refuge from the toxic atmosphere your partner creates.

"I am going to find a healing path that fits me."

Sexual Self-Expression

Today it's time to think about what you want and what you don't want regarding sex with your partner. Depending on your partner's style, you may spend a lot of your mental energy on trying to figure out how to keep him happy sexually, or on managing his sexual demands. So when do you get to think about what *you* want?

Begin by reflecting, and writing some in your journal, about what you *don't* want. Intimacy should never be an obligation, and no woman should ever have to participate in any sexual contact that she finds demeaning, physically uncomfortable, or just plain a turnoff.

Then spend some time thinking about what you *do* want sexually. What kind of lovemaking would feel desirable and satisfying to you? What makes you feel sexy? What are your sexual needs? What would help you to feel sexually safe and sexually free?

Depending on your partner's style, you may feel like "Well, I can forget that. Those positive things are just not going to happen with him, except maybe three or four times a year." But it's important to get in touch with these aspects of who you are even if they don't have any clear avenue for expression right now. Knowing what you want is as important as knowing what you don't want.

Sexuality is a crucial part of the human spirit. Pondering who you are sexually will take you another step toward being able to figure out what to do about the relationship you are in currently.

"I have a positive, joyous sexuality within me."

Women as Enemies

Women are your natural allies. Women should be there for each other, stand by each other, and, in some sense, be on the same team.

Is your partner setting you up to see women as your enemies? Consider whether he does any of the following:

- Does he flirt with women, make you feel like other women are more attractive than you are, or cheat on you? Does he compare you to other women, perhaps including past lovers of his, with respect to your attractiveness, sexuality, or personality? Does he claim that other women are after him and that they are trying to break the two of you up?
- Does he try to get you to mistrust your women friends by telling you that they are using you, that they are too much in your business, or that you are naïve about what they are really up to? Does he try to make you feel that other women are trying to hurt you or compete with you?
- Does he make your life miserable when you spend time with women friends? For example, is he cold or nasty when you come back from going out with people? Does he accuse you of caring about other people more than him? Does he accuse you of telling your friends things about him or about your relationship that are too private?

Any of these behaviors can, over time, make you come to feel that you need to keep other women away from you.

Notice if this is happening, and look for ways to move back toward viewing women as potential allies and sources of support. Don't let him split you off from the women in your life.

GUIDING CHILDREN

Bigger Is Not Better

Many of our efforts to get our children to do what we want them to do sound something like this:

- "Be a big girl and sit up straight."
- "Oh, look, you're wearing your big boy pants!" (instead of diapers)
- "Big boys don't cry."
- "You helped me so much with putting the groceries away. What a big girl!"
- "That's great! You're acting so grown up!"

Almost all parents seem to do this. And I recommend that we give it up.

Here's why: These statements are sending kids the message that *bigger is better*. That means that the older kids in the family have a higher value than the younger kids (a belief that fuels fighting among siblings). And it says that adults are better than children, and that children's goal in life is to be more adult-like.

But children should be children.

And what if one of your children grows up to be quite small? Statistically speaking, your children have about a fifty-fifty chance of being below average height as adults. Why teach them to devalue being smaller?

Finally, the reality is that until at least their teenage years, your children are going to feel quite small as they look around themselves at the world. Don't you want them to feel okay about who they are? Or even better, to actually appreciate being small?

So let's drop "big" (ditto for "grown-up") from our parenting vocabulary.

What is it we really mean when we tell our children to be "big"? The words that come to my mind are things like: responsible, kind, flexible, helpful, fair, reasonable, and concerned for the needs of others. Use these words instead, and let your child feel good about being whatever size or age he or she is.

$\mathcal{H}$

"My height and age are just right,
and I will encourage my children to feel
the same about themselves."

EACH NEW DAY

Slow Down

The world has gone mad. We rush around now at breakneck speed, packing every minute of the day full. Rush to get out the door. Fight our way through traffic, cursing at the other drivers who are in our way. Count the minutes. Meet the deadline. Try not to arrive late. Move on again soon. There's so much we need to get done.

The hurrying just goes on and on. Meanwhile we struggle with high blood pressure or hypertension or heart palpitations. It's all too much. And the more we try to squeeze into our lives, the faster the years seem to go by; more turns out to be less.

See if you can step off of this crazy conveyer belt that is propelling the human race, perhaps combining with pressure that your partner puts on you about things. Stop to take a long look at a tree in blossom. Look up at the clouds and watch them move and change. Sit at a table before a candle and watch it flicker. Take deep, relaxed breaths and let your heart rate slow down. Let the world go rushing by while you draw yourself back to center. Everybody needs these times of peace.

"I don't have to be flying forward all the time.
I need to remember to breathe."

The Man Who Everyone Thinks Is the Greatest

When you met your partner, he probably seemed like the most wonderful guy in the world. The first time he showed his selfish side, or suddenly didn't give a damn about your thoughts or feelings, or called you a demeaning name, you were shocked. But, tragically, his dark side turned out to be a central aspect of who he is, and it has kept reappearing over and over again. You can tell now that it's not going to go away, at least not anytime soon.

Everyone else, however, tends to still see only the exterior, that man you fell in love with at the beginning. He may be a smooth talker, a man who gives compliments and does favors, a real people-pleaser. It's hard to swallow when someone says to you, "Oh, he's such a good guy, you're lucky to be with a man like that."

If only they knew.

That two-faced quality, that split between his public and private selves, is an aspect of his abusiveness. Putting on a front to mislead the world is part of how he controls you, how he controlled his past partners, and how he gets away with it all.

You are not alone. There are so many women out there who have suffered abuse at the hands of a "great guy." You will be able to find people who can understand what you have been living with.

"He has no right to go around making other people think he's so wonderful while he treats me like this."

Financial Abuse—Part 2

Last week I alerted you to some economic rip-offs that controlling or abusive men sometimes pull on their partners. I encouraged you to look at your financial situation and see if any of the concerns I listed might apply to your situation.

Now it's time to plan for how you can protect yourself from your partner's financial maneuvers and build your economic independence.

Begin by taking steps to inform yourself about finances and how they work. There are learning guides that are designed specifically for women in abusive relationships; take advantage of the fact that these are available. (See "Resources" at LundyBancroft.com.)

Talk to other people, such as your relatives or even a professional financial advisor, about economic decisions that your partner is making. Don't assume that he is right, no matter how much he pressures you to do so; in fact, you should *especially* not trust him if he insists that you should. Any excuses he comes up with for being mysterious or secretive about financial dealings should make you suspicious.

Look at ways to separate yourself financially from him, especially ways that he might not become aware of. See if some of your money could be in a private account, and if you could have some cash hidden in your home or held by a friend. If he is using secrecy to gain power, you may have to use secrecy to protect your rights.

Don't wait until you know for sure that he's harming you financially. The best time is now to start informing yourself, and to involve other people in the decisions you and your partner are making about money.

⤳⸙

"I can empower myself financially.
I don't have to depend on him."

HEALING

Your Body Belongs to You

Does your partner ever act as if your body is somehow his, to do with as he chooses? Tragically, the controlling or abusive man seems to look at his partner as if she were a piece of land—a thing, in other words, not a person—and that he somehow has purchased the mineral rights. This outlook leads him to feel justified in pressuring you and invading you. He may say that you owe him a certain frequency of intimacy, or certain kinds of sexual contact, because you are his partner. And if you resist, he may use sleep deprivation, verbal abuse, or physical force to take what he wants.

He is deeply, deeply wrong. In fact, these sexually entitled attitudes and behaviors are among the most selfish, dehumanizing, and immoral acts that an abusive man can carry out.

Your body belongs to you, and to you alone. No matter how long you have been together with your partner, no matter whether you are married, no matter what he claims his "needs" are, no matter what he has done for you, no matter what he claims are your obligations according to the Bible; you *never, ever* owe him any kind of sexual contact. Sexual intimacy is an activity that only rightfully takes place between fully consenting adults who are desiring the interaction. Pressure, guilt, force, religious obligation—none of these ever has any place in sexuality.

It may take some time for you to find a way to get free of your partner's sexually intrusive behaviors. But know inside of yourself that he has no rights over you. Don't give up until you have recovered your full freedom to control and determine everything that happens to your body.

"Every bit of my body belongs only to me,
all the time, every day, no matter what."

Practicing Honesty with Yourself

One of the ways to manage the pain of an injurious relationship is to convince yourself that the problem is not really that bad. You can tell yourself that your partner doesn't really mean any harm, he just "loses it." You can try to believe that his behavior is not being absorbed by your children at all. You can decide that there's something wrong with you, so that you don't have to face that something is seriously wrong with him.

These soothing fantasies can help you get through the day. But over time they lead to a dead end. The reality of life with an abusive man is that you can't save your own life until you are prepared to look at the true nature of the problem. Your partner has destructive behavior patterns that are not going away. And they are taking a toll on you over time.

The first step toward getting well from the harm he has done, and thus the first step toward regaining control over your life, is to develop a strict practice of being honest with yourself. Don't pretend this isn't happening. Don't pretend you can handle it emotionally without outside support. Don't pretend he is going to change, when he has proven over and over again that he will keep returning to his old ways. Stop selling yourself on ideas that you know aren't true.

It isn't your fault that you have developed habits of glossing over the truth; your relationship is a traumatic experience, and every trauma survivor does some pretending. But it's time to recognize that your self-deception habit is a product of your partner's unhealthy behavior, and that you need to step out of it.

You need to be your own best friend, and best friends tell each other the truth.

> "No one has the right to take my life away
> from me. I'm going to look squarely at
> what's happening and find a way to
> take my life back."

Are You Telling People the Truth?

Most people who have destructive partners don't. It's so much easier to gloss over what's really going on, and to avoid revealing his drinking or his intimidation or his put-downs. But down the road you will regret not having talked about it more. And the longer you go without talking about it, the harder it will be to start.

Let's look at what gets hard about telling the truth. When your partner and you were first falling for each other, you probably brimmed over with excitement about him, telling people how terrific he was. It can feel embarrassing now to admit to people that his behavior is a serious problem. You may feel like people will roll their eyes at you, or look down at you for having been so thrilled about him before.

With some people, you may face an opposite challenge: You may fear that some of your friends or relatives will refuse to believe you because they are so wowed by your partner. They might tell you that you're blowing problems out of proportion, or that nothing is ever good enough for you, and that you should just make the relationship work.

Lastly, you are most likely quite unsure regarding what you want to do about the relationship. You may worry that anyone who knows what is happening will start pressuring you to break up with your partner, and won't understand the powerful mixed feelings you have.

I respect these concerns. You may have to make some careful choices about which people you tell the full truth to and which ones you don't, based on which people you believe are most likely to give you a sensitive and supportive response. But don't allow the outcome of these concerns be that you tell no one the truth. You've got to find someone you can tell the full story to, and ideally two or three people. Don't leave yourself alone with any of it.

⚬⟞ ⟩⟅

"I can find someone whom I can
trust with the full truth."

Boys Will Be Men

The title of today's entry comes from a bumper sticker I saw. It is a response to the often-used phrase "boys will be boys," which gets used as an excuse to do nothing about their selfish, overly aggressive, or irresponsible behavior. The bumper sticker is telling us that the attitudes and behaviors that boys are developing now will determine the kind of men they will become.

What kind of boys do we want to raise? Ones who are sensitive and caring, who can speak up for their needs but also take into account the needs of others, who take pride in contributing to their family and community, who are prepared to fight for what is right, and who honor females and treat them with respect.

These are not radical goals. But we can't expect to suddenly instill these values and capabilities in males when they reach age eighteen. We need to bring our rearing of boys into line with our values.

What could we do differently?

- Stop telling boys that they can't cry and have feelings. If we don't allow them to be sensitive now, we can't expect them to become sensitive, caring men.
- Increase the physical affection we give to boys—more hugs, more cuddling, more companionship at bedtime.
- Firmly—but not meanly—stop tolerating it when boys disrespect or exclude girls, when they order their mothers around, when they hoard food and toys without considering the needs of other kids, when they make messes and leave them for others to clean up, and when they minimize each other's accomplishments instead of celebrating them.

It's not true that boys "just are that way." The behavior and outlook of boys varies from nation to nation, and from generation to generation, depending on the leadership that adults take. We need to give boys more love, more exercise, and firmer limits. Watch how quickly we'll see positive results.

>⌒⌇⋇

"Each day is another step toward
manhood for my boy."

Retreating to Your Core

Some days there is just no peace. Your partner is having one of those days when he finds something wrong with everything you do. Your head aches and your back is sore. You make some error at work and your supervisor is crabby about it. Your children are screaming and demanding all day.

Is it possible for a woman to find her center while living in this onslaught? Let's work toward it. The first step I'd like you to take is to develop, today, an image that represents your core. Think of a place that you love. It might be: a spot by a stream, a field surrounded by trees, a fountain in a park, or a special sitting place in your house or at a friend's house.

If no spot comes to mind, create one from your imagination, perhaps from a book you've read or a movie you've seen.

Now, I want you to close your eyes and think to yourself: "That place is my spiritual home. That is where my soul dwells."

Don't ever tell your partner about this place. If no one knows about it, no one can ruin it for you.

Take a minute each day to mentally visit this home. On a bad day, go to it many times. This place contains the truth about the beauty within you.

*"I have a beautiful spot inside me
that belongs only to me."*

When You Can't Figure Out What Just Happened

Do you ever come out of an argument with your partner feeling terrible, but you can't put your finger on why? You're thinking, "I can't figure out what just occurred, but I feel so *messed with*. Maybe it's just me."

It's probably not "just you." Sometimes the most subtle forms of control or manipulation can be the most injurious. I wish sometimes that women could have recordings of their arguments with their controlling partners; if you could play it back a line at a time, you'd be able to identify the tactics he was using.

When your head is feeling like it just went through some kind of threshing machine, here's some of what it may be about:

- He kept taking what you were saying as if you had said something completely different.
- He kept implying that you had bad intentions behind the things you were saying.
- He kept turning everything back on you, twisting the subject to be about *your* actions and *his* feelings. You were the one who had reason to be hurt, but *he* kept acting victimized by *you*.
- He kept using a superior tone as if he was burdened by how unreasonable and muddy your thinking is. (But if you complained about his condescension, he jumped all over that as proof of how unreasonable you are!)

When you come out of an interaction feeling messed with, trust your perceptions. When you have had some time to pull yourself together, you can start identifying what he did, and that will help you stay well.

"Sometimes I feel so hurt and furious, but I don't even know what to call the things he just did."

Couples or Marriage Counseling

Can a good therapist get him to realize how he treats you?

Before I answer this, let me say that there are some issues in relationships that couples counseling is well designed for. It can help when two people have unproductive communication styles and find themselves tied up in knots. It's effective when people have grown distant and need help rebuilding closeness and intimacy. It can help couples find ways to work through conflicting sets of needs. And it can guide people in negotiating clashing religious beliefs, incompatible sexual styles, or conflicting values about how to raise children.

But at the same time, couples counseling can do little or nothing about situations where one partner chronically disrespects the other, looks down upon her, or treats her as a servant; one partner refuses to listen to the other and doesn't consider her opinions worth taking seriously; or one partner bullies or intimidates the other.

In short, couples work doesn't help when the main problem is that your partner treats you badly. Shared therapy is for shared problems. Control and abuse are the sole responsibility of the person who does them, not a problem *between* the two members of the couple. If you try to "work on it together," the abusive person keeps blaming his behavior on you. It happens every time.

It's natural that you want to find some source of hope for your relationship. But I have never seen couples counseling lead to lasting improvement in the behavior of a selfish or abusive person. For him to change, he has to recognize that his behavior is his own problem and you are not the cause of it. And then he has to be willing to get help for it on his own, without making it in any way your responsibility.

✼

**"I can't make him deal with his issues;
that's going to be up to him."**

HEALING

Your Partner's Reactions to Your Anger

When people ask me if my abusive clients have a problem with their anger, I say, "No, they have a problem with the *woman's* anger. They don't believe she should feel or express anger, no matter what he has done." Your partner may well believe that women's anger is silly. He sees himself as being above reproach, and since your anger is drawing attention to something he did that isn't okay, he won't allow it. Further, he finds your anger irritating because it makes it harder for him to ignore your opinions, which he likes to do.

There is one more crucial reason why he is determined to squelch your anger: Anger has power in it. The anger of people who are being mistreated gives them energy to fight back. It fuels their hope. It builds up their courage. It helps them to believe that they deserve better. It keeps them from giving up. That's why your partner wants to drive your anger out of you. So he insults and humiliates you for being angry, imitates your voice, walks away from you, or puts you in fear.

If he is scary or cruel, I realize you may have no choice but to hide your anger from him sometimes. But don't give your anger and outrage up on the inside. It's your lifeline to freedom.

> "The worse he reacts to my anger the more that
> shows how important my anger is."

Looking at Your Ways of Coping—Part 1

To get through the day while being involved with a destructive partner, a woman tends to develop a collection of survival mechanisms. Here are some examples:

Thinking about him all day long, trying to figure out how to make things go better and what to do about him

Blaming herself for what goes wrong

Drinking alcohol

Taking her stress out on her kids

Telling herself that her partner really loves her and that he's going to start behaving better

Forgetting what he's like during the bad times

These ways of living are tempting, because they make daily life less painful. If you blame yourself for your partner's actions, then you can take what he does less personally. If you focus on what's frustrating you about your children, that distracts you from the pain of your relationship with your partner. If you keep holding on to signs of hope that he'll change, that shields you from feeling your grief about how destructive he has turned out to be. But these approaches all come at a cost that isn't good for you in the long run.

Spend some time over the next couple of days observing the ways in which you are managing your distress. Evaluate how these coping mechanisms are affecting your life. See if it's time to make some changes in how you deal with the pain of your partner's patterns.

✂━❃❦

> "I'm going to reflect some on whether my
> partner's behavior is taking a bigger toll
> on me that I've been realizing."

STAYING CONNECTED

Nurturing Your Helpers

It isn't easy to find people who really "get it," is it? I hear from women how difficult it has been for them to describe what life is like with a controlling or abusive partner. So when you find allies who are truly on your side, it's important to keep them around. How do you get your support system to hang in there with you, instead of giving up and walking away in frustration? How do you avoid falling back into isolation?

Consider it one of your missions in life to *take care of the people who are taking care of you*. Here's how to do it:

1. Express appreciation and gratitude for the help you are given. Do so with pride and dignity; people want you to thank them, but they feel awkward if you thank them too much. Keep it simple and sincere, yet make it clear that you do not take them for granted.

2. Accept what people can't do. Even when you feel panicked, avoid getting angry at people who can't come through in the way you wish they would. You might need those people later, so don't alienate them now.

3. Take the help you are given and use it to make positive things happen in your life. People are happy to help when they see you taking steps and moving forward; whereas they grow reluctant to stay involved if they feel that you keep asking for assistance with the same issues so that they feel like their help doesn't really do any good.

4. Give back. You want people to feel that the help they give you is mutual and rewarding, forming an equal relationship over time. Ask them what is going on in their lives and listen supportively, rather than always talking about your own struggles. Return child care favors, lend money to people whom you have borrowed from in the past, put together a great birthday party for a friend.

Follow these guidelines, and you will have people delighted to be there for you. Not only that, but you'll increase your own sense of dignity and equality by handling your relationships in this way.

"People are eager to help when they see that their assistance is valued and used well."

Competitiveness Between Siblings

"I can run way faster than you can! You wouldn't have a chance against me!"

"Why can't you do that puzzle? Jeez, it's so easy, I did it in like twenty seconds!"

"You thought that joke was funny? Come on!"

"You liked that movie? It was so boring."

Siblings can get competitive about who's faster, who's smarter, who owns better stuff. They can compete about who is more "grown-up." They can compete about who is cooler, including who can look down on other people's humor and who can be the most bored. (Nowadays kids consider it cool to be apathetic.) Your partner may be feeding this problem by creating an atmosphere heavy with criticism, put-downs, and sarcasm. He may also compare the children, such as by saying, "Why can't you be more like your brother?" Comparing kids is divisive, contributing to competitiveness, infighting, and distance among them.

Your best bet in countering these dynamics is to work to create a family ethic that runs the other way. Make statements such as:

"I want this to be a family where we take pride in each other's abilities."

"Let's be excited about one another's successes."

"This is a family where we notice what we do well, and feel good about that."

Another angle is to keep asking children about *feelings*. For example, when a child says, "I'm way better at that than you are," we are tempted to say, "Hey, don't talk to your sister like that!" Try instead asking, "How do you think it makes your sister feel when you say that?" Then ask the target of the statement how it felt to hear it. Some kids don't mind getting "in trouble" with Mom; they may even find it stimulating and get hooked on it. But no child wants to keep getting confronted with the hurt feelings their behavior is causing their siblings.

"I can train my kids to have each other's back,
instead of working against one another."

"The Opposite of Dysfunction Is Dysfunction"

Once again, the title of today's entry comes from a bumper sticker. Here's what it means to me.

One of the keys to happy living is flexible thinking and action. We need to be able to consider each situation, each person, each challenge as unique. But in the flood of complexity and distress that comes our way in life, it gets tempting to find simple formulas and rigid rules to give our lives a sense of structure and direction. We can feel especially drawn to believing that the cure for an unhealthy way of thinking or behaving is to adopt its opposite.

For example, many people go through life spreading criticism and negativity around like garbage, passing harsh judgment on other people with no understanding of what those people are actually dealing with.

It's tempting, therefore, for the rest of us to decide that everyone should be "nonjudgmental," meaning we shouldn't take stands on what other people do.

But this is no solution. People who are selfish or manipulative thrive in "nonjudgmental" groups, getting away with a lot of harm because no one wants to call them out on what they are doing.

Then what is the answer? What we need to do is not try to flip negative characteristics into their opposites, but instead develop completely new approaches. Think of yourself as a creative person—even if that clashes at first with your self-image—and look for fresh attitudes to the challenges life presents you with.

> "When one approach hasn't worked
> for me in the past, behaving in an
> opposite manner isn't the solution.
> I can find a new way."

Being Furious Respectfully

The destructive partner's favorite excuse for his behavior is his anger. "Yeah, I know I yelled and called you some names, but I was really pissed off!" In other words, he thinks his emotions give him a free pass to be disrespectful.

Is it possible to be enraged yet still behave with decency? Absolutely. It's not only possible, it's his responsibility to do so. The respectful partner expresses anger in the following ways:

- He speaks more loudly than normally, but doesn't yell.
- He may pace around or wave his arms with some agitation, but he doesn't become scary, doesn't stand too close, and doesn't tower over you.
- He describes what you did that he didn't like, and explains the effects on him. In other words, he expresses anger at what you *did*, not disgust at what you *are*. This is the crucial distinction.
- He doesn't call names, imitate your voice, or refuse to let you talk.

When your partner blames his actions on his anger, remind yourself that he could have expressed it in a healthy way instead. When he uses demeaning or bullying behavior, that is his *choice*.

"Anger and disrespect are two completely different things. He is behaving abusively because he's disrespectful, not because he's angry."

The Bad Times Make the Good Times Great

The abusive and controlling man is like two people; you can feel almost as if he has a split personality. One side of him is the person you first fell for. He was charming, attentive, and crazy about you. The other side took a while to reveal itself; that aspect of him spews what looks like hatred, not love, and seems determined to hurt you any way it can.

Those periods of nightmarishly bad treatment from him have an important backwards effect: They sharpen the happy times, making them appear to be just amazing. He starts to seem like an incredible person because he's so great during the good times.

Except, he's actually not that great during the good times; it just seems that way because you're so hurt from his abusive periods. He's actually creating a kind of addiction in you as he swings back and forth between his extremes. You're left longing for the good times, and then so excited and relieved when they come back for a while.

And you'll notice that, over time, the good feelings you get from his kind periods fade faster and faster.

The next time he's in the Mr. Great stage—or at least the Mr. Half-Decent stage—try not to feel dazzled by him. Remember that many of your positive-seeming feelings are actually coming from how injurious he is the rest of the time. That perspective can help you not to get as crushed the next time he goes back to tearing you down. Work in this way toward the goal of keeping yourself centered emotionally, unhooking yourself from your partner's unhealthy ups and downs.

"I can start to notice when
I'm getting dazzled by him."

HEALING

Making Big Changes Is Scary

When people talk about bad circumstances that they were stuck in earlier in life, they often comment on how afraid they were to break away. As much as they hated the way they were living, leaping into an unknown future seemed even worse. The result was that they chose to stay with what was familiar for a long time, until a day came when the fear was not enough to hold them back.

This fear of what will come next sometimes leans heavily on a woman whose partner is harming her. She worries about:

- Whether she can really make it on her own—especially since he has tried to convince her that she can't do anything right
- Whether she will survive economically
- Whether she will be lonely
- Whether he will hurt her even worse for having left him

In this context, it's easier to keep complaining to yourself and your friends about what's wrong than it is to take action to change your situation.

Life is precious. Not a single woman who used to have an abusive partner has ever said to me, "I wish I hadn't given up on the relationship so soon; I should have stuck around longer to see if he would change." But hundreds have said to me, "I wish I could have those years back that I poured into being with him and suffered."

Some of your fears are about real dangers—such as how explosive he may be after you split up—but other aspects of your fear come from ways that he has indoctrinated you to believe in your own incompetence. Confront both sets of fears now. Start making plans for how you will address the real risks, and how you still step through the other fears, the ones that are not based in reality.

Don't let years go by that you will later wish you could reclaim.

"The time to start facing my fears is now."

Looking at Your Ways of Coping—Part 2

Last week we started looking at some of the behavior patterns you could be developing as a way to manage the stress of your partner's behavior.

These ways of coping with your distress can cause more problems than they solve, especially as time goes by. Forgetting what he's like during the bad times sets you up to be badly hurt over and over again. Being hard on your kids hurts them, and it hurts you because you start to feel like a bad mother. Drinking too much leads to your life becoming increasingly out of control.

For most women, this isn't a conscious process. They don't notice the connection between their emotional distress and these unhealthy behavior patterns, and they don't notice where these patterns are leading them. It's important to tune in to your internal world to see if the dynamic I'm describing feels familiar.

Don't blame yourself if you are coping in some ways that aren't good for you. But do start breaking out of those patterns. Strive to become more aware of your own stress, and work toward handling it in more constructive ways, such as writing in your journal, talking to a friend, calling a hotline, or taking a brisk walk. Keep applying the principles you are learning in this book, moving toward healthier coping approaches.

"I can pay more attention to
what's going on inside me."

Taking a Fresh Look at People

We're wading into tricky waters here, with some crosscurrents and rip-tides. On one hand, your partner is trying to get you to think badly about people and not trust them. But on the other hand, he may be planting negative thoughts about you in the minds of people around you, so that some of them may truly be starting not to be trustworthy. On one hand, you need more people in your life who can counter your partner's toxicity. On the other, you may need to pull away from people who share his disrespectful attitudes and ways of treating people.

In this swirl, it can be confusing and scary to figure out how to continue. But you can sort it out. First, stop looking at people through his eyes. Instead, form your own impressions and conclusions. Some people whom he finds disgusting you will decide have real value, and at the same time, some of his favorite people you will come to recognize as bad news. Despite how authoritative he sounds when he passes his judgments, the reality is that he has huge blind spots about people's character. (This is true of all abusive people.)

Second, draw upon what you've learned (the hard way) from being involved with your partner. His behavior and attitudes demonstrate all kinds of ways *not* to be; he is teaching you about selfishness, about manipulation, about twisting things into their opposites. As you become more able to recognize these qualities in him, you will notice them more in other people. Depending on your social surroundings, this growing awareness may mean that you decide it's time for some big changes; some women have told me that they realized they had to do a pretty big housecleaning as they started to face up to how many toxic people they had around them.

"I'm going to turn this experience into a positive, by moving more and more toward healthy people."

Feeling Pressure to Medicate Your Kids?

Psychiatric medicating of kids is skyrocketing. The drug companies are making billions of dollars by putting kids on drugs while common sense, safety, and kids' rights are disappearing in the piles of money. And long-term use of psych meds with kids simply isn't safe.

Parents who are reluctant to medicate their kids can meet with disapproval from school officials and child welfare workers, and courts sometimes punish parents who don't want to drug their children. This pressure is not scientific. The evidence from research points to the conclusion that psych meds can do more harm than good for kids in the long term. (I encourage you to read the book *Anatomy of an Epidemic* by Robert Whitaker, especially the two chapters on the lasting effects of these powerful drugs on children and teenagers.)

And think of the message we're sending our kids. As adults, we're telling kids, "Don't take drugs, that's no way to solve your problems," but then we turn around and say, "Well, actually, you *should* take drugs to solve your problems." If we want kids to learn constructive ways to overcome depression, anxiety, and loneliness, we're going to have to really get in there with them and help them fight it through.

I saw the play *Distracted*, by Lisa Loomer, about the pressures a mother goes through when the doctor and the school want her to put her son on psych meds. The play illustrates the fact that you will have to do some digging in order to get information about whether or not to medicate your child, to find alternatives to medication, and to get support for making up your own mind. (See "Resources" at LundyBancroft .com.)

You are not a bad parent for having reservations about putting your kids on drugs. Reach out for information and support. And if you do decide that a period on medication is in your child's best interests, make sure to combine that approach with other avenues to healing; drugs are not a good long-term solution even in cases where they are the right choice for now.

"I am the parent, and medical
decisions belong to me."

EACH NEW DAY

The Power of Exercise and Movement

One way to make things go better in your emotional world is to increase your physical activity. Modern life involves far too much time spent sitting or standing. Like most other animals, we were built to spend most of each day moving around looking for food and chasing after our children. Our spirits naturally decline if we stay still too long and too often.

Exercise, sports, dance, and other ways of putting your body in motion have proven to be among the most powerful mood regulators available. Studies have found, for example, that regular exercise, such as vigorous walking for twenty-five minutes a day, is more consistently effective at combating depression *than any antidepressant medication so far developed*. In other words, a doctor or therapist shouldn't even talk to you about psychiatric medication until you've tried an extended period of vigorous physical activity several times a week.

Your partner's treatment of you can send you into a downward spiral, where his actions feed your depression and then the depression feeds your difficulty in figuring out what to do about him. You can help to break this cycle with a good half hour of movement three to five days per week. Walking and running are two of the easiest activities to build into your day. Equally accessible is vigorous dancing, which you can do by yourself with music. There are also opportunities to dance in group classes like Zumba and Jazzercise. You might also consider joining a women's volleyball, soccer, or other sports team through your town's recreation office. Look online for hiking clubs or exercise partners.

Seek a form of movement that feels fun rather than being drudgery. Whatever approach best fits you, find a way to get out there and move.

"In motion, I can feel my spirits lift."

Your Partner's Hard Life

Compassion is a great thing. It's important to care about the painful childhood your partner may have had, or his mean boss, or the friend that once betrayed him. Being there for each other about the hard aspects of life is one of the gifts that partners can give each other.

At the same time, watch out. These "hard life" stories, which almost everyone has some of, can play an unhealthy role when they are coming from the mouth of an abusive man. The distinction between healthy and unhealthy depends on what he's looking for when he shares these experiences. His sharing is *healthy* if:

- He wants your support and understanding.
- He wants to talk his experiences through so that he can heal from them.
- He wants to figure out how to keep these kinds of misfortunes from happening to him again in the future.

His sharing is *unhealthy* if:

- He is saying that, because of his hard past, you need to stop complaining about his behavior.
- He's claiming that you don't understand how bad the things are that he's been through.
- He wants to convince you that the world has always been unfair to him and that nothing that goes wrong in his life is his own responsibility.
- He keeps placing a higher value on the hard things he has endured than on the challenges or sadnesses you have faced in your life.

The bad breaks he has had are no excuse for him to be mean or explosive now. They have no business pushing your needs out of the picture so that only his needs matter.

*"I'm not the cause of his hard past,
and I'm not going to pay the price for it."*

Who Is Using Sex as a Weapon?

A controlling man twists things around. The sexual realm is one of the places where he may try to claim that reality is the opposite of what it is. For example, when he wants sex but you aren't in the mood, or he's pressuring you for specific sexual acts that you don't like, he may say that you're using sex as a weapon against him. You may come out feeling confused, because when he rejects you sexually, it does feel to you like he's using sex as a weapon. So are you doing the same thing he's doing?

I don't think so. The critical distinction has to do with *intentions*. When you say no to sex with your partner, you do so because you are exhausted and need to sleep, or because he's been treating you badly and your emotional wounds make intimacy with him feel bad, or because he's being sexually crass and demanding, which is such a sexual turnoff. There's no reason why you would want to make love at times like these.

When he turns you down sexually, on the other hand, he's doing it to punish you for some way you stood up to him, or because he knows he gets power by leaving you starved for affection, or because it's part of his overall pattern of tearing you down and making you feel bad about yourself. He's using sexual denial to hurt or control you.

He may continue to insist that you are out to hurt or control *him*, projecting his intentions onto you. But don't buy it. Keep holding on to the truth inside of yourself. There's a vast distinction between using sex as a weapon—which is what he does—and turning away from sex because your partner is bullying you, which is what you do.

⟡

> "I have rights sexually. He has no business playing the victim around it."

Starving for Things We Needed Long Ago

We all carry scars from the past. Some of those scars are not about bad things that happened; instead, they are about good things that *didn't* happen. By the time we reach adulthood, we are carrying stored emotional injuries regarding times when we needed attention and companionship and it wasn't there; times when people around us ignored us and didn't care about what we were dealing with; times when no one was (appropriately) physically affectionate with us; and times when we didn't receive love. Those old unmet needs are frozen inside of us.

This accumulated emotional hunger can create distress for us in the present. Often when we have powerful desires or longings, we are actually responding to those old hungers. That's why people will, for example, work for months or years saving up to buy something, looking forward to it constantly, and then when they finally buy it, the excitement wears off almost immediately. Similarly, part of what traps people in relationships that aren't healthy for them is that, without realizing it, they are trying to fill big empty spaces inside of themselves that aren't from the present.

And that's why you can come out feeling that you "need" somebody who clearly isn't good for you.

Start to explore the places inside of yourself where old starvations dwell. You can train yourself to recognize the ways in which those longings are luring you into present-time decisions that aren't the best—such as waiting on and on for a partner to change when deep inside you know he won't. Once you learn to see that dynamic, you can break the hold it has on you.

"My feelings of overwhelming need are
actually left over from the deep past."

Your Strongest Point

Today I want you to spend a few minutes remembering the time in your life when you felt the strongest.

Begin by doing a brief mental scan of your life, looking for the good parts. See, for example, if you can remember one of the following:

- A time when you were part of a good group of friends, where you knew you belonged and you all looked forward to spending time together

- A period when your school or work life fell into place, and you were feeling good about what you were doing and the people you were around
- A phase in your parenting life when you felt close to your children and you were enjoying each other
- A skill that you had that brought you pleasure, whether artistic/creative, athletic, academic, social, or any other kind

Form a mental image of what you were like at that high point, whether it lasted two hours or two years. How did you walk? How did you feel about yourself? How did you react to a nice view or a kind word from a friend? How strong did you feel to confront any challenges that came up?

Give that image of yourself a location. Did you feel happiest and strongest at home? At school? At a friend's house? Walking by yourself? Writing in your diary? Picture yourself in that place.

In your journal, describe what that woman or girl was like—that version of you from another time in life. The description doesn't need to be long; four or five sentences might be enough. Just try to capture the essence of her strength, her energy, and her belief in herself.

Now the last and most crucial point: This image holds the truth about who you are. *She is the real you.* Carry her around inside of you like a stalwart friend. She is your guide through all the confusion and distortion that life sends your way.

"Deep inside me exists the person
I have always really been."

Is Anyone Trustworthy?

Perhaps the single most common effect of being in a destructive relationship is that women find that their ability to trust people is damaged. I hear many variations on the following experience:

"I thought he was great, and he turned out to be so awful to me. That really shook up my sense that I know how to judge people. And to make things worse, a couple of my closest friends turned on me while I was with him, and one of them won't even speak to me anymore. So even with women, I don't feel like I can tell anymore who is okay and who isn't."

You can sort this challenge out by learning the signs of trustworthy people. Then broaden your base of support, so that if one friendship does fall apart—as friendships sometimes do—you won't be left feeling alone in the world.

Look for these qualities in people you decide to let close to your heart:

They don't focus on finding what's wrong with people. Fault-finding is a sign of insecurity and of the need to build oneself up. And a person who is a fault-finder may praise you today, but farther down the road she'll be focusing on your faults too.

They practice what they preach. Look for consistency between a person's values and her actions. If she keeps having to explain or excuse what she does, that's not a good sign.

They can own their part in things. The healthiest people are the ones who can look honestly at their own mistakes and can apologize, but at the same time aren't constantly apologizing and blaming themselves for everything.

They listen well. Good listeners are hard to find, but they are worth it. Look to people who focus their attention well, who ask questions about you, and who don't keep switching the subject back to themselves.

They make you feel valuable and seen. A good friend speaks appreciatively about you and makes you feel like you matter. She also gets who you are as a separate individual, rather than assuming that you are just like her.

⤚❧⤙

"I can find good people; I just need
to know what to look for."

GUIDING CHILDREN

Alternatives to Medicating Kids

Last week I wrote about the pressures a mother faces in trying to decide whether to put her child on psychiatric medication, along with the difficulty of getting accurate information about the risks and benefits of those drugs. At the core parents are often reluctant to go this route, and most kids hate it.

So what other solutions exist? The research points in a number of directions. The biggest help is *time*; the crises that children and teens go through tend to pass. We are an instant-solution culture, and so we're reluctant to let kids struggle through difficulties for a couple of years, but that's actually what usually works best.

Next, kids need *exercise and motion*. Our schooling system requires kids to sit for about six hours a day, which is unnatural and unhealthy for them. Before there were schools, kids were moving and active all day long, mostly outdoors, and this is what young and growing bodies are actually designed to do. Parents have two roles here. The first is to pressure schools to give kids more opportunities to move around. The second is that when our kids aren't at school, we need to insist that they be active. They need to get off of video games and Twitter and go exercise their bodies.

Kids need homes where there is physical and emotional *safety*, where they aren't torn down or violated and they don't have to witness their siblings or their mothers being abused. Unfortunately, you as their mother don't have the magical power to require your partner to behave appropriately; I wish you did. But you can offer your children support and understanding about what they are going through. (For detailed advice about how to help them, see my book *When Dad Hurts Mom*.)

You can help your kids work their way through life's challenges and its painful periods. You have so much to offer them.

"I can figure out what my children need.
I am their mother."

EACH NEW DAY

Where Does a Happy Life Come From?— Part 1

Happiness is not as mysterious as it sometimes seems. The people who find the most enjoyment and satisfaction tend to have certain elements in place in their lives. Some of them have partners and some don't, by the way; a primary relationship is not the "be all and end all" to happiness that many of us assume it is.

Here are some of the qualities that the most contented people have present in their lives:

Rewarding work. The fulfillment we get from our work is not determined by how much money we make. We need work that is interesting, challenging, and that benefits the world. Raising children and tending a home and garden, for example, can be profoundly meaningful work if you are doing it by choice, and if you feel that the people around you *place a high value* on what you do. What matters most is that we all need to feel that we are contributing.

Loving relationships. We need close people in our lives whom we look forward to spending time with and who we know appreciate us. Everyone counts: friends, relatives, coworkers. A partner is not the only source of love, or necessarily even the most important one.

A good relationship with themselves. Strive to be loving toward yourself and to hold a high self-opinion. Your relationship with yourself is your most important connection.

You may often go through the day feeling that your partner's moods determine whether your life is good or not. See if you can start to turn that around, making it up to *you* what your quality of life is.

⚜

"I can take charge of building a life that works
for me, regardless of whatever he does."

Passive Aggression

Bullying behavior often disguises itself as something else. For example, does your partner ever make everything grind to a halt? You might be getting ready to go somewhere, for example, and he gets mad at you about something so he suddenly stops moving and deliberately lets the hour get later and later. You might be trying to get an important answer out of him—"Have the children had lunch?" for example, or "Did your parents decide to come over or not?"—and he just won't say anything.

Or does he have subtle, unspoken ways to get you back for something you said? For example, you might ask him to stop leaving his messes around the house, so he makes a point of strewing his clothes and junk around even worse than he normally does. Or you might ask him not to feed the kids so much junk, so the next time he's looking after them he takes them out for doughnuts.

These are all examples of passive aggression. The behavior isn't loud or violent, and may not involve words at all. But if you look at the impact that these kinds of tactics have on your life, you'll see that they can have just as negative an effect as screaming or calling names would. In some ways passive aggression can be even worse, because then when you get upset about how he's acting, he responds manipulatively by saying, "What's your problem? I didn't do anything!" *Trust your perceptions.* You can tell when he's using a passive-aggressive technique as a way to get at you.

"Hidden bullying is still bullying.
He doesn't have to make a sound."

"How Do I Make Conflicts with Him Go Better?"

You have perhaps noticed that I haven't written about how you can resolve conflicts with your partner more constructively. That's no accident. I don't believe that a woman can make things go better with a controlling or abusive man by changing how she argues with him. Some people may say that you should bring things up with him in a very diplomatic, nondemanding manner, almost like you're asking him a favor. Others will tell you the opposite: that you should be firm and no-nonsense with him, setting clear limits and boundaries about his behavior. You may be advised to talk just about how you feel, so that you don't sound like you are criticizing your partner. Some people believe that you'll reach him more successfully if you give him lots of reassurance that you love him and that you're just trying to make your relationship go better.

Some days, one or more of these approaches may seem to actually work. But it's an illusion. Within a few days or weeks he'll be right back to his usual behaviors. *This is one of the ways you can identify the fact that your partner is abusive*: There simply is no "right way" to talk to him.

It makes sense to improve your own behavior, but for a different reason: because it will help you build your own self-respect, and it will help your children. It won't change him.

※

"There's no way to improve communication with
an abusive or controlling partner. It's a dead
end to pour my energy in that direction."

Play

Adults forget how to play. We mistakenly decide that playing is "child-ish" behavior, and get embarrassed or uncomfortable about participating in anything that doesn't seem grown-up enough.

Your partner may not even want the children to act like children. He may get bent out of shape when anyone in the home seems to be too happy or having too much fun. He'll say that they're making too much noise, they should be doing their homework, they're going to break something, or whatever else he can come up with to find something wrong with their high spirits.

But kids need to play and be loud and rambunctious. *And adults do too.* Many behaviors that get defined as "immature" or "silly" are not only harmless but are actually healthy and life-giving. Do you ever play? Do you ever run around, or get silly, or put loud music on and dance around the living room? Do you ever get down on the floor with your kids and push the trains around, put your scissors to those doll cutouts, or build fairy houses?

When your partner isn't around, look for chances to "act like a kid." If you get embarrassed by it, giggling and laughing will relieve the embarrassment. Who cares what other people think? You'll be amazed what it does for your spirit when you just let loose and play.

And if you have kids, they will love to have you join the fun.

"Playing is for adults too.
I'm going to let my playful side loose."

Feeling Certain

You have great knowledge and wisdom within you. We all do. Sometimes that wisdom is buried away, lost under layers of rage and hurt, covered by abuse and oppression, but it's still there. There is so much that you know, so much that you see.

Your partner tries to sow doubt in you. He wants you to believe that your mind doesn't work right, or that you are alone and confused in your outlook, or that you aren't very bright. Getting these messages from him enough times can make you start to doubt your intelligence and even your sanity. You can start to wonder what is your imagination and what is real.

This insidious process can be stopped and reversed. You can get back in touch with your faith in yourself.

Try this exercise: Close your eyes, and then say to yourself, either aloud or in your mind, in a firm, definitive, and slightly angry tone, *"There are things that I know."* Repeat this phrase many times. Reach for a tone that communicates the following: "There are things that I am absolutely certain about, and no one is going to drive me into self-doubt."

You know the truth of who you are. You know the truth of what has been done to you. You know the truth of what you have tried to accomplish. (And whether you feel it to be true at the moment or not, the reality is that you have accomplished many important things in your lifetime and have had great triumphs. Try to remember them.)

꜀꜀꜀

"There are things that I am certain of."

Not Writing People Off

It's tempting to paint people with a broad brush. We can fall into making overarching judgments, and then use those as reasons to axe people out of our lives. We justify our actions by saying, "I realized what he/she is really like."

But one bad quality does not completely define a person. We all have our good aspects and our not-so-good aspects. We all have done many things that we can be proud of, but also some things that we shouldn't have. You can't judge a person by one action or one facet of his or her character.

I'm not encouraging you to keep people in your life who are toxic to you. But reach for a balance in how much of a chance you give people, avoiding extremes. At one extreme you may give certain people too many chances, setting yourself up to be hurt over and over again. At the other extreme, perhaps you reject people too quickly, based on the one time they acted like a jerk or hurt your feelings.

Aim for the middle ground. Your partner is perhaps someone to whom you have given too many chances. But there may be other people in your life to whom you have given too few. Consider whether you are judging people too harshly, and as a result cutting yourself off from possible sources of friendship and support. Make sure you've given people a chance to apologize, to clear up misunderstandings, and to make things go better.

"I need to watch out about closing
the door on people too soon."

Noticing the Goodness in Your Children

There was a time when parents viewed children as being full of selfish and irrational tendencies that needed to be stomped out of them. It was considered the job of parents to be constantly vigilant for any indications of weakness or evil in their kids, and to drive those tendencies out before they could grow and fester. Children were seen as just a series of bad intentions, of terrible accidents waiting to happen.

And though this negative outlook is a little less rampant than it was a few decades ago, it's still widespread.

But couldn't our job be primarily to cultivate the good in our kids, instead of defending against the bad?

The reality is that children want, on a deep level, to head in a loving and constructive direction. They of course won't seem like that every day; you'll see lots of frustration, anger, and yearning that aren't coming out in a very good way. But that's all surface stuff; it doesn't change what kind of person the child is in his or her core.

Your partner's hypercritical style can be contagious, creating a family culture that's about finding fault with others. If you see that happening, make a conscious decision to step out of it. Ask your children to do the same. When your partner isn't around, for example, say often to your kids, "I want this to be a family where we support and encourage each other. Let's focus on what everyone is doing well, and express our appreciation for the strengths that we see."

Model this approach for them. Every day look for things that they do well, ways that they have been kind or generous, funny things they have said, times when they have made you feel good. Tell them what you appreciate about them, in a tone that sounds more like a caring friend and less like an "approving" parent, so that they learn to use that tone with each other. The atmosphere in the home is yours to create—at least when your partner is not around.

"I am going to bring my children's wonderful
qualities to light every day."

Where Does a Happy Life Come From?—Part 2

Last week we began examining some of the key elements that make up a fulfilling life. Here are a few more that play a key role in how things go:

Spiritual connection. People are happiest who feel connected to something bigger than themselves. They may believe in God—or in many gods and goddesses—or they may not; what seems to matter most is that their beliefs give them a sense of beauty and unity. A surprising number of people find their path to spiritual connection through science; it doesn't matter how you get there.

Enjoying our bodies. Feeling centered in our physical beings helps us enjoy life. Find movement that pleases you, whether it's hiking, studying dance, or doing a sport. Soak in the bath. Hug people you love. Feel the sun on your skin. Love your body and what it can do.

Fun. Find something you deeply enjoy. You are never too old to need fun, and to need it often. If you've forgotten how to play, start learning again.

Start noticing people who seem to feel content and fulfilled, and see if you can discover what is making life work so well for them. Perhaps come right out and ask them. We can all strive to create a foundation for contentment; happiness doesn't come through pure luck. And that means you can work your way there.

✕⟶⟵✕

"I can build a happy life, so I'm going to."

His Attachment to Payback

Women who are in unhealthy relationships struggle with the question "Is my partner's behavior normal?" You may wonder whether the problem is that you're just too sensitive, or that your expectations are unrealistic. One way to get clear on the nature of your partner's problem is to notice when he *gets you back* for doing something he doesn't like. Payback is not normal in a couple. People in healthy relationships get upset with each other, of course, but they don't get *revenge*.

Each time that he uses verbal abuse toward you, or the silent treatment, or intimidation, or emotional cruelty, ask yourself, "Is there something he is punishing me for?" You will find that the answer is usually yes. He's getting you back for:

- A way you stood up to him
- A way you didn't cater to him as if he were a master and you were his servant
- A way you tried to have your own life
- A way you didn't live up to some absurd ideal he has

The attachment to payback toward his partner is one of the central reasons why an abusive or controlling man has the problem that he does. The more you can recognize the times when he is getting you back for things, the easier it will be for you to avoid getting sucked into believing that something is wrong with you. His vengeful acts show that he is the one with the problem.

"In normal relationships, people don't get each other back for things."

Lack of Sleep

If you go day after day, week after week, not getting enough sleep, the toll on you can be big. Lack of sleep can clog up your ability to think clearly, and can make you raw and sensitive emotionally. The effects tend to be cumulative, so that the longer you've been having trouble getting enough rest, the greater the impact on your life. Some people report starting to have depression, hopelessness, or even a sense that they are losing their minds. You can start to just plain feel shaky, physically and mentally.

If you feel as though you're falling apart, maybe you really just need sleep.

Being involved in a destructive relationship can make sleep hard to come by. The stress and emotional pain of being mistreated, plus worrying about what your partner will do next, can keep you awake. Maybe he doesn't allow you to sleep, either to punish you for something he's angry about or to force you to have sex with him. Sleep deprivation is a serious form of physical abuse—yes, *physical* abuse—though it is often not recognized.

If you have young children, that adds more challenges to getting sleep, especially if your partner is leaving you with almost all of the parenting responsibilities.

Keep some notes about how much sleep you get, tracking your rest patterns over a few weeks. Keeping this record will help you to see whether lack of sleep is actually one of the contributors to the struggles you are having.

><%>

"If he's not letting me sleep, that's one of
the worst things he can do. I'm exhausted."

Guilt

If you are plagued by guilty feelings, you aren't alone. One of the typical dynamics of abusive relationships is that the man is the one who behaves destructively, yet the woman comes out feeling as if she's the one who did something wrong. See if any of the following dynamics feel familiar:

- Your partner sends you the message that you are at fault for bad things he has done to you. As a result, your pain from his behavior gets *interwoven* with the ways in which he blames it on you.
- Voices in your own head blame you for what has happened because

"you picked him" and because "you're choosing to be in this relationship." Neither of these points actually makes you responsible for your partner's actions, but guilty feelings don't follow logic.

- His behavior triggers feelings from experiences you had early in life when you were made to feel guilty for bad things that happened to you or around you. Some parents, for example, lay heavy loads of guilt on children over everything from broken dishes to the parents' own unhappiness in life.
- Your partner's behavior seems to make no sense, so you end up feeling that you must have done *something* to cause it. Otherwise, how do you explain where on earth it came from?

Write in your journal about these feelings to help you get perspective on them. Guilt can eat away at you inside, and you don't deserve to carry that weight. Noticing when you are feeling guilty will also help; then when those feelings come up, you can ask yourself, "Have I really done anything wrong? Or am I actually feeling bad because of what *he* did?"

><DK

"His unhealthy behavior doesn't
make me guilty of anything."

"I Can't Stand the Way I'm Acting"—Part 1

In a number of the reflections in this book I've explained that your partner doesn't get to blame his abusive behavior on you. But what about when the roles are reversed? What happens when you are the one calling him names, or swearing at the top of your voice, or slapping him? Do you get to say that your behavior was caused by his abuse toward you?

I'm going to encourage you to begin by looking at this question through two different lenses:

1. What kind of atmosphere do you want your children to live in?

If you have kids, you don't want them to grow up with the distress of hearing their parents saying horrible things to each other. You also don't want them to learn that such behavior is normal and acceptable. They need at least one parent who doesn't use those tactics, so that they'll know right from wrong.

2. Has this relationship become more than you can handle?

A woman who is in a destructive relationship often tells herself, "I'm doing fine, I can manage this, it's all going to be all right." But if yelling and name-calling and degrading have become part of your own behavior, that's a sure sign that you *can't* manage the relationship you're in. Being involved with an abusive partner takes a serious toll on a woman. If his behaviors are creeping into yours, that's a glaring sign that he's harming you on a deep level.

"If I don't like my own behavior,
it's time to reach out for help."

Longing to Connect with Him

He's in there somewhere. You know he is. Behind all the coldness and criticism, behind the snarls and the insults, behind his looks of impatience and disgust, is the man you once knew and loved. You feel like you see a gem that has fallen into dense thorn bushes, and that if you could just find a way to reach through all those nasty, twisting, razor-sharp tangles, you could pull it out into the light of day and keep it there.

From time to time his old self shows itself for a while, and these periods make your longing even more intense. You ask yourself, "Why would he go back to all that ugliness? Why would he choose to live in that atmosphere instead of in the fun and loving days we are having now?"

The painful truth is that the controlling or abusive man cannot deal with his partner's humanity—with her womanhood—and if a good period goes on too long, her humanity becomes unavoidable. So he escapes it by going back to treating her like a *thing*.

Your longing for closeness is natural. Your faith that goodness still exists within him is admirable. But the sad truth is that as long as you keep reaching for that gem, you are going to keep getting torn to pieces by all those thorns.

Much more important are the gems inside of *you*. Make your day today be about reaching for the best in yourself—and in other people you love—not in him. Bring *those* wonderful qualities out into the light.

⚶

> "There is so much goodness in people that
> doesn't come at a high price."

Dealing with Tantrums—Part 1

It's "one of those days." Your child is pitching fits, and they are mounting in intensity. Finally, he or she "loses it" and starts screaming and throwing toys everywhere, running wildly, and perhaps hitting you. Your child looks like an enraged little monster. You are furious and ready to wring a neck, and your heart is racing with frustration, especially over how openly you are being defied.

Does it feel like this craziness is unique to your parenting experience? Actually, tantrums are common in kids, and most parents have to deal with them at some point. For kids who are living in circumstances that bring extra stress—kids whose moms are being abused, for example—tantrums can get more frequent.

I'm going to propose a dramatic change in how you respond to these eruptions that can dramatically reduce stress for both you and your child. Almost all parents think of tantrums as terrible behavior that must be snuffed out sharply and instantly. This effort fails, however; the more intensely and negatively we react, the more the tantrum escalates. So here's the key point: Although a tantrum *may* include bad behavior, it doesn't automatically. When children stomp their feet, yell, run angrily around, and pound things (without breaking them), they aren't actually doing anything wrong. *You don't have to make a tantrum stop*; that's not your job. Understanding this concept will save both you and your child so much anguish.

So what is your job?

1. Keep the child safe.
2. Don't let the child hurt you or anyone else.

3. Don't let the child damage anything important.

4. Let the child know that he or she is not alone, that you are present and caring.

Believe it or not, that's all you have to do.

> "I don't have to make a tantrum stop.
> I only need to prevent harm."

The Temptation to Have an Affair

Other possible partners may be looking pretty good these days. Most women who feel bullied by their partners have days when they dream of being with someone who is kind to them, who cares what they think, who finds them sexy and beautiful. You're not a bad person for having some fantasies; it's a natural reaction.

But is it a good idea to act on those urges? Perhaps there's a man in your life who is giving you pretty strong signals that he's interested, and you're wondering what to do. Or there's someone you'd like to pursue. So should you?

My answer is that in most cases you're better off not doing it. I've heard a number of women speak about their affairs with regret:

"I ended up feeling even worse about myself than I already did. I don't like feeling sneaky and dishonest."

"I didn't really want to hurt him; I just wanted his abuse to stop."

"It left me feeling empty inside. I realized I don't want an affair, I want a good relationship."

"It didn't solve anything."

And if your partner has a violent side, he may get dangerous if he finds out.

At the same time, the truth is that I have spoken with a number of abused women whose affairs had a positive impact. I've heard:

"It was so good to be treated in a loving way, instead of with hatred and put-downs."

"It helped me to see that he was wrong when he said no other man would want me."

"It helped me get the strength to get out of the relationship."

The bottom line is: Whatever you decide, don't put yourself in danger, and don't violate your own principles in a way that leads you to feel bad about yourself.

$$\rightsquigarrow$$

> "I'm not a bad person for craving kind,
> loving, and sexy treatment."

Feeling Caught Between a Rock and a Hard Place

Earlier in this book, I wrote about how important the dynamic of payback is in understanding how abusive men think and behave. Now let's consider the effects on you. Because your partner uses payback, much of your energy goes into anxiety about whether he will explode if you defy him or even do something "wrong" accidentally. The result is that you come out feeling trapped between bad choices, such as:

"It's really going to hurt my life if I don't finish school, but if I stay in school he's going to make life hell for me."

"Spending so much time alone is messing up my head, but he tears me to pieces when I try to see friends."

"He's destroying our financial situation, but when I try to talk to him about money he goes ballistic."

"I'm really going downhill from being in this relationship, but if I leave him I think he might kill me."

Take a few minutes to write in your journal, reflecting on the binds your partner creates for you. And notice the wrongness of what he is doing.

> "I feel so trapped sometimes. And that makes sense, given my partner's punishing style."

When Crying Seems to Only Make Things Worse

Crying long and hard is one of the most powerful healing forces, helping to relieve and reshape emotional anguish. But it doesn't work for everyone all the time. Some people report that crying doesn't seem to discharge their sadness; they just weep on for hours and hours and nothing feels any better, or they even feel worse than they did when they started. If you sometimes experience prolonged crying that doesn't bring you relief, here is one of the most likely reasons: You are sitting on a pile of *rage* that you've been stuffing away for years, or even for your whole life. Crying won't work because first you need to be pounding couch cushions, screaming into pillows, stomping your feet, or throwing tantrums in the woods.

Releasing anger is not as much about yelling and screaming as most people think; it's even more about getting your body into it, flailing your arms around and grabbing things and throwing them and making wild motions.

Don't release your rage with your children around because it will frighten them, and don't do it around your partner because he will use your tantrum against you to humiliate you. It's best to be alone, or with a trusted friend.

There are additional ways you can work with anger, though the ones above often work best. Tell a loved one the truth about the outrages that have been done to you, especially if you've never told anyone. You may find it cathartic to write furiously in your journal, or compose enraged poetry, music, or art.

Don't keep all that anger inside of you; it needs a safe and constructive, but forceful, way to come out.

⁂

"My rage is beautiful and necessary.
Here it comes."

Feeling Like You'll Never Get Over This

After enough times of being torn apart by your partner's cruel side, you can come to feel like nothing could ever put you back together again, and like the pain will never go away.

But it will. You aren't always going to feel this bad. Healing is a long process, especially when you've been harmed by someone you love. But the injured places do grow back together.

One thing that emotional wounds and physical wounds have in common is that they take triply long to heal if you keep getting hurt again in the same spot. So you may not be able to heal well from your partner's mistreatment of you unless you put emotional distance between yourself and him—and perhaps physical distance as well. Your spirit needs a chance to bounce back. It may be time to put yourself in an environment where healing can happen.

It's true that some women have to get stronger before they can get out of their relationship, but for other women the opposite is true— they have to get out of their relationship before they can get stronger. Consider which one might be more true of you.

✳

"Healing well requires safety. When I find
a way to get myself to a safe place, my
spirit will start to grow whole again."

"I Can't Stand the Way I'm Acting"—Part 2

A week ago we started looking at the question of what to do if you're bothered by your own behavior. Perhaps you are yelling or swearing with increasing frequency, or you are calling your partner names and trying to demean him. I asked you to reflect on the kind of surroundings you want your children to be raised in, and also to consider whether your partner's behavior has become more than you can handle. Now I'd like you to reflect on a third question:

3. What kind of person do I want to be?

If you are involved with a controlling partner, then he undoubtedly attacks your self-opinion in all kinds of ways, forcing you to fight to maintain your sense of self. But if your own behavior is going against your beliefs, you are contributing to harming your own dignity and self-esteem. Don't do his dirty work for him. It is critically important to improve your behavior so that you can stay in touch with your goodness and decency, with the truth of who you really are.

Blaming your actions on him won't help, even if you are reacting to years of being controlled and torn down by him; it will just add to your feelings of helplessness. And although adopting his behaviors may feel like a way of standing up to him, it actually just sucks you deeper into his control. Don't kid yourself; an abuser wins even when he loses.

"I need to stay clear of his way of
thinking and behaving."

Withdrawing When You Feel Hurt by People

Learning how to deal with hurt feelings is key to having successful relationships with friends and relatives. Hurt feelings are inevitable; it just isn't possible to have connections with people that have depth and substance without having times when those people do things that make you feel bad. (And there will, in turn, be times when things that you do feel hurtful to them.)

And when you are in a relationship with a destructive partner, you are likely to feel raw and sensitive much of the time; as a result, people will hurt your feelings more often than usual, and they won't necessarily have any idea that they made a mistake.

When you feel wounded, it's tempting to pull away. It's natural to have thoughts such as "They should have known what they did would hurt me. That was so insensitive. They don't really care about me."

Try not to let these kinds of reactions compel you to cut people off. Give yourself space to feel those feelings, but then bring yourself back to center, remembering that communication is essential. As soon as possible, tell the person that you are feeling hurt, and explain why, rather than blowing up at him or her. Try to have faith that you and a person you care about can work through some tensions.

$\rtimes$ᐧ᠎

"Just because my partner is impossible
to talk to about my hurt feelings
doesn't mean other people are."

Dealing with Tantrums—Part 2

The big secret about tantrums is that they actually help kids feel better. Observe the difference in your child's mood before and after a big fit. What you will discover is that, just like a big sobbing cry, a tantrum wears off after a while and leaves in its wake a happier, more cooperative child. Children are easier to reason with after the tantrum than they were before it started!

The tantrum will actually make the rest of your day go better, if you can just get out of the way of it and let it happen. Your goal is to support your child during it, rather than sending the message that he or she is being a bad kid.

Now, you may be thinking, "That will never work here. When my kid has tantrums, I end up black and blue from being kicked in the shins, toys get smashed, glasses get broken. I can't just let that go on." But you can teach your child to separate the bad behavior from the tantrum itself. At a time when your child is calm, sit and talk about what's okay during a tantrum and what isn't. "You can yell and stomp your feet, you can pound the cushions on the couch, you can run back and forth. But if you hit me or break things, here's what the consequences are going to be." And then impose those consequences as you would for any other misbehavior.

What many parents report is that children who are permitted to have their tantrums—meaning they aren't required to choke them off—can learn to have them in nondestructive ways. When the voice inside your head says, "I can't let my kid get away with acting like that!" respond by asking yourself, "Which parts do I really have to make stop, and which parts are actually harmless?" You'll be amazed how much easier your life gets when you let the tantrum go; in fact, you can actually support and approve of it as long as it doesn't hurt anything or anyone. Your child will revel in your ability to accept and respect the powerful emotions he or she feels.

I can teach my child to have safe tantrums.

The Goal: An Abuse-Free Life

Where you end up in life depends to some extent on the direction you aim yourself in. So point yourself toward a life that is free of abuse.

Think for a moment about what your wishes are for the relationship you are in. That your partner will stop criticizing you and putting you down so often? That he will trust that you are faithful instead of accusing you of cheating on him? That he'll stop getting scary or violent when he's mad at you? The problem with wishing for these things is that they are so much less than what you need and deserve. In effect, these wishes are saying, "I'm hoping not to be treated quite as badly in the future as I am now."

Set your sights much higher. You should never again be called a demeaning name by an intimate partner. You should never again be pressured for sex you don't want. You should never again be made to feel worthless. In fact, you should feel that your partner is on your side, supporting you to get what you want.

Your reaction to my words may be to think, "But that's completely unrealistic! No man is going to be that good to me."

Those voices in your head aren't telling the truth. Many, many women live a life where they don't get harmed, emotionally or physically, by their partner's words or behavior. There are men who consistently behave responsibly and respectfully in their relationships with women—even when they are really pissed off.

And there are also women who are very happy being single, which is another valid route to an abuse-free life, but one that is not often mentioned.

From where you are now, the road to a life where you don't get torn down in any way by your partner—whether it's your current one or a future one—may seem impossible to travel. But if you make that your goal, you will find a way to get there eventually. Don't settle for less than everything you have a right to as a human being.

"Why should I be happy with things being
only a little better than they are now?"

When He Doesn't Get His Way Sexually

No one, male or female, is always in the mood for sex. And sexuality is only a positive, loving experience when both people are into it. A woman whose partner is abusive tends to have complicated feelings about sex. On the one hand she craves intimacy because of how cold and rejecting he often is; but on the other hand his touch can feel violating to her because of the way he insults, devalues, and bullies her so much of the time.

When an abusive man doesn't get what he wants sexually, he may punish his partner in a number of ways: giving her the silent treatment, accusing her of cheating on him, calling her names such as "frigid" or "lesbian," keeping her awake, or telling her she doesn't love him. Some men become threatening or assault the woman.

Your partner has no right to retaliate against you for the sexual choices you make. Your body belongs 100 percent to you, and 0 percent to him. And a marriage certificate doesn't change that.

If your decisions about when to have sex with your partner are being shaped by your fears of what he will do to you if you say "no," then what he is doing is not lovemaking, it's sexual assault—whether it appears violent or not.

"My body belongs entirely to me, every
minute of every day, my whole life long."

Why Is It All Your Job?

The saying goes, "A woman's work is never done." But the reason why it's never done is that there is a man who is making the rules about which jobs are yours and which are his, and he's leaving you with way too much work to do.

If he complains about the food, it would be fair to ask, "Why don't you do the shopping? Why don't you make more of the meals?" If he complains about the mess in the house, it would be fair to ask, "Why can't you clean the house this time? When do I get to put my feet up and declare that I've been working hard all day and have to rest?" If he complains about the children, it would be fair to ask, "How much quality time have you spent with them? How many of their messes have you cleaned up today? How many of their behavior problems or their conflicts have you helped solve?" (And he doesn't help solve anything by yelling at the kids.)

I realize you may not be able to actually say these things aloud to him because he would get you back for it. But you can at least say them to yourself to maintain your clarity.

Let's look at a list of what is typically thought of as "women's work": clean the house, wash the dishes, do the food shopping, prepare two or three meals a day (which can be endless work in itself), do the laundry, schedule the kids' appointments, fill out school forms, drive the kids places, spend quality time with the kids, change the sheets, buy curtains, buy clothes for everyone, get medicine for the kids and remember when they have to take it, read to the kids and put them to sleep, get out of bed when the baby is crying (sometime several times a night), clean up the children's vomit, and on and on and on.

Who gets to say that this is all your job? Why does he get to decide who does what?

Here's the simple formula: He has no right to demand that you work more hours in a day than he does. Paid and unpaid work count the same. (And if he claims that his work is "harder," he's using a classic excuse that abusive men rely on for treating women like servants.)

*

"I have the right to take on a fair share
of the work and no more."

"But I Still Love Him"

There are few decisions in life that are as difficult as making up your mind about whether to leave a relationship that you're not happy in. Giving up hope about being with someone you cared a lot about can feel overwhelmingly sad; in fact, when people do try to break up with their partners, the weight of grief is often what drives them back into the relationship. In addition, you naturally struggle with the question of whether there might still be some way to make the relationship work.

Many women with abusive partners say to me, "He's been so awful to me so many times, and he's even had affairs, and maybe you'll think this is crazy, but the thing is I still have feelings for him."

I don't think it's crazy. In fact, it's completely natural to still love someone who has mistreated you, because you have seen other sides to him and you know the person he could be.

But the mistake is to think you have to stop loving him before you can leave him. Waiting for your feelings to change is a mistake. You may love him for the rest of your life. The huge question, though, is whether this is how you want to spend that precious life. Aren't there all kinds of people whom you love in this world but you wouldn't want to be the partner of? Well, your current partner may be one of those people.

Once it has become clear that the relationship you are in is not good for you, and that your well-being is deteriorating, it's time to leave. As one woman who divorced an abusive husband told me, "I realized I was never going to stop loving him, but I also knew I had to get away from him because he was toxic to me."

"Once I know this has become unhealthy for me, it's time to move on, whether I still love him or not."

Believe in Your Capabilities

When I have a conversation with a woman who has a controlling partner, I notice how many of her sentences start with expressions such as:

"I can't possibly . . ."

"I know I don't have what it takes to . . ."

"I admire the things you do, but I could never . . ."

Her partner's voice has wended its way inside of her, so that she has internalized his outlook. To her all kinds of steps that other people might take have come to seem out of the question, because he's made her believe that she isn't capable of very much.

Reflect for a moment on whether this dynamic is playing out in your life. Are you finding yourself giving a lot of reasons and excuses for why a better life is out of reach for you? Has your partner colored your image of yourself to the point where his view has started to feel like the real one?

Notice what he communicates through his behavior, not just in words. For example, he may say that he thinks you are smart, but when he puts down your opinions, ignores what you say, or tells you to quit school, those actions send the opposite message.

You are intelligent and capable. See if you can start your sentences with "Maybe I can," or "I'm going to really give it a try." Reclaiming power over your life begins with believing in yourself.

"I can do so much more than I feel like I can. I'm going to stop listening to those negative voices."

Daring to Ask for Help

Reaching out for help can be a scary business, especially if you have been burned in the past by people you thought would assist you. You may encounter people who "don't want to get involved," blame you for your predicament, or refuse to believe that your partner is capable of exhibiting the kinds of behavior that you are trying to tell them about. It can be even trickier if you live in an area where everyone knows everyone else.

But there's another side out there. There are people of integrity who will listen carefully to what is happening in your relationship. There are people eager to help, wanting to feel that they are making a difference in the world. You can find ones who will believe you and take your challenges seriously.

And it can be a gift to other people to allow them to help you! You are giving them the opportunity to contribute to another human life and to improve their community. Every time a woman who is being mistreated receives good assistance, the overall quality of life rises for everyone who lives anywhere nearby, for many reasons.

Your partner may have tried to keep you from looking for assistance. He may say that no one will believe you, or that you don't deserve help because you are actually the one with the problem. He may work to turn people against you so that they won't help. He may have made up bad things to tell you about programs for abused women so that you won't want to call them.

Don't believe what he's telling you. Find out for yourself what is out there (check out the "Resources" section in the back of this book as a starting point).

꒰ ꒱

"I can find people who will be on my side. I deserve assistance and people will see that."

Dealing with Tantrums—Part 3

Parents worry about what will happen if they don't stop their kids' tantrums. They say to me, "I can't allow my children to behave that way, or they'll never learn to respond appropriately when they are upset. If I let them pitch a fit, they're going to learn that they can do that every time they don't get their way. They'll turn into spoiled little brats."

It's not true. Here's where the confusion lies:

1. If you make the mistake of giving children what they want in order to settle the tantrum down, then, yes, they will learn to use tan-

trums strategically. And then their spoiled tantrums will become a big problem.

2. But if you let them have their eruption and then, when they come back to earth, you still don't give in, they will learn that tantrums don't get them any reward. The message from you, spoken aloud and demonstrated through what you do, is: "You can use tantrums to get your rage and fear out, but you can't use them to get your way—it won't work."

The proof of the value of this system is, of course, in the results. I can assure you that if you follow this simple formula:

1. Support the tantrum lovingly for as long as it takes to blow over by itself
2. Don't give in to the child's demands

then you will have a child who gradually gets easier to deal with around the clock, not just at tantrum time.

One final point: The belief that if you let kids have tantrums, they'll never learn more constructive ways to express their emotions, is a myth. Children who are permitted to have tantrums—as long as they are required to behave acceptably during a tantrum—actually learn *more* quickly how to channel their emotions in positive directions. Try it and see.

"I can actually support my child through
a tantrum, and we'll all be happier."

When Abuse Feels Natural

Some women come from backgrounds where abusive behavior is most of what they have known. They grew up in homes where the adults swore and put the children down, where the kids got hit and threatened, where children's boundaries were violated by a relative. Where they grew up it was normal for kids to devote their energy to being mean to each other. As teenagers they hardly knew any decent guys; their relationships were marked by pressure for sex or by violence from the guy, beginning with their earliest days of dating. They can hardly imagine what a loving relationship would look like.

If this is what your history has been like, you may find it hard to even figure out which of your partner's behaviors are normal and which ones are unacceptable. You may ask yourself, "Well, doesn't everybody act that way?" And you may use abusive behaviors yourself quite a bit, so your inner voice says, "If he's abusive, then so am I."

I recommend that you stop trying to figure out what's normal and what isn't. Instead, decide how you want to live. You are not condemned to follow the pattern that your history has established for you. Every day there are more people who reject their unhealthy pasts and head off in a completely new direction.

Living separate from abuse can feel strange at first. When you come from a rough background, being kind and patient with people can seem stupid and fake. You can feel suspicious of people who are being good to you, assuming that they are just setting you up to take advantage of you. You may feel that if you don't keep a hard exterior, people are going to come crashing through your boundaries left and right.

These are natural reactions to the shift you are trying to make. I've heard women say that it took them years to adapt to a life where people treat each other well; but they were so glad they stuck with it until it came to be the new normal. You can do it too.

"I can reforge my life in a new mold;
the past does not determine and control me."

Dealing with His Promises to Change

If only your partner could always be like his better aspects, the way he was when you first knew him. Right? You fell for him for a reason; he was fun, you liked his style, he was crazy about you. You had no idea he could be so insulting, so hateful, so mean. He didn't seem anything remotely like that back then. And even now, on his good days, his ugly side can seem far away.

But his destructive moods and behaviors keep coming back and back, like waves on a shore.

So one day you get up the courage to tell him that you can't live with this kind of mistreatment, and it may be time to break up. His reaction is to do some deep soul-searching, and he ends up apologizing for how he has been behaving and promising he's going to change. So now what do you do?

The catch is that promises, no matter how sincerely meant, don't lead anywhere. Deep personal change requires *hard, honest work* over a period of *years*; nothing else works. All quick transformations that people undergo, based on a new philosophy or a book they read or a sudden profound awakening, fade away before long. Their old habits, attitudes, and behaviors return.

Is he willing to back up his promises with extended serious effort? One way to find out is to use the chapters called "Men's Work Part I" and "Men's Work Part II" under "Articles" at LundyBancroft.com. Print those two chapters out for him and ask him to start doing the reading and assignments. If he actually sticks with it, then maybe his promises will take him somewhere.

And if he isn't willing to do the work, or goes a little way into it and then quits, or starts to get angry at you about having to do it, then you have your answer.

><>

"I'm not going to be swayed by promises
anymore. I want and need to see action."

"Why Do I Keep Going Back to Him?"— Part 1

So it's one of those bad periods again. Your partner is cold and distant; he snaps and criticizes. Nothing you do is right. He's back to his double standards, where he can behave any way he wants but whatever you do is under a microscope. Everything feels ugly. And once again you are asking yourself, "What am I doing here? Why didn't I just stay away the last time we split up? When will I ever learn?"

Let's take a look at what happens when you split up. At first, no doubt, you feel a sense of relief to be away from the tension and mistreatment. But close behind that follows a period of mounting sadness. You start to miss your partner's better side. Even more than that, though, you miss the feeling of being in love. And that's why you get back together with him even though it makes no sense to do so; you are in pursuit of something that feels like it's in him, but actually is in you. What you are chasing after is already yours.

You have the capacity already in you to feel deeply loving, and deeply loved. Your partner does not give you that. You feel love for certain friends or relatives. You feel love for certain special places. You love some precious objects that belong to you, crafts or seashells or photographs. If you believe in God, or in some overarching force toward beauty and truth in the world, then you feel that spiritual, all-encompassing love sometimes.

And there are people who love you, whose lives you have touched. There are people eager to see you and spend time with you (though not all of them have had the courage to tell you so yet).

Your partner is not the source of love in the world. Work on growing your ability to feel love all around you, to notice and take in what is there. The more you can expand that awareness, the less you will feel that his mistreatment is just a price you have to pay for love.

꒰ꫛ꒱

"I live surrounded by love. I can learn to
tap into that more and more each day."

Avoiding "New Year's Resolution Syndrome"

I've been told that January is the month of the year when fitness clubs sign up their largest number of new members, because so many people make a New Year's resolution that they are going to get in shape. By February, unfortunately, gyms see fewer people as they start to lose their motivation.

This pattern is actually a year-round challenge. All of us have times when we resolve to make certain changes in our lives, or to start working toward goals or ambitions that matter to us. But more often than not we lose steam before getting very far.

The way to break out of this pattern is to add a number of additional steps; just making the resolution is not enough. Here's how to make it work:

1. Tell a trusted friend that you have decided to work toward an important goal. Explain why the goal matters to you and how long you think it will take you to get there. Then ask the person to call you at least once a week to check in on your progress. That person's job is to encourage and support you, without criticism.

2. Make a plan for what kind of progress you want to have made toward your goal a year from now. Take a piece of that and set a target for three months from now.

3. Now break your goal down into even smaller steps, the smallest ones you can think of. If you want to go back to school, for example, make your goal for this week something like "I will make two phone calls and check out two websites to get information about school programs for myself." In other words, choose a piece to do this week that you know you can succeed at.

4. Work toward your goal with one step per week. At the end of three months, evaluate how you are doing and set your course for the next three months. Don't spend much time thinking about your one-year target; once you've set that, keep your focus on what you need to do this week.

This approach actually works. The key to success is breaking your dreams up into really manageable steps. Give it a try.

✤

"I can get to where I want to be, one step at a time."

Projection

Here's an interesting irony: People who have recurring patterns of behaving destructively tend to also specialize in identifying what's wrong with everybody else. They often criticize in others exactly those qualities that are worst in themselves. Gossipy people run around complaining about how gossipy this person or that person is, greedy people look down on other people's lust for money, explosive people complain loudly about people who go berserk for no reason.

In some cases they are perceiving other people's issues correctly—while of course remaining blind to their own. But much of the time they are seeing things that aren't even there. The man who is exclusively focused on his own needs, for example, tends to call his partner "selfish," and some of the most controlling men in the world call their partners "control freaks." (Sound familiar?)

In the field of psychology, this process is known as "projection"; the person unconsciously projects their own issues onto other people, so the faults they believe they are seeing in others are actually in themselves. The more destructive and unpredictable an individual's behavior is, the more projecting that person tends to do.

And here's the ultimate irony: The man who does a lot of projecting sometimes tells his partner that she's the one who is projecting! In other words, if he has heard about this concept, he'll use it to discredit her when she points out how terribly he treats her.

Next time your partner starts to list off your supposed faults, see if you can get some emotional distance from what he is saying by telling yourself, "There he goes again, pouring out his projections." His insults are about him, not about you.

"When he is putting me down, none of what he says
is about me. In fact, most of it is about him."

Why Did So Many People Side with Him?

On some days the following thoughts may rattle around inside your head: "Okay, I can kind of see his friends backing him up, because they only hear his side of the story. And some of them are kind of like him anyhow—that's why they're friends with him. But why have people I trusted taken his side? My own good friends? My brother? Our pastor? People who'd been neutral before? What happened?"

Go back in your mind to the first several months of your relationship with your partner. Remember how convincing he was, how persuasive? Remember what a great guy he seemed to be? Remember how he made you feel bad for him when he told you about other people who had done wrong to him (including previous partners of his)? Abusive men tend to be skillful manipulators. Unfortunately, the same skills he used with you he is now turning on other people.

Additional factors play a part. In tightly knit communities, such as some towns and churches, people want to avoid anything that could tear their cozy network apart. They'd rather decide that a woman is lying about being abused than to take the scary steps involved in addressing the problem.

Some people are working hard to not face what's happening in their own relationships, so they don't want to think about how your partner has treated you—it's too close to home.

And finally, we are a society that blames women more than men for what goes wrong in relationships.

So even though I'm outraged that they've turned on you, I'm not surprised. Do your best through this painful time to remember that they are the ones with a problem, not you. They should come up with the courage and common sense to look squarely at what has actually happened. Perhaps someday they will.

"I can keep my sanity even though
everyone else is acting crazy."

Good Secrets vs. Bad Secrets

Sometimes you may need your children to keep secrets from your partner, for your safety or for their own. Suppose, for example, that you have a talk one night with your kids about your partner's rages. You explain to them that it isn't okay for him to get scary like that. The children then open up about how upset they get when he explodes at you. Such a conversation would be a very positive event; children need to know that abuse is wrong, and they need to know that it's okay to talk with their mom and with each other about disturbing incidents that they have witnessed.

But what will happen if they decide to bring up this conversation with your partner? What if they tell him that you all talked about it and agreed that the way he was acting was wrong? If he's like most abusive men, there is going to be hell to pay for you and for the kids.

You want to teach your kids not to keep secrets, but now you have one that you need them to keep. What do you do?

The answer is to teach your children the difference between a good secret and a bad secret. The characteristics of a *good secret* are:

- You *want* to keep it; you aren't being told by someone else that you have to.
- Keeping the secret helps to keep you safe or to protect people you love.
- You have people you can talk to about it; you aren't left all alone with the secret.

A secret is a *bad secret* if any of the following things are true about it:

- You were told you had to keep it; the person said you would be punished or hurt if you told.
- Keeping the secret feels bad; you don't want to have to keep it.
- Keeping the secret is making you more likely to get hurt, not less likely (such as keeping a secret about something a bully did to you, since the secret will allow the bully to keep hurting you).
- You are all alone with the secret; there is nobody you can tell.

These are good concepts for every child to understand, so teach them to your kids even if there isn't any immediate need to.

꒦꒷

"My children need to know when it's
okay to keep secrets and when it isn't."

The First Step of the Day

The tone of your day can be set by what happens during the first hour. Once you have established a certain mood, and a posture or energy in your body, a momentum is created that can carry on until you fall asleep that night. If you start out tense, or lonely, or hopeless, that atmosphere can be hard to shake. On the other hand, if your day begins with some energy and self-confidence, you can get yourself on a positive roll that will be hard for anyone else to knock you off of.

Here are a few strategies for getting off to a strong start. Begin with at least a few minutes of vigorous physical movement. You might go for a run or a walk, or spend a few minutes dancing, stretching, or doing yoga. If you have children and need to focus on them right away, engage them in some wrestling or roughhousing so that you are active. Strong blood flow and deep, regular breathing are crucial first thing in the morning.

See if you can make contact with someone who is consistently positive. If you have children, focus on a fun, loving morning connection with them, and remember to laugh together. If you have a close friend or relative, make a quick call or send a quick morning text to them, even if it's two sentences. In this way you bring someone you love into your heart early.

Finally, eat good food. Don't start your day with pastries and coffee; sugar and caffeine set you up to feel discouraged and irritable by mid-morning. Instead get some eggs or other good source of protein, a cooked or raw vegetable (yes, even at breakfast), and some kind of probiotic (yogurt, a fermented food, or a probiotic capsule). The right foods can have a positive effect on your attitude and energy level, which in turn determine the tone of the day.

⟡

"I am going to create momentum for a good day."

CLARITY

Defining Reality

The controlling man can adopt a tone that lets you know that he considers himself The Absolute Last Word. To his mind, anyone who disagrees with him—especially if anyone is you—just isn't facing the facts, which he is the expert on. He's fond of expressions such as, "It's obvious that . . ." and "Everyone knows that . . ." and "Anyone with a brain in their head can tell that . . ." When he's in this mode, his voice is steeped in superiority, impatience, and disgust. You know that if you don't agree with him he's going to insult you.

This way of speaking is known as "defining reality."

It's hard to defend yourself against him when he's using these mental control tactics, because he twists anything you say around and uses it to make you feel stupid or ignorant. But you can defend yourself *inside*, invisibly to him, protecting the health of your spirit.

The first step is to name silently what he's doing. Next time he goes off in his "no sane person would disagree with me" tone, repeat to yourself in your head, "There he goes, 'Defining Reality' again."

Next, as soon as you are away from him, in a different room for example, check in with yourself about what your true beliefs and opinions are. *Trust your gut instinct, and hold on to what you know.* Your partner can sound so right and be so wrong.

Of course your thoughts should evolve and grow over time; everyone's should. But this process should happen through respectful engagement with other people's ideas, through thoughtful disagreements, through the sharing of perspectives. Don't change your mind easily, and don't do it because someone speaks arrogantly.

And if he were so full of wisdom, he wouldn't be a bully; the proof of the clarity of people's thinking is in their actions.

"He doesn't get to define
what's true and what's real."

"Why Do I Keep Going Back to Him?"— Part 2

So you're back with your partner after breaking up with him for a while, and you're asking yourself why. You wonder, "Do I just want to be treated like this? I must be a glutton for punishment."

No, you're not looking for pain. Women get stuck for different reasons. We started looking at some of those last week. Here are some additional common traps:

His love feels more powerful because it's so hard to get. When a partner is cold, distant, or mean, the periods when he turns loving just seem like the most dazzling experience in the world. You might compare it to how delicious a meal will taste if you're starving when you sit down to the table.

His show of pain draws you in. Maybe he pours his heart out telling you how bad he feels about himself, including how terrible he feels about how he's treated you. Maybe he tells you that he gets off track drinking or chasing other women, but then he realizes that your love is the one thing that really matters to him. You look at him and he just seems so hurt and vulnerable, and you just want to wrap him in your arms.

You can't bear the loneliness when you try to leave him. Breaking up is always a sad experience for people, but leaving an abusive relationship tends to bring up even more intense feelings of loneliness than other breakups do. The loneliness can be further accentuated if your partner has driven you away from other people.

You felt afraid of how he was reacting to the breakup. If he has been volatile or violent with you in the past, leaving him is extra hard because you can't keep an eye on his moods and escalations. It can get scary wondering what he's thinking and planning.

Rather than dumping on yourself for being back with him, start working on how you are going to address these challenges, both inside yourself and in your life. You can prepare yourself so that the next time you leave you'll be able to stay away.

✴

"I can build my strength so that I'll be able to go
through with ending things with him."

"Bragging"

If you ever said anything positive about yourself when you were a girl, you probably got told, "Stop bragging!" The effect of this criticism may have been to make you feel as though you should never take pride in yourself out loud.

But bragging is not the same thing as appreciating yourself or showing pride. Bragging is when someone adopts a superior tone about his or her accomplishments or abilities, or goes on too long about them. In other words, it's when the person talking is sending the message that other people's strengths are less impressive or important. You might also label it "bragging" when a person talks proudly about what they *own*; why are possessions something to be proud of?

But appreciating yourself is another matter. Speaking proudly about the ways in which you have been courageous or honest or hardworking or kind is not bragging. When you appreciate yourself aloud, you actually strengthen yourself to grow more and do even better. You are also doing a favor to the people listening to you, because you are inspiring them to believe in themselves.

Take a journal or a writing pad in hand, and put down as many things as you can think of that you like about yourself or that you do well. (Try to silence your partner's voice in your head while you do this.) Here are some areas you could consider:

- How you treat other people, how you treat animals
- What you do well as a mother
- What skills you have
- What kind of friend you are, how you have "been there" for people
- What things you work hard at
- What areas you are smart about (everyone has some)

Try not to hold back or slip in negative comments about yourself; make what you write 100 percent self-appreciation.

"There is a lot that's good about me."

Being "Alone"

Part of what keeps women trapped in unhealthy relationships is the fear of being single. Our society seems to have a negative outlook on the lives of women who don't have partners. We assume that the woman is lonely; in fact, we refer to being single as being "alone," as if she spends all of her time by herself. We tend to think of her as not quite complete. Where is "her man"? Where is her "other half"?

The reality is quite different from the societal image. Having a partner is not the key to happiness in life. Many single people are quite content, and many people in relationships are miserable. Single women are certainly much happier than women who have abusive or controlling partners.

I have an older friend—in her seventies now—who was married and divorced when she was young, with two young children. She simply decided at that time that she preferred to be single, and has kept her life that way all the decades since. There are famous female artists and writers and actors who, too, chose the single life as being the best one for them.

Being coupled off is neither a necessity nor an obligation. Having a partner is a *choice*, an option to exercise when it makes you happy. And being single does not mean being "alone." Many single women live lives of abundant close and affectionate connection to other people. They can be far less isolated than a woman who lives with a controlling partner. Joy in life comes from many sources.

>◦<

"I'd love to be with a good man, but I can have a great life without one."

Where to Get Help When Everyone Sides with Him

Sometimes it just becomes too painful to keep trying to get the people around you to see the truth. When people are impressed with your partner and convinced that he's a great person, your efforts to get them to see won't always work. They don't want to believe they idolized a false icon, so it's easier to blame the victim.

So sometimes you're better off letting go of trying to open their eyes. Instead, look elsewhere for support, validation, and safety. Some places you might turn to include:

- Friends and relatives who don't live close by, so they haven't been swayed by your community's mythology about your partner
- Websites for women who have faced abuse by influential abusers (such as NotToPeopleLikeUs.com) or where you could seek out women whose experiences are similar to yours (such as VerbalAbuse.com)
- A hotline or support group for abused women (see "Resources")

A day will come when you can get yourself into circumstances where people validate and support you. You will be able to surround yourself with friends who don't know the man who abused you and haven't been indoctrinated by his allies. I recognize what a painful journey it can be to get there, but you will make it. He will not succeed in controlling you forever.

⁂

> "Eventually I will build a life away from all this
> toxicity. I can do it."

His Relationship with the Kids Is on Him

Our society sends messages to women that it's a mother's job to create a close connection between her children and their father. She's supposed to ease the tensions between them, convince the kids to think well of their father even when he's behaving badly, and give them ideas for how to spend time together.

This is all wrong. A father's relationship with his children is his own responsibility. He should be the one working out his conflicts with them. He should be the one planning activities with them—and then coming through on what he planned. He should be the one remembering important events in the children's lives. He should be the one understanding their feelings. Why should all these responsibilities fall on the mother, who has an endless list of her own tasks to deal with?

These societal messages become even more problematic for a mother whose partner is selfish and self-centered. You can't solve the problems that are arising from his failure to make the children's needs and feelings a priority, and no one should expect you to. If he wants to be a good father, he will have to do the hard work and make the sacrifices that good fathers make. He will also have to be capable of some self-examination; it's impossible to be a good parent without that.

Your children need to know that you recognize the problems in how your partner behaves. Don't make excuses to them for his actions; the kids will misinterpret that as meaning that you don't care about how his behavior is hurting them. You're going to have to let their father clean up his own messes.

> "He can have a good relationship with our
> kids if he chooses to; it's up to him. I can't
> make it happen, and anyhow it's
> not my responsibility."

Respect Is What It's All About

Abuse and respect are opposites. You can't respect a partner that you abuse. The destructive man may insist over and over again that he respects his partner, but if he did, he wouldn't treat her in the demeaning and unfair ways that he does.

What he is refusing to look at is that respect is a profound orientation toward another person, not just a superficial set of polite behaviors. When we view another person with respect, we recognize that the person is just as fully human as we are. We see that person as *equal* to us in value—this is the most critical point of all. We also recognize that the person has important strengths and capabilities, even if we don't know what they are; we just take it for granted that they are present inside the person. Finally, we recognize that the person suffers pain just like anyone else.

There are two additional points about respect that I especially want to draw your attention to. First, notice that none of the items above says that we need to have warm feelings toward the person, or even like him or her. In fact respect is just as important, and in many ways more important, when we are dealing with someone we resent, disapprove of, or find irritating. Being furious at someone, or even knowing that the person has done bad things, is no excuse for demeaning that person. We have to learn to call people out on bad behavior without treating them as less human.

Secondly, no one can lose his or her right to be respected. I emphasize this point because of the number of times I have heard an abusive man say about his partner, "I can't respect her because she's not *worthy* of respect." In other words, he has convinced himself that she is disgusting, so he can treat her however he feels like treating her. But the only thing disgusting is his behavior. All human beings are worthy of respect.

✂ ✑

"I have always deserved respect,
and I deserve it now."

Feelings Are Not an Excuse for Behavior

The definition of adulthood is: the time when we are ready to be fully responsible for our actions. Children do make choices, but not to the same extent that adults do; their feelings often overwhelm them and take over their behavior. For adults, however, our feelings are no excuse for our behavior.

The controlling man typically hides behind his feelings to avoid being answerable for what he does, with claims such as:

"I couldn't help how I acted; you made me too angry."

"I go crazy when I feel that jealous, because I love you so much."

"What do you expect me to do after you hurt my feelings like that?"

"There's only so much a guy can take."

Your partner may blame you for his actions because (he says) you caused his feelings. Now, it's questionable whether you even caused the feelings that came up for him—controlling men often have emotional reactions that make no sense—but even if you did, you didn't cause how he decided to *act* on those feelings; that's on him.

The reality is that feelings do not cause behavior. Even actions that look like instant, spontaneous reactions are governed by choice. Our feelings can certainly give us the *urge* to do certain things, but they don't control us.

So what does determine our actions? The answer is our *values, attitudes,* and *habits.* If we consider violence or threats unacceptable behavior, then we don't use them no matter how angry we get. For example, most men never hit or threaten to hit their partners, even when they are enraged. If we are honest people, we don't start lying when we're upset. If we don't believe in abusing alcohol, then we don't start getting drunk daily after a painful loss.

And that means it isn't his feelings that need to change; it's his attitudes.

"If he blames his actions on his feelings,
that's just another excuse."

"Why Do I Keep Going Back to Him?"— Part 3

Do you feel like the victim of your own emotions? Over the years, many women have said to me, "I just keep getting back together with him. I don't know why." These women felt almost like someone else was making their decisions for them while they watched from the sidelines. They had stepped outside of themselves and were watching themselves keep returning to misery.

Does this feel familiar?

Your emotions do not have to run your life. You can make decisions based on what you know in your mind is good for you. Start basing your actions on your best thinking, on your deepest wisdom, not on your painful emotions and unmet cravings. *This is the key to a happy life.* Ironically, the more we allow our pain and longing to govern our decisions, the more those choices cast us into pain and longing! The only way to actually get what you need is to start being good to yourself and true to yourself. When you make a deep enough decision that you deserve better, you'll find a way to get it.

"My emotions don't rule me;
I choose my actions. I can choose to
stay true to what I know is best for me."

Don't Be Afraid of Your Strengths

I have two tasks for you in the week ahead. They may feel a little uncomfortable, but on a deeper level they will feel good.

The first is: *Accept compliments.* Whenever someone tells you something good about yourself—you're smart, you're pretty, you're kind—I want you to say, "Thank you," and smile, *and that's all.* The crucial part of this exercise is what you *don't* say; you don't say, "Oh, not really," or "Ha, ha, I wish that were true," or "Oh, please." You also don't compare yourself to the other person, as in, "I'm not nearly as good at it as you are." Just graciously accept the compliment, whether it rings true to you or not, with no negative comment about yourself.

This applies, by the way, if someone says something nice about how you look; no responding by pointing out some other aspect of your hair or body that you don't like.

It's important to learn to handle being complimented. You're strong, you can take it.

The positive things that people point out about you will almost always be true. But the critical voice in your head (especially your partner's voice in your head) will claim that they aren't. So keep saying to yourself, "I need to just work on taking this compliment in."

The second task for the week is: *Tell someone else something you like about yourself.* This step may be even harder than the last one, but during the next few days, do it at least once with a friend, or a coworker, or a sibling. You can draw from that list you wrote in your journal several days ago. Start a sentence with, "I'm really good at . . ." or, "I'm proud that I . . ." or, "I like it that I . . ." Once you've done it, you'll feel good.

Maybe it will become a habit. Perhaps you'll even spread it to others, so that people around you start to speak positively about themselves.

When Praise Becomes a Weapon

We all know that you can control people by putting them down. But can an abusive partner control you through the opposite technique, using compliments? Actually, it's possible. So despite what I wrote yesterday, you might have to be a little cautious about praise when your partner is the person it's coming from. Consider whether any of the following dynamics have gone on in your relationship:

He built you way up early in the relationship, which now makes you feel like you've fallen really far in his eyes. When you were first involved, he may have talked about you as if you were the most amazing, perfect woman he'd ever known. But now he seems to see nothing but faults in you much of the time. And his criticism has extra power over you because of the way he idealized you before.

His praise is focused on who he wants you to be, not on who you want to be. In other words, he only compliments you about qualities that serve his goals, as if he's trying to mold you into his own creation. And some of the qualities that you consider the best aspects of who you are he never mentions in a positive way. He focuses on praising things that are less important to you, or that aren't even really true about you.

He uses compliments to get you to do what he wants. Praise can be manipulative. For example, your partner might say that you are too intelligent and mature to be hanging around with the friends that you have. In this way he tries to drive you away from people you care about.

He rarely gives praise, so you become addicted to hearing it. A partner who doesn't give compliments much, but once in a while suddenly pours them on, can get you hooked on trying to win his approval.

Pay attention to the spirit in which his compliments are offered, and to the actual impact they have on you. When a controlling man uses praise, it can have a backwards impact.

> "I'm not going to let him define what my strengths are; I get to decide who I am."

Protecting Your Relationships from Him

I want you to place a high value on your relationships with loved ones, whether friends, relatives, teachers, coworkers, or members of your spiritual community. To protect those precious connections, be alert for your partner's capacity to create divisions between people; controlling and abusive men tend to be splitters.

The best defense is to talk openly with people about your concerns. Tell them, for example:

"I'm concerned that my partner may have habits of causing problems between people." Ask them to watch for any signs that he is trying to turn you and others against each other.

"Please don't allow him to involve you in keeping secrets." One divisive tactic your partner might use is to take people aside and say quietly, "I want to share something with you, but I need you to agree not to tell my partner about this." This is a toxic maneuver. Friends and relatives of yours need to respond to him, "Don't tell me anything you don't want her to know, because I'm not going to be involved in keeping secrets from her."

"Please check with me about bad things you hear about me." Your loved ones need to know how important it is to get your side of every story, so that your partner can't plant destructive seeds that will bloom later.

"Please don't talk to him about things you are upset with me about; please bring your issues directly to me." Controlling men often try to get people around the woman to open up about their grievances or concerns about her, and then try to feed those complaints. Ask loved ones not to participate in talking behind your back, and to be honest and direct with you.

To take these steps, you'll have to break the habit of pretending with people that everything is fine in your relationship with your partner. And that too will be a positive step for you.

"I need to protect my relationships
from him, just in case."

Spoiling a Child Is Not What You Think It Is

The process through which children come out spoiled is widely misunderstood. Spoiling children does not come from giving them too much of what they need. It comes from giving them too much of what they *don't* need, combined with overlooking their genuine, deep cravings. You cannot give children too much love, kindness, patience, understanding, or attention. (With one exception—which is if you are forcing these things onto a child who does not want them, failing to respect his or her need for space, privacy, and independence.)

So what have spoiled children received?

- Too much material stuff (toys, gadgets, exaggerated comforts)
- Too much favoritism
- Too much license to be rude and disrespectful toward adults or other children
- Too much escape from responsibility and accountability, too many excuses made for them
- Too many things done for them that they could have done for themselves
- Too much license to demand and expect service, to be waited on hand and foot
- Too *little* experience of being genuinely and deeply seen and understood

It is common for a controlling man to tell his partner that she is spoiling the children because she picks them up and cuddles them when they cry or get scared, or because they love to sit in her lap, or because she gets down on the floor and really plays with them, or because she keeps helping them with things they have a hard time with. He's wrong. Being a loving, present, safe parent is *good* for kids; it's exactly what they need you to do. (His real issue is that he wants you to focus at all times on doing everything for *him* instead of the kids. He's the spoiled one.)

And, by the way, no matter what your partner may say, you can't spoil a baby. There's no way to do it.

"I'm going to love my children with all my heart. He has no right to make me hold back."

The Meaning of "Consent"

Today's topic can be a triggering one for many women, so you might want to take a couple of deep breaths. The question is what the concept of "consent" means when we are talking about sexuality.

Sex is only sex when it's 100 percent voluntary. And that means your partner is using zero pressure, zero guilt-tripping, zero dishonesty, zero telling you it's your duty as a wife, zero keeping you awake, zero doing paybacks after the times you say no. Otherwise what's taking place is sexual abuse, not sex.

When we think of sexual abuse, we typically imagine either an adult violating a child or a man physically forcing a woman. But sexual abuse comes just as commonly in the form of a woman being pressured into unwanted sexual contact. Or maybe she did want to be sexual, but then the man bullied or manipulated her into particular sexual acts that she didn't want.

The opposite of sexual abuse is consent. Consent means that you wanted the contact to happen, and you let the other person know you felt that way. Consent does not have to happen in words, but it is an *active* act; a woman shows her consent in how she moves her body, in the kinds of pleasurable sounds she makes, in the initiative she takes. If she just lies still and doesn't resist, that is *not* consent. Irresponsible men will say, "Well, she didn't say no," or "She didn't fight me" after having sex with a woman when she obviously was not into it; these men are justifying rape.

If you feel bad sometimes after sexual contact with your partner, consider whether you were truly a voluntary participant. Even if you "let him do it," he's still abusing you sexually if you didn't send him a message that you wanted what was happening. *Being sure that you are fully consenting, with no pressure from him, is his responsibility.*

"If I don't fully want the contact,
what's happening is not lovemaking."

CLARITY

He's Been Working Hard All Day

It's quite common in a male-female couple for the man to be working more paid hours per week than the woman does, particularly if the couple has children. If your partner is a controller, he is likely to seize on this fact and say that he works much more than you do. He may also insist that his job is more pressured, more important, or requires more physical effort, so he supposedly needs more rest than you do.

Meanwhile, he isn't even counting unpaid work, such as cooking, shopping, cleaning, and raising the children, which he does far less of than you do.

What this often comes down to is that the controlling man asserts that he shouldn't be bothered when he is at home because he's "tired." He means that you should keep the children quiet, stay out of his favorite chair, don't ask him to help clean up or fix things around the house, and don't expect him to play any role in producing meals or cleaning up after them. He's the king of the castle with his feet up on a stool.

Maybe that's how his father acted, maybe that's how men have behaved for generations, but none of that is any excuse. You have at least as much reason as he does to be tired. Wouldn't you just love to sit in a recliner or lie in the bath? Wouldn't we all? Why does he get this privilege?

Because he's demonstrated that he's prepared to make your life hell if he doesn't get it. That's why. Not because he has earned it; he hasn't earned it any more than you have.

A man who respects his partner doesn't put his feet up at the end of the day and declare that he has done too much.

"I deserve rest at the end of the day as much as he does. Women do 70 percent of the world's labor."

His Affair "Didn't Mean Anything"

Infidelity causes tremendous pain. Anyone who pretends otherwise is trying to cover up a serious issue. It is common for a woman to identify her partner's affairs as the single most injurious thing he has done, even in relationships where he has hurt her in a lot of other ways.

Later in this book we'll look in detail at the issue of cheating. For today I will just examine one aspect: the ways in which the man who cheats tries to minimize the harm he has done. This effort typically begins with claiming that the affair didn't "mean anything" to him. He may say that it was "just a physical thing," or that it was caused by alcohol or emotions that "got out of hand." He may suggest that you're taking it too seriously, though at the same time he throws in some apologies.

Let's look at what he's saying. First, if it's true that the affair had no meaning for him, that's just as bad. He's willing to hurt you that much over an insignificant thing? That says a lot about his self-centeredness.

Second, the line about it being "just a physical thing" is no less injurious. Would he be okay with you having sex with another guy as long as he knew it was "just physical"? Of course not; if anything, that would make him feel worse.

Third, his excuses are absurd. Alcohol and runaway emotions don't cause him to stab himself in the eye or jump out of a third-story window, do they? Well, if he can choose not to hurt himself, then he can choose not to hurt you.

> "There's nothing wrong with me for feeling deeply
> hurt; what he did was deeply wrong."

HEALING

Getting Your Legs Back

Ending a serious relationship is hard. When it comes time for you and a partner to part ways, whatever the reason may be, you need to draw on your deepest reservoirs of strength. A woman at this time needs to believe in her own capabilities and competence and have self-confidence. She needs to have friends or relatives she can draw on for emotional support. She needs to have money to live on and a good opinion of herself.

And she needs to believe that she is attractive and that a new partner will want her (unless she's prepared to abandon relationships forever, which most people aren't).

Unfortunately, the strengths I just listed are precisely the things your partner has been attacking in you for a long time. So leaving an abusive relationship is actually harder than leaving a non-abusive one.

I recommend two pieces of reflecting work. First, spend a minute looking over the above list of strengths. Has your partner moved you backwards in any or all of these areas? If the answer is yes, then what does that tell you about whether this relationship is healthy for you?

Second, how could you start working on building yourself back up? What steps would you need to take in order to be ready to leave him if you decide you want to?

Don't wait until you decide you want to leave. You need to recover these strengths just as much if you choose to stay. This process does not have to be visible to him; if this is a bad time to confront him or create tension, then focus on secretly rebuilding these pieces inside you.

"I will rebuild the pillars I need to be an independent woman, whether I choose to leave or stay."

YOUR OWN BEST FRIEND

Be the One to Define Who You Are

Does your partner insist that he's the one who knows what you are "really" like? Is his distorted image of you getting under your skin, shaping how you view yourself? You are the only person who gets to decide the truth about who you are. Your identity is yours to define. And it's never too late to discover who you really are.

Be aware that you can't form a healthy identity by just deciding what you are *not*. Your controlling partner can get you focused on fighting off his way of defining you, so that you tell yourself, "I'm not stupid, I'm not ugly, I'm not selfish." These defensive messages are important, but they need to be followed by positive thoughts about what you *are*.

Think of this period in life as an exciting time of self-discovery. Your partner has interfered with your ability to get to know yourself, but now you are going to cast his interference out of the way (even if you have to do it secretly, inside of yourself). You are going to explore the "real" you. You are the only one who can know her.

Get out your journal, and write as many statements as you can about who you are, avoiding saying anything about what you're not. Here are just a few questions to help you write: What are your interests? What are your beliefs? How do you treat people? What do you enjoy? What have you studied or learned about? What kind of work do you do (including homemaking)? What are you good at? What culture are you from? What do you dream of for the future?

"I am the only one who gets to say who I am."

Love in Its Many Forms

A mother and child walking in the park holding hands. A clergyperson speaking with a parishioner who has been part of the congregation for years. An uncle taking his niece to the water park. Siblings spending the afternoon fishing together. A woman meeting her best friend for dinner and drinks. A trip a few hours away to see a cherished grandparent.

This is love. These connections are as feeding to the human heart as the love of an intimate partner. But we chronically put less value on love in these myriad other forms. How many songs do you know about love toward grandparents, best friends, children, schoolteachers, pastors, mentors? Maybe a handful. But about love in the romantic sense? You could think of hundreds.

Take a minute to reflect on these questions: Who are the people whom you most love in your life, and who love you? Who are some important people you tend to forget, or you've dropped out of contact with? How could you place a higher value on those connections?

For the next week, focus on noticing the love in your life and in your heart. Tell the people you care about how much you appreciate them. Say "I love you" to someone you haven't told before, or to whom you haven't said it in a long time. Decide to have all forms of love in your life matter as much as your partner does.

"There is so much love around me if I can tune in to it. Romantic love is just one kind."

GUIDING CHILDREN

Practicing Patience

When an angry and controlling man lives in the house, his demeanor can set the tone for everybody. His outlook at home is focused on judgment, criticism, and demands. The message he sends is "You should be doing better! Something is wrong with you! You need to be hammered into a better shape!"

A woman living in this atmosphere is pushed toward adopting an outlook on her children similar to the one the destructive man takes toward her. She can start to view her kids as bundles of problems and faults that need to be fixed. She may spend the day yelling and criticizing. She works doubly hard hoping to mold her children into people who will please her partner so that he won't yell.

If you see yourself in this picture, reflect on where your partner's control is leading you. It's natural that you want to keep the children from upsetting their father, but you don't want his tyranny to creep inside you and make you become like him.

So work to step outside of the tone that he sets, and give your children the kindness and patience that, deep down inside, is really how you want to be raising them.

※ ✎ ⟩⟨

"My children and I are on the same team. Whether
today is a hard day or an easy one, I'm going
to keep reminding myself how much my
love and kindness mean to them."

Overcoming Barriers to Writing

There is no path to clarity for a woman with a destructive partner more powerful than writing. If you haven't gotten a journal or notebook yet, get one today.

Why is writing so crucial? First of all, putting your ideas down allows you to see them from a different perspective; it's like having another person to talk to. As soon as you put your experiences on paper you are less alone. Second, writing allows you to look back weeks or months from now and remember what you were seeing and feeling. This ability to remember is especially important for an abused woman, so that she can see the *patterns* in what her partner is doing.

You may tell yourself, "I have no time to write." But you don't need a large amount of time; if you have your journal open for five minutes a day, you'll feel the difference. Just get one or two thoughts down.

You may tell yourself, "If he finds what I'm writing, he'll kill me." But you can think of places to hide your journal where he won't find it. He can't look everywhere. If necessary, have a friend or relative help you figure out a good hiding place.

You may tell yourself, "I can't afford to buy a journal." But you don't need a nice $15 journal; you can get a 99-cent notebook at the drugstore.

You may tell yourself, "I have no private place to write." In that case, write sitting in the bathroom.

The point is: write, write, write. Your thought processes will grow and change through the process of putting your experiences and feelings down on paper.

"Keeping a journal is the most important step
toward taking my life back."

Does God Give Him the Right to Punish You?

Your partner may sometimes lure you to pour boatloads of effort into fighting him on the wrong questions.

Let's look at how this principle plays out with arguments about religious beliefs. The controlling man sometimes says to his partner, "The Bible says that a wife should not deny her husband sex." You could make several good points in response:

- The Bible was talking about a loving relationship, not one where the man is cruel and cutting.
- The Bible meant that sexuality is part of a healthy relationship, but that doesn't mean you can demand sex from me when I'm not in the mood.
- You can't pick and choose the parts of the Bible that you feel will help you to get what you want while you ignore all the rest.

These are strong arguments, *but I don't recommend pursuing any of them with your partner.*

Why not? Because in the context of your relationship, they will serve as distractions. You don't want to help your partner avoid the only question that actually matters for your situation, which is:

Where in the Bible does it say that he gets to insult you, intimidate you, make fun of you, force you, or assault you when you don't do what he believes the Bible says you should do?

The answer? *Nowhere.*

So whenever he goes looking in the Bible for excuses for mistreating you, he's revealing another layer of his abusiveness. Don't let him convince you that your supposed sins give him any right to harm you verbally, physically, or sexually.

"My partner is not God's deputy, but
some days he seems to think he is."

For the Woman Who Just Can't Leave

Nowadays the world wants to believe that every abused woman has the option to get out of the relationship she's in. But I talk to quite a number of women for whom leaving is simply not possible, at least for the time being. Here are some of the reasons why a woman finds herself trapped:

She has absolutely no way to survive economically and provide for her children (and she's tried everything).

She knows he will go for custody, and he has enough money, connections, and dirt on her to win, plus he'll be charming and persuasive in court.

Her family, friends, or community have all sided with him, so she has nowhere to turn for help.

The police or the courts in her area are protecting him, not her.

Child welfare officials have turned against her, labeling her a bad mother, and they are treating him like he's the one who is okay.

She has a physical or mental disability that severely restricts her.

She can tell he would hunt her down and kill her.

If you are one of the women in this type of situation, I want you to know that you are not forgotten. I am not one of those people who assume that all abused women should, or even can, leave the abuser. You deserve support and understanding from your community and the wider society; the situation is not your fault. I am behind you in your effort to keep building the best possible life that you can with the hand that you've been dealt. I hope one day a way out emerges, but I get it when you say that there's no escape right now.

✺

"My life challenges have no easy answers, but I will keep working my way daily toward the light."

HEALING

Post-Traumatic Stress "Disorder"

Living as the target of an abusive man can shake a woman to her core. The negative effects can be even deeper if the man's abuse includes violence or threats, sexual mistreatment, or crazy-making behavior. Many women have said to me bluntly, "After being with him for a few years, I was really messed up."

Many of the effects of abuse are similar to what anyone goes through who has had a traumatic experience, especially if the trauma was caused by another human being. Psychiatrists have created the diagnosis of "post-traumatic stress disorder," or PTSD, to describe these predictable impacts. (I wish they wouldn't say "disorder," because that makes the person sound broken; words like "injury" or "response" would make much more sense.)

Consider whether you have suffered some of the following difficulties:

- Experiencing nightmares of being chased or attacked by your partner or another man
- Having trouble concentrating, so that you keep losing the thread of a conversation, "spacing out" at work, or reading the same sentence over and over again
- Frequently finding it unusually hard to sleep at night, and feeling exhausted during the day
- Starting to have big overreactions to little upsets during your day, being unable to regulate the normal emotional ups and downs of life, crying all the time
- Feeling depressed and lonely in a way you didn't feel before your relationship
- Constantly feeling anxious that you are going to do something wrong

Recognizing these effects as symptoms of trauma can help you to not feel that you're crazy. You are having similar reactions to those of people who have been traumatized by earthquakes or floods, or who have witnessed shootings, or who have been in combat. There is actually nothing wrong with you; you just need safety, kindness, and time to heal.

꧁ ꧂

"My symptoms are actually totally
normal for what I've been through."

A Day to Be the Center of Your Own Thoughts

Take a day off from thinking about your partner, gently redirecting your thoughts each time you notice that he is in them. When the voice in your head says, "But I've *got* to think about this problem involving him because I've got to figure it out," remind yourself that you can figure it out tomorrow. You're just taking a one-day break.

So what can you think about instead? You may be in such a channel of thinking about him all the time that it's hard to know where else to go with your mind. Here are some ideas:

"What would I want to get out of this day if I were just thinking about what was good for me?"

"Who are my most important friends and relatives? Today I'll reflect on them and on what's going on in their lives."

"What are my dreams? How could my life be doing more to move me toward those dreams?"

"What are my strengths? What's good about me? What do I have to offer?"

"How could I be closer to my kids?"

"What brings me joy in life, or interests me the most? I'm going to spend some time today reflecting on those things."

You deserve a life that revolves around you, not around your partner. Begin now to take a small step in that direction.

"Today I'm going to make myself
the center of my thoughts."

Putting Your Caring for People into Words—
Part 1

"I like you."

"You're a really good person."

"I think you're great."

No one has ever said, as the end of life approached, "My only regret is that I wish I hadn't expressed my fondness to so many people. I said 'I love you' too often, exaggerated how important people were to me, and expressed too much gratitude for what other people had done. I wish I could take those words back."

Of course not.

Get in the habit of telling people the positive feelings you have toward them. Your friends, your relatives that you are close to, your children, and whoever else your favorite people might be—put your caring into words.

You might even make a particular effort to show your fondness to people that you "don't know well enough" to tell them; in other words, tell them anyhow.

Will you make people uncomfortable sometimes? Perhaps occasionally. But they'll still remember happily what you said once their embarrassment subsides. You'll never regret a positive comment, and it will help to counterbalance the negativity you are living with at home.

⁊⟋⟋

"I'm not going to hold back my caring for people."

Keeping Kids Connected

Children crave to grow up in a tribe. They like to have a lot of people around, of all different ages. They may fight with their friends and siblings, they may roll their eyes about spending the afternoon visiting their grandparents, but at the same time they very much want those people in their lives.

The modern child spends far more time at home than kids used to. This change comes from the amount of homework children are assigned, the tendency of relatives to live far apart, and the weakening of communities. Technology is also a factor; children now spend the bulk of their free time in front of screens instead of interacting with each other.

Your partner's behavior can further isolate your children. For example, he may create a tense atmosphere that makes you uncomfortable inviting people over. He may say negative things about your friends or your children's friends. He may get grumpy when you go out to have fun with the kids. And the secrets that you and your children are keeping about his behavior can make you feel distant from other people.

In this context, *one of the most important contributions you can make as a mother is to work daily on helping your children have social contact and success-ful relationships.* Pull them away from their screens and take them to the park to play with other children. Help them constructively resolve their conflicts. Ask them about their friendships and demonstrate that you value those relationships. Help them schedule times to get together with people. And talk to them about your own friendships so that they have the model of seeing that you make your own connections a high priority.

"I'm going to do everything I can think of to keep
my partner from cutting us off from the world.
We can find ways to stay connected."

EACH NEW DAY

Your Goal in an Argument

It's extremely difficult to get an abusive man to admit that he's wrong. You tend to get hurt in the process of trying to convince him, because the more wrong he is the dirtier the fighting tactics he uses. Ironically, he uses his most demeaning tones, and his most cruel and insulting words, when he is the most off-base in what he's saying.

If your goal in an argument is to get him to change his mind, you're going to come out feeling awful. He has a comeback ready for anything. And if you make your points so clearly that there's no way for him to escape how right you are, he'll just roll his eyes and walk away, or tell you to shut up.

So what can you do? *Shift your goal.* Make the object of the argument three things:

1. To know inside yourself that you've expressed your point, even though he refused to hear it
2. To maintain your dignity
3. To refuse to agree to things that you know are wrong

Point one means that you don't base your success on how well he "gets it," only on how well you said it.

Point two means that no matter how demeaning or insulting he behaves, you try to avoid screaming or yelling, you keep your head up, and you keep breathing, staying as centered as possible.

Point three means that you hold your ground no matter how superior he acts; you avoid backing down. (Unless he's getting scary, so you're forced to pretend to let him win.)

By applying these three principles, you can come out of arguments with him feeling less terrible and keep your own thinking on course. It's all about having faith in yourself, regardless of what he thinks.

"What matters is that I stay true to myself."

His Comments About Your Weight

There is no other issue that women get hounded about by their controlling partners as much as their weight:

"My, honey, looks like you've added a few pounds."

"Are you really sure you should be eating that right now? Shouldn't you be watching your waistline?"

"You need to work out more often, and bring down that weight."

"Where's the beautiful girl I fell in love with?"

I'll put the most important point first: Whether it is true that you've gained weight or not, he has no right to be hounding you and putting you down about it. How would he feel if you frequently made comments about his body and how it looks, and kept telling him what he needed to do to improve it? He'd go berserk. But he thinks it's okay to do it to you.

Point two: When has making a woman feel bad about her weight *ever* helped her to take better care of herself? Never. In general, the worse you feel about your body, the harder time you will have treating your body in a loving way. The world is full of women (and men) who have unhealthy habits regarding food and exercise precisely because of how bad they feel about themselves.

For a man to pester a woman about her weight is abusive—plain and simple. It is among the most emotionally toxic things he can do.

≫❁≪

**"My partner is not invited to make critical comments
about my body. I'm setting up this boundary."**

"How Much Should I Stand Up to Him?"—Part 1

If people that you care about have noticed some of the difficulties that are going on in your relationship, you may have gotten a lot of advice. (It seems like we're all better at solving everyone else's problems than our own, doesn't it?) Although people who are trying to help you have good intentions, you may find their advice contradictory, with one person advising the opposite of what someone else suggests. Here are some of the mixed messages you may get:

"You really should leave him."
followed by:
"You should give him another chance, you have so much history."

"You need to figure out what's bothering him."
followed by:
"You can't fix him—it's his own issues."

"You really push his buttons."
followed by:
"You're not to blame; he's responsible for his own actions."

"You're as bad as he is."
followed by:
"What difference does it make if you're not perfect? That's no excuse for how he treats you."

"You should stand up to him more. Don't let him treat you like that."

followed by:

"You need to back off and leave him alone; he just gets madder
  when you challenge him."

The only solution is to listen to *yourself.* No one's advice is going to
be as valuable as your own thoughts and reflections. No one's desires are
as important as what you desire for yourself. No one knows the right
path for you. You are going to find your own way.

✂╼

"The most important opinions
about my life are my own."

HEALING

Drawing from Nature

You are connected to all of life. Scientists not only observe similarities
between human beings and other animals, they are finding striking
ways in which humans are like plants and other life forms. All living
things are relatives.

Tuning in to that connection can be a source of sustenance. Standing
still for a few minutes and gazing at a tree in the morning sun can remind you that the world is carrying on, and that beautiful forms of life
are growing and developing. You remember something about your own
strength and beauty while you stand there, because the tree sends messages about qualities that you have in common with it.

Power in nature does not reside only in the larger plants and animals. Lichens can cover huge exposed rock faces that no other life form

could hold on to, and survive there off the tiny fragments of dirt and rock that they collect. Given enough time, grasses push their way through asphalt and concrete. Ants invade homes despite every human effort to keep them out. These tenacious little fighters can remind you that every living being has the potential to take its stand and assert its right to exist and thrive. And that includes you.

Build into your life some time to let nature fill your spirit. Take a walk in a grove of trees or stand for a few minutes at the edge of a field. If you live in a city, make your way to a park and look up to see the tree branches set against the sky. Stop to watch a flock of birds. Tend to the plants that you share your home with.

Nature is a powerful healing force, bringing you back to the truth of who you are.

> "I am part of the beauty of the whole world.
> What is true about the most beautiful
> spot in nature is true about me."

"Why Can't He Just Accept That I Need a Break?"

Figuring out what to do about a relationship can be overwhelming. Sometimes it just isn't possible to think it through while living in the midst of daily conflict and bad feeling, surrounded by layers of tension-filled silence. You may not be considering breaking up with your partner; but you know at least that you can't tolerate the current atmosphere. And you can tell that you aren't going to find solutions unless you can get away from him and clear your head.

The controlling man sometimes agrees at first that some time apart would be a good idea. But soon after the separation begins, he starts working on his partner to give the idea up. He calls when he's not supposed to call; he shows up when he's not supposed to show up; he sends fifteen texts a day. He starts drinking heavily to make you worry about him. He has a life crisis all of a sudden (he's about to lose his job, his mother is in the hospital, etc.) and lets you know that right now he really needs you. One way or another, you can't have your break.

Why can't he give you the space you are asking for?

Because on a deep level he knows that he isn't treating you well. He senses that if he leaves you in peace you are going to grow stronger and harder to control. You will attend to your inner voice, build self-confidence, and see through the confusion that he specializes in creating.

In short, he's afraid that you will come back from the break prepared to stop putting up with his outrageous behavior.

Don't listen to all the excuses he comes up with. The break is essential to your well-being. If he can't respect that, he doesn't respect you.

"He doesn't like the break because he can't stand
not being able to control me. And that's all the
more reason to take some time off."

Putting Your Caring for People into Words—Part 2

Last week I encouraged you to stop holding back from telling people how much you care about them. Let your friends, your close relatives, your children, the people in your faith community know how happy you are to have them in your life.

One way to make your caring words even more meaningful is to work at telling people in a specific and detailed way what exactly you appreciate about them. The more thought you put into what you say, the more your comment is likely to touch the person. The goal is to have the person think, "Wow, she must really mean what she said, because it was clearly about *me*, not just something generic she'd say to anyone."

Consider the following examples of specific appreciations:

"I've noticed how much you remember about things I've told you before. You really listen."

"You go way out of your way to do favors for people."

"You're good at noticing when a situation needs some humor, and bringing it in."

"I like how affectionate you are."

"I've noticed how you stick up for people that others are scape-goating."

See how concrete these compliments are?
I don't mean that you should stop giving general appreciations such

as, "You're a good person," or "Thank you for your contributions." Say those things, but then go on and add the specifics. People will feel good knowing that you are truly seeing the person they are working to be.

*.⁆

"I'm going to let people know in detail
what I appreciate about them."

Listening Carefully

Children are sponges. They absorb far more of what is going on around them than adults realize. A woman recently told me how surprised she was when her six-year-old said to her, as they were leaving a visit with relatives, "Dad would never help you the way Uncle Paul helps Aunt Renee. He would just yell at you to go get it yourself." She knew that her daughter got tense when she and her husband were fighting, but she had no idea how aware the girl was of the actual dynamics.

One of the things the children are taking in is that you don't get listened to. They are noticing that your partner disparages much of what you say, that he twists your words around, that he rolls his eyes and walks away. In the face of this dynamic, kids start to have internal questions: Should I listen to Mommy, or should I ignore her too? Should I listen to my siblings, or should I just respond with insults to whatever they say? Is anyone ever going to listen to *me*?

In this context, it becomes crucial for you to listen to your children well, and really hear what they're saying. Adults often misunderstand what children are saying to them, or dismiss their comments as unimportant. Our responses to children can invalidate their feelings, such as when we toss little sayings at them like "Life isn't fair," or "Things could be so much worse."

Children who have a bad role model in the house urgently need a counterexample. They need a model from an adult who listens carefully and respectfully, makes room for their feelings, and doesn't throw simplistic solutions at complicated life challenges. Take your children seriously and really hear what they are telling you.

✧

> "My children's voices are as important as the voices of any adult. I am going to let them know that I value what they are sharing."

Operating from Choice

Your partner strives to take your choices away from you. In many ways this goal—to narrow his partner's options—is the central force driving the behavior of an abusive man. Dealing day in and day out with his control, you can gradually come to feel like nothing is up to you; that all decisions are in his hands, and all you can hope to do is have some small influence over what he decides.

The reality, however, is that you continue to have choices. Your partner is brainwashing you to believe that you don't. But you do.

Start noticing how often you say one of the following things to yourself:

"I wish I could take certain steps, but I can't get myself to do it."

"I wish I could do [fill in the blank], but he would never allow me to."

"If only I could [fill in the blank], but I know I can't."

"I don't know why I keep going back to him after leaving."

Unless your partner is dangerous to you or your children—and perhaps even then—you have a much greater range of options than you feel like you do. So stop yourself when you hear these messages in your head, and replace them with some of the following alternatives:

"It's time for me to make some different choices."

"The risks of leaving him may be smaller than the risks of staying with him."

"I don't have to let my fears and longings control me."

"I can operate from choice."

Helplessness becomes a habit, and it's a habit your partner keeps pushing you to fall into. (Though he then turns around and criticizes you for not taking enough action.) You can break out of helplessness by becoming aware of the choices you are making and owning those choices. As you develop this new habit, you'll get to the point where you can choose to take your life back.

***

"He's convincing me that I have
no options, but he's wrong."

Does He Mean It When He Apologizes?

One of the questions that abused women most ask me is "How can I tell whether my partner is sincere when he says he's sorry? He sounds like he really feels bad, but it's hard to tell."

Here's my answer, which may surprise you: *It doesn't matter.*

A destructive man who feels bad after he mistreats you isn't any more likely to change than one who doesn't. Why? For several reasons:

- He feels sorry for the wrong reason; he's upset that he made himself look bad, not that he caused you pain.
- He believes that an apology gives him the right to do the behavior again, or do something similar, after "enough" time has gone by, whatever that means.
- He thinks that since he feels bad, that obligates you to leave him alone about the wrong that he did.
- In order to chase away his guilty feelings, he is going to spend the days ahead ruminating about why his behavior was your fault, and this view will gradually take over in his mind.

So instead of trying to read how much genuine feeling there is behind his apology, focus on the far more important questions:

- Is there a distinct change in how he is treating you?
- Is he giving you room to be upset, and to stay upset for as long as you need to be?
- Is he continuing to own his behavior, or instead is he sliding back toward justifications and excuse-making?
- Is he doing actual reflecting on the attitudes and choices that led to

his injurious behavior, such as his selfishness or lack of respect, or instead is he keeping it all kind of vague, as in "I need to not lose it the way I did"?

Saying he's sorry, whether he means it or not, does nothing. Real work looking at himself—and especially looking at his attitudes toward you—is the only thing that matters.

~꙳

"I need to stop getting my hopes up so much when he apologizes."

SURVIVING TO THRIVE

"How Much Should I Stand Up to Him?"—Part 2

Because of your partner's patterns of making you pay when he doesn't like something you do, you are forced into a position of having to decide, over and over again, how much hell is worth it. When should you give in to him, and when should you just go ahead and do what you want, and damn the consequences?

Here are two questions to evaluate in making up your mind whether to challenge him or not:

"How much harm will come to me by obeying him?"

Yes, standing up to him leads to harm—in the form of his abusive punishment. But it's important to notice that *not* standing up to him leads to harm also. If you give up seeing friends, that isolates you. If you give up school or work, that harms your financial future. If you give up involvements that are important to you, that makes you more dependent on your partner. If you give up your true opinions, you start to lose your sense of identity and your confidence in who you are.

So you can't afford to look just at the consequences of defying him; make sure you also consider the costs of not defying him. There are prices to each.

"How important is this to me?"

It's hard to figure out what you really want when a big part of your brain has to be focused on how your partner will react to your decisions. In fact, your fear of being punished by him can make you unconsciously convince yourself that you don't want what you really want. And this is the beginning of allowing your partner to take control of your mind.

Most important, make clear decisions inside yourself. Then, if you have to abandon your choices because of your partner's abusiveness, at least you'll know that the reason your life is not progressing is because of him, not you.

"Deciding when to stand up to him is really hard.
I'm going to make the best choices I can."

HEALING

The Pros and Cons of Getting a Mental Health Diagnosis

If you decide to seek counseling from a therapist, or if you go to a psychiatrist for assistance, the provider is going to raise the question of assigning you a "diagnosis" so that they can bill your insurance for the services they give you. They will have to assign you to one of the categories of mental health difficulty that insurance companies recognize and are willing to pay for.

The pro, of course, is that insurance will pay most of your expenses. The downside is that the fact that you've been given a mental health diagnosis could be used against you later; for example, your partner could bring it up in court as a weapon if you ever end up battling him over child custody or visitation.

If you can pay for services out of pocket, you can avoid this dilemma, but few women can afford to do so. So the best path is to work with the provider on what diagnosis he or she will give you, and don't continue in the counseling unless you are comfortable with the one chosen. The diagnoses that are least likely to come back to haunt you are "post-traumatic stress disorder (PTSD)" or "adjustment disorder." Both of these categories make reference to difficult conditions in your life that you are having trouble dealing with; that way it's harder for someone who learns about your diagnosis to claim that you are "crazy."

One other advantage of the PTSD diagnosis is that it can be defined as a disability, which may allow you to qualify for certain kinds of additional services or special accommodations.

Move carefully into the realm of mental health diagnosis, and don't allow yourself to get saddled with a label that could be used to hurt you or discredit you later. Be a well-informed client and advocate for yourself.

⁕

"If I'm going to seek mental health assistance,
I need to be sure to protect my rights."

Believing in Your Worth

Life with a controlling partner can become a vicious circle of working harder and harder to prove to your partner that you are a good person worthy of his love. The more you look to him to validate your value, the worse you feel about yourself. Why? Because he only gives positive attention in small doses, with lots of criticism or subtle invalidation in between. His silence, or his ignoring of you, or his sneering at your opinions and accomplishments, are having a much greater impact on you than his occasional praise or approval.

You are always in risky territory when you become dependent on other people's confirmation to feel that you are a good person. Praise or appreciation from other people should be a nice boost to your day, but not more than that; it shouldn't determine your value or your sanity. It's especially risky to base your self-esteem on the reactions you get from a self-centered, moody, hypercritical individual, no matter how loving and positive he may become on certain days.

Strive to decide, deep inside of yourself, that you are okay, no matter what anyone else says. Notice your strengths, and remind yourself of them frequently. Be the last word on who you are. Be gentle and forgiving toward yourself, and have faith that you are sane, smart, and generous. Look to yourself for approval—and give it generously—rather than looking to him or to other people.

꒦꒳꒦

"I don't need him to tell me that I'm okay;
I'm the one who knows best about me."

Avoiding People When You Go Back to Him

See if the following dynamic feels familiar.

First, you find yourself mired in one of those periods when your partner is being rotten to you day after day, and you feel like you can't take it anymore. You rant to some of your closest people about what a jerk he is, and they are right behind you on it. You say you're done with him, and they cheer you on to give him the boot, helping you to plan how you'll do it. You're all a team.

But over the ensuing days or weeks you start to feel less sure. Ending your relationship starts to feel overwhelming, and the loss seems too great. Your partner know that you are leaning toward the door, so he becomes kind and loving and he promises to make big changes.

The upshot is that you decide you are going to give the relationship another try.

Now comes the tricky part. You've been bonding with loved ones about how awful he is, so how do you explain to them that you're staying?

And something else starts to happen, which is that the crisis of your relationship almost coming apart makes you and your partner feel closer. He's being sweet, and you're feeling a little resentful toward people around you for being so negative about him. You tell yourself that they don't really understand him, or understand you for that matter; in fact, you feel like he's the only person who really gets you.

So now you and he have become a secret society, a special team together against that hostile, uncomprehending world out there. You have a deep connection with each other that they just can't grasp.

In short, you have two reasons to keep them all away; you are a little ashamed in front of them, but at the same time you are feeling that you and your partner are a little bit above them.

But what is really happening is that you are growing more traumatized and more isolated. Your partner is drawing you into a traumatic bond and leading you away from your support system. Your secret society is not a healthy place to be. It's an illusion, and a destructive one.

Your people love you. Don't cut them out. Whatever you decide about how to handle your relationship, keep reaching back toward the hands that are reaching out to you.

"I can't ever let my partner come between me and my people. I have to see this for what it is."

Dealing with Sibling Rivalry

Do any of the following outcries sound familiar?

To you:
"You gave Addie more than you gave me!"
"You always let Anna have what she wants!"

To each other:
"Ha ha, I got more than you did!"
"Hey, that isn't fair! You got to play with the new cars longer than I did!"

Siblings can become preoccupied with who is getting more presents, who has bigger portions of food, or who got to use toys longer. They can come to define "fairness" as meaning "everybody gets exactly the same thing." But actually it wouldn't be good for kids to all receive exactly the same things and in the same amounts (even if that were possible somehow) *because their needs are different.* Besides, the more the parents try to keep everything exactly even, the worse the children's preoccupation with the issue becomes, so a different solution is needed. We don't want to discourage children from caring about what is fair, because that's a positive characteristic. But we need to help them have a broader sense of what fairness means. Here is where the book *Siblings Without Rivalry* (by Adele Faber and Elaine Mazlish) comes in. The authors advise parents to send the message:

> "What we want in our family is for everyone to get what they need, not for everyone to get the same thing. That's what is the most fair."

If a child is complaining that someone else got a bigger portion of food, reassure her that she'll get enough. (Unless there's truly a shortage of food—that's different.) If a child gripes that a sibling got more time with a toy, ask him, "How could we work it out so that you get to play with it enough, instead of worrying about whether it was more or less than someone else?" The more kids feel that their needs are being watched out for, the less obsessed they become with what their siblings get.

✕·🔔

"I can switch the focus from everyone having
the same to everyone getting enough."

Feeling Like You've Changed

I couldn't count the number of times that women have said to me, "My partner is always telling me that I've changed, that I'm not the girl he married. I guess in some ways he's right. I did use to be more kind of happy-go-lucky, and I'm not in those kinds of moods much anymore. I'm more serious, or even kind of crabby. He complains that I used to want to go out and do things more, and it's true that mostly I just feel like staying at home. And he's right that I'm not as up for sex as I used to be."

But is your partner perhaps the cause of these changes? Maybe you've gotten short-tempered because of living with his criticism and negativity for so long. Maybe you've lost your interest in sex because his treatment of you makes him so unappealing. Your loss of energy could come from feeling depressed. And you might have a hard time being playful when he suddenly turns nice to you, because you can't just block out all the hurtful things he has done.

Could part of the issue also be that you're growing up but he isn't? It's common for people to be less interested in going out to party as they get more involved in creating a home and raising children. Abusive men can be reluctant to move into a more responsible lifestyle because they only want to focus on themselves.

Take a few minutes to think about how *you* feel about the ways you've changed, and forget how he feels about them. If you are remaining true to yourself, then there's nothing to worry about. But if you are losing pieces of yourself that matter to you, that's worth reflecting on.

$\rightarrow$

"I need to shape my future self
and not have him shape it."

Naming His Behavior

When you sit down with a friend and try to describe your partner's behavior, you may find it difficult to put it into words. Each day seems a little different; he has a range of different ways that he gets upset, and many issues set him off. You might think, "Where do I begin to explain what it's like?"

One starting place is to work on developing names for his actions. Look for a moment at the following list:

- Silencing you (making it hard for you to say or express what you are trying to)
- Controlling your opinions, desires, and tastes
- Demeaning you, tearing you down verbally, insulting you
- Controlling you sexually, putting you down sexually, pressuring you into unwanted sex
- Intimidating you, hurting you or putting you in fear that he could hurt you, towering over you, blocking your way
- Ripping you off financially, controlling money, taking away your say over money
- Harming the children in order to upset you, using the children to hurt or control you
- Causing isolation and division (not letting you go out, cutting you off from friends or relatives, being a jerk so no one wants to come over, making jealous accusations)
- Imposing double standards (making you live by a completely different set of rules than he does)
- Treating you like a servant, expecting everything done for him
- Turning things into their opposites (such as claiming that you are

the abusive one, calling you selfish, or saying that your behavior shows *you* don't care about *him*)

Think back on a few recent examples of hurtful behaviors of his. Find a place on the above list where each incident fits. See how his behavior follows patterns? Get in the habit of categorizing his behavior each time he is being bad to you. Your clarity will grow rapidly.

"I can recognize what he is doing."

Beware of the 5 Percent Solution

Today we're going to look at a natural human reaction that happens also to be a trap.

The more hurt or emotionally starved you are, the more grateful you will feel for any kindness that comes your way. If you haven't had a hug for a week, a little physical touch feels almost electrifying. If you've been working nonstop for hours, even five minutes of sitting down with your feet up on a chair can feel like the most blessed rest of your life. If your boss is grouchy and rude but today she happens to smile and say something positive about you, your heart fills with gratitude toward her.

This dynamic—which happens to everyone—can keep a woman grasping at signs of hope that her partner will change. The more years of mistreatment that have gone by, the more excited you feel when he finally moves even an inch in the right direction. You think to yourself,

"This tiny progress must be significant, because in the past he's never made any at all."

Your reactions are natural, but they also hook you in. If it has taken your partner ten years to move 5 percent of the distance that he needs to go, then it will be two hundred years before he's a decent partner. You will sacrifice the rest of your life waiting for him to overcome his issues.

When you feel excited or hopeful because he gives you one-twentieth of what you deserve, that is your trauma speaking through you. Learn to recognize those feelings as traumatic reactions, and don't act on them. Just watch the feelings go through you, be gentle with yourself, and work your way back to center.

And from now on when he makes tiny improvements, remind yourself, "There goes that 5 percent solution again."

"The more time that has gone by, the more his steps
need to be huge ones to be worth bothering with."

Grief Needs Space

Have you gone through a number of cycles of breaking up with your partner and then getting back together with him? If so, there's a good chance that you're getting stuck in your own grief. Women who leave destructive partners tend to get overwhelmed by sadness. The woman's loved ones sometimes don't understand this natural emotional reaction, so they don't always give her the support she needs.

The reality is that you will feel at least as sad when you break off a relationship with a man who has treated you badly as you would if the relationship ended for a completely different reason. *Being abused is one of life's saddest experiences.*

Ironically, your grief over your partner's treatment of you can drive you back *toward* him, because you try to relieve your sadness by deciding to give him another chance to treat you right. The sad result is that you keep getting hurt over and over again.

What's the solution? The single most important step is this: When you separate from him, you need to go at least two months, and maybe longer, with *absolutely no contact with him*; no texts, no phone calls, no Facebook. Zero. None. You need space and peace to grieve, to go through what you have to go through inside yourself. If you have children, make arrangements for his visits with them through third parties so you don't have to see him or talk to him.

If he won't respect this break in contact, you need to block his number and his email address, including any way he would send you Facebook messages. You might even need to consider getting a restraining order.

Carve out space for yourself to do the grieving you need to do, and you'll be able to make decisions that serve your true interests better.

><)≈

"I have to take space to be with
my grief and let it wash through me."

"Am I the One Mistreating *Him*?"

Life with a controlling partner can become a twisted world where bad is good, down is up, and wrong is right. Many women over the years have said to me, "My partner tells me that I'm the one abusing *him*. How do I know if it's him or me?"

Read the following concepts, taking a deep breath after each one so that you can absorb it.

One: You are not responsible for his behavior. You do not make him do things. His actions are his own choice.

Breathe.

Two: You deserve to be treated well even when you make mistakes, and even if you make them a lot.

Breathe.

Three: Setting firm, clear limits for how your partner is allowed to treat you is not the same thing as controlling him, and should not be called control.

Breathe.

Four: Choosing to not always put your partner's needs ahead of your own does not constitute hurting him, wronging him, or being selfish. You have the right to give substantial priority to your own needs and desires.

Breathe.

Five: If you scream and yell once in a while, that does not mean that you are crazy or abusive. It depends on whether you are yelling degrading things, whether your partner has reason to be intimidated by you, and whether you are yelling to control him (versus yelling to resist his control).

Breathe.

These five concepts will cover most of the situations where your partner tries to turn the tables on you. Digest each point and your partner will stop being able to convince you that you are the one with the problem.

⁓

"I am not responsible for my partner's behavior.
I am responsible for my own."

Combating Isolation

Being the target of chronic hurtful treatment by your partner is a lonely experience. Your connection to him is obviously gone during the times that he's being mean. You might turn to other people you care about, but it's uncomfortable to tell them what's going on, so you often don't. Plus he may be causing harm to your relationships with friends and relatives, or not letting you see people at all.

Isolation can creep up on you; you may not even be aware that you are getting cut off from people until the damage has gotten quite deep. And by that time you may feel discouraged enough to give up on social contact, especially if your partner makes you miserable any time you try to see people.

But isolation is a huge threat to your soul. Don't give up; you will find a way to reestablish your connection to the world. It's never too late. He may have convinced you that no one would want to be your friend, but it isn't true.

Look for ways to reach out to people. You may have to be secretive and cunning about it, but don't give up. If your partner monitors your telephone, look for ways to send emails and then erase them after they're sent. If he watches all of your electronics, see if you can get in conversations at the grocery store, or see if you can slip a handwritten note to someone who might be able to help you. If he lets you go to medical appointments, that might be your opportunity to tell someone what is happening at home, or to make a friend in the waiting room. Look for a chance to call a hotline and talk.

Keep making any kind of human connection that you can. Little by little those moments of interaction will build you a path to freedom.

୬ଽଽ

"I don't have to give in to isolation. Connection is
the most important way to sustain my spirit."

GUIDING CHILDREN

Raising Self-Confident Girls

If you have daughters, they need a whole lot from you. Any girl needs a lot from her mother, but there are two reasons why your girls need extra.

First, they are living with the stress of your partner's behavior. The ugliness of his words and actions makes them need extra affection, patience, and encouragement from you to keep them whole. His behavior is affecting them even if they never hear or see what he does.

Second, they are having to sort out whether it is dangerous to be a female in this world, because they sense that you sometimes don't feel safe. So they are looking to you for indications of how securely they can move through the world.

You can be a *huge* help to them in managing these challenges.

Begin by thinking of yourself as an island, a rock-solid home base for them. They will head off each day to manage the waters, which will be calm some days and stormy others, and each day they will return to the solidity and security of being with you. Show them each day—don't tell them, *show* them—that they have a special place in your heart and that you are watching over them.

Next, give them support for their fears and upsets. Don't minimize or gloss over the hard things they go through, don't tell them, "You'll get over it" or "Life isn't fair." Instead, show them that it matters to you when they are having a hard time.

Last, make it clear to them that you believe they are going to be fine and that they will be able to claim their place in their world. Show them that you see their strengths and their abilities. Tell them, "You can do this," about whatever it is they are trying to take on. Radiate confidence in them, even when—or perhaps especially when—you don't feel that same level of confidence in yourself.

Your girls can make their way, and make it well. All they need is for you to be their rock.

~ ✫ ~

"I'm going to make sure my
girls know I am behind them."

Making an Altar

An altar is a spot you create in your home, or outdoors right nearby, where you can sit or kneel for a few minutes when you need to gather strength.

To create an altar indoors, find a surface on a small table, a shelf, or your dresser. Lay pretty material on the surface, a weaving, a doily, or a nice piece of fabric. Organize a display of a few items that have some meaning for you. You might place polished rocks, figurines, dried flowers, seashells. Items gain power if they connect to specific people; you could include a gift that a loved one gave you, or a trinket that represents that person to you. You can set out photographs of some of the individuals closest to your heart, living or passed away. Choose also a couple of pieces that relate to happy memories—a natural item you collected on a special picnic, or driftwood from a day you spent near a lake or the ocean.

Caring for your altar by adding or subtracting pieces, or by changing the arrangement, becomes another way to draw sustenance from your chosen objects.

If your partner will ridicule or harm the altar, think of a secret place you could create it, perhaps outdoors. An outdoor altar can include the same setup as an indoor one, minus items that would be destroyed by weather. An outdoor altar can have some special magic to it. Find frequent quiet moments to visit your altar. Take deep breaths as you look over your layout, and then spend a minute with your eyes closed. Feel the power of the scene flow into you, and carry that energy away with you.

"I can create a spiritual center for myself
right where I live, and let it feed me."

When the Problem Isn't "Him," It's "Her"

Are you a woman who sometimes or always forms her intimate relationships with other women? Have you been reading this book saying to yourself, "I'm being mistreated by my partner, but my partner is 'she,' not 'he.' Does this all apply to me?"

The answer is largely yes. People who abuse or control their same-sex partners tend to follow many of the same patterns as men who abuse women. And the partners of those destructive people find themselves in similar binds and similar confusion, though with the additional challenge of having to sort out what this all means in the context of a same-sex relationship.

Your partner may try to tell you that what she is doing is not abuse because she's not a man, and a woman can't abuse another woman. But actually plenty of people bully, demean, and financially exploit their same-sex partners, including some who use physical or sexual assaults. The mistreatment you are experiencing is real.

She may also tell you that no one will believe you and no one will support you. Again, ignore what she is saying. Yes, it may take you a little longer than it would take a straight woman to find someone who really "gets it," especially if you live in an area where there is still a low level of acceptance of gay and lesbian relationships. But there is help out there. Most programs for abused women, for example, are fully welcoming to anyone who needs support, regardless of the gender of the abusive partner. There are websites specifically devoted to supporting victims of same-sex mistreatment in relationships. You can find a safe place to reach out.

*"If I'm being mistreated by a female partner,
I deserve the same support that any woman
should get who is being abused or
controlled in her relationship."*

Dealing with the Onslaught of Lies

Men who control and disrespect women lie and lie and lie, often without entirely realizing it themselves. Your partner lies to you about what kind of person you are, about what your body is like, about what other people think of you, about how the world works, about what the "smart" people believe, and on and on. He'll draw you whatever picture of reality best supports his desire to wield power over you.

Keeping these lies out of your head is difficult because he keeps repeating them, and because he sounds so knowledgeable. Stop taking his word for things, no matter how sure he sounds. Seek out other sides to the story that don't come from him. Ask your friends and relatives their opinions about issues, read websites, go to your town library. Call professionals and ask their advice. Go out there and get the story for yourself, *and come to your own conclusions.*

Finally, be careful of the partner who presents his lies and distortions in the guise of trying to "help" you navigate the world. Notice how following his "guidance" isn't working very well? It's time to go back to following your own.

*"I don't need my partner to explain the world to me;
I can go out there and discover for myself."*

Sexual Healing—Part 1

Of all the emotional wounding that people carry, sexual injury is often the deepest. The use of sex as a way to hurt the woman is a widespread pattern among abusive men, because it gives them so much power over her.

Sexual wounds can heal, but they take time. When I talk to the women who are feeling the worst about themselves, and who are feeling the most debilitated by being in a destructive relationship, their stories almost always turn out to include sexual mistreatment by the man, and commonly they haven't talked to anyone about it.

To begin down the path of sexual healing, take a look at whether you have been hurt in any of the following ways:

- Your partner has cheated on you sexually.
- Your partner has insulted you sexually. This could include, for example, insulting your attractiveness or saying bad things about the sexual parts of your body, insulting your sexual preferences or desires, or insulting the way you make love.
- Your partner has humiliated you sexually. This could include telling other people sexual information about you, or making supposed "jokes" to people about your sex life. It could also include private

behavior, such as getting you sexually aroused and then suddenly turning that into something to hurt you about.

- Your partner has pressured, guilt-tripped, or badgered you into sex when you didn't want it, or into specific sexual acts that you found unappealing.
- Your partner has raped you or committed other forms of outright sexual assault on you, such as grabbing you sexually when you didn't want to be touched, forcing you to have sex with other people, getting sex through threats, or not letting you sleep until he got sex.

Spend a few minutes now reflecting on this list, and write your thoughts in your journal. These kinds of experiences are painful to remember and write about, but by entering into this realm you open up great potential to heal and free yourself emotionally.

"I need to spend some time taking in
the ways he has hurt me sexually."

YOUR OWN BEST FRIEND

Avoiding Contagion

Being around a sick person can make it hard to keep yourself healthy. This principle applies just as much to being around a person with unhealthy attitudes or twisted behaviors as it does to avoiding pneumonia or the flu.

When you live with someone who periodically turns ugly or dictatorial, or who gets superior and cutting when he's angry, or who blames other people for messes he has made, or who flies off the handle about nothing, you can come over time to feel that the toxicity is in you.

Create a daily ritual to maintain your connection to your individuality. You might stand in front of the mirror, look out a window, or walk around the block—whatever helps you get focused for a few minutes. Then repeat to yourself:

"I am not him. I am my own person."

"I am not going to become like him. I know the kind of person I want to be."

"I am going to stick with myself through this."

By making time to reconnect with these sentences every day, you will help to keep his toxicity from creeping inside of you. Picture yourself creating an invisible barrier that protects your spirit.

✦

"His toxicity exists in him, not in me. I'm different."

Desperation Can Lead to More Desperation

In times of crisis, you need close people in your life. But the challenge is that if people experience you as too needy, they may start to pull away, and then you'll feel even more desperate than you did before.

The solution isn't to deny that you feel overwhelmed; it's best to tell people the truth about how you're doing. But look carefully at how you approach people for support or assistance. Here are some steps you can take to not scare people off:

1. Monitor how long you talk about your situation. Talking endlessly won't make you feel any better (really, it won't), and it will exhaust your listener. Make yourself stop after a while, and talk about some other aspect of life, or, even better, ask the person you are with to tell you about what's going on with him or her.

2. Force yourself to maintain an interest in other parts of your life. Your hobbies, your children, your spirituality, your political beliefs are all a continuing part of who you are. Keep your mind involved in thinking about these things, and let that be reflected in what you talk about with other people. Your emotional distress is only one aspect of who you are.

3. Try to see yourself as strong, and present yourself that way to others. The best way not to come off desperate is to not view yourself as a helpless, panicked person. See yourself instead as a smart, tough, capable woman who stumbled into a bad situation and just needs some help and support.

4. Before calling professionals for help, practice telling a one-minute version of your story. You may feel that if you tell people more details about how bad things are, they'll be more willing to help. But actually the more you tell them the less likely they are to help, because they'll worry that you are going to take up more of their time than they can afford. Be succinct.

Practice these principles and people will be happy to be there for you.

"I feel desperate some days, but that's not the full story of who I am."

Keeping the Children from Thinking Like Him

Women with controlling partners (or ex-partners) often worry about their children following in their father's footsteps. You may see signs that your kids are absorbing some of his negative social attitudes, such as his tendency to be a racial bigot or to look down on females, common traits in abusive men. Or he may tell them lies about you. It can be distressing to hear your children say things like "Women are just out to take men's money," or "Mom, there you go being way overemotional again," and you knows where they're getting these ideas from.

You need to counter this tendency, but carefully. When your partner tries to get the children to think like him, it won't work for you to respond by pressuring them to think like you do; he will win this competition. He is skillful at manipulating the kids, by withholding all praise from them except when they are being just like him, making them feel stupid when they disagree with him, and getting them to feel that being on his "team" makes them superior. You can't beat him at his own game.

So what is the alternative? Two approaches matter the most.

First, teach children to think for themselves. The best defense against bad messages isn't good messages; instead, it's learning how to evaluate messages yourself. Keep asking your kids questions like "What do *you* think about that?" and "Does that make sense to you?" and "Why?" Guide them to use their analytical skills and trust their own thinking, rather than following what they are told.

Second, keep the focus on being loving and kind with them. You want to send the message "What matters in this family is how we treat each other, not what goes on in our heads. Opinions are always secondary."

"My children will figure out what's right."

Is It Okay to Be Traditional?

From time to time I meet a woman who says that she really prefers the more "traditional" role of being a homemaker and mother, and doesn't really want to take a job outside the home. She may not particularly want to mow the lawn or change the oil in the car, and would rather have her husband do those things than help her cook dinner. She sometimes adds apologetically, "I know this isn't very feminist of me."

You have every right to choose the life that you enjoy and that works well for you. That's actually what equality is supposed to be all about. It's regrettable that so many people have come to perceive feminism as meaning that women should want to live the way men do, trading one set of rigid requirements for another.

The only question that really matters is, who gets to decide? If a woman is doing "women's work" because a man has made it the rule that she has to, that's not tradition, that's oppression. But if that's what she herself enjoys and values, more power to her. Whatever way of life a woman chooses freely deserves our validation and support. No one gets to tell you what your proper "role" is, whether as a full-time mother or as the CEO of a corporation. The life that brings you joy, connection, and a sense of purpose is what matters.

*"I am proud of the version of womanhood
that I choose for myself."*

Abuse from a Female Partner

Women who fall in love with other women are unfortunately not abuse-proof. As I wrote about earlier, there are women who bully and intimidate their female partners.

If you are involved with a woman, or married to one, it is important to listen carefully to your deep feelings and intuitions about how you're being treated in the relationship, just as a straight woman needs to do. Don't let yourself believe in myths, such as "Intimidation and violence are just male characteristics" or "Women don't abuse other women." Your experience is real.

A woman who is being mistreated by her female partner can be even more likely to blame herself than a straight woman is. You may say to yourself, "If I weren't so messed up, she wouldn't treat me like this." Or you might think, "It's not her fault. She has such a stressful life and has lived with so many emotional attacks during her life." Another voice in your head might say, "I must be blowing this out of proportion in my mind; it can't really be that bad since my partner is a woman." The reality is that women who abuse their female partners use many of the same tactics and exhibit many of the same attitudes that are found in abusive men. They can be highly manipulative, they can use sexual assault, and they can be dangerous. Take your situation just as seriously as you would if your partner were a man.

There's nothing wrong with you. You have a right to be with a woman who is kind, respectful, and responsible. Don't let your partner convince you otherwise.

"Whether I go out with a woman or a man,
and no matter whom I marry, I have the
right to live free from abuse."

Feeling Guilty About Leaving Him

He's going to be all right if you leave him. But that also shouldn't be the main question.

Let's look at two pieces:

1. "He's really depressed."

It's no surprise that he's depressed, since he has habits of blaming other people for his problems and expects to be taken care of like a baby. He can't be happy until he accepts responsibility for his own life.

Here's a crucial point to grasp: You cannot help him with his depression while he's mistreating you; it's impossible. Depressed people can't receive effective assistance from people they disrespect. There is some chance that he will decide to seek help to get himself well *be-*

cause you leave him; but he won't do it because you stay, even if he claims he will.

2. "I can't leave him at this point in his life."

Maybe he just lost his job, or his mother is sick in the hospital, or some other challenge makes this a really bad time. But if you want to end the relationship, don't delay your exit by more than two or three months due to his life circumstances. If the crisis in his life continues beyond that, you need to move on and trust that he'll manage. Remember that although this may be a bad time in his life for you to leave, this is also a bad time in *your* life for you to stay. His mistreatment of you is every bit as serious a problem as his lost job or his sick relative. (Yes, it is.) Your needs can't keep getting sacrificed to his; and that's what will happen endlessly if you stay put.

$\sim$

"I'll do more help to *both of us* by getting
out of this relationship, since
I know it's time to go."

Sexual Healing—Part 2

Last week I wrote about the fact that sexual wounds can run deep, and asked you to consider whether your partner has been sexually injurious to you. Today I'd like you to begin looking at what kind of toll his behaviors in this realm may have taken on you.

Read over this list, which gives examples of common struggles that women have when they have been sexually abused by their partners:

- Depression, difficulty getting yourself to do anything, feeling suicidal
- Self-hatred, self-disgust, a desire to escape your own body
- Nightmares, recurring memories of what he did (sometimes playing almost like a tape in your head), waves of bad memories of events from earlier in life that may or may not involve him
- Feeling raw and vulnerable so that everything in life seems more painful, as if you were missing layers of skin
- Feeling full of bottled-up rage
- Feeling more dependent on him, needing his reassurance more about things, being more preoccupied with his moods
- Finding that the joy or pleasure goes out of sexuality

Spend some time reflecting on these effects and writing in your journal. Are these struggles going on for you? Do you see ways in which they are connected to your partner's sexually abusive behaviors? Are there other ways you have been affected that aren't on this list?

Women (and men) sometimes underestimate how wounded they have gotten sexually. They also can feel isolated because this subject is an uncomfortable one to talk about even with close friends. You are not at fault for your partner's sexual mistreatment of you, and for the harm it may have done.

"It's natural that I'm going through
some of the struggles that I am, given
how he has harmed me sexually."

Choosing the Opposite

Usually, I tell people not to direct their lives at avoiding what's bad; it works better to set your sights in a positive direction, toward building the life you do want. And instead of working on getting rid of your faults, put your energy into developing and growing the best aspects of yourself.

But today let's come at things from a different angle. Taking the opposite side isn't always bad. When you've spent big chunks of your life with a toxic individual—a parent, a boss, a partner—consciously choosing to cleanse yourself of their influence can be healing.

Begin by taking stock of the characteristics in your partner that bother you the most, probably including some or all of these:

- He's hypercritical (of you, and maybe of other people too).
- He's arrogant, always assuming that he knows more than other people and that his opinions or tastes are better.
- He doesn't trust people.
- He's insulting to you or to other people, but then he's super-nice to people when he has a reason to want to be in good with them. (Two-faced, in other words.)
- He's dishonest.

Now for the next few days focus on being everything the opposite of what your partner is. If he finds fault in people, look for their strengths and tell them what you appreciate. If he's always rushing, take your time. If he is suspicious of people, give people the benefit of the doubt and assume they have good intentions.

You don't need to let this process be visible to your partner. The goal is to prove something to yourself, not to him. You are not like him, and you don't have to be. The more you work on being different from him the better you will feel, and the more your self-opinion will improve. Shake off the toxicity.

"I'm going to show myself that I'm not like him."

Are There Rifts That You Could Repair?

When you live with a partner who has two dramatically different sides, your relationships with friends and relatives tend to suffer. He may be rude to people in your life or make it hard for you to see them. He may do the opposite, charming and impressing your loved ones and then working to turn them against you. He may lie to you about them, or lie to them about you. He may convince you that their intentions are bad, or that they control you too much. He may be insanely jealous of your connections, not just to men but also to women.

And you may pull away from people of your own accord, because you find it hard to talk about what is going on between you and your partner.

But maybe your relationships with people can bounce back. Consider the following:

Is there anyone you could apologize to about anything you've done, even if that apology would be hard? Could that be a way to create an opening in a relationship that has grown strained?

Is there anyone you could open up to about your partner's issues, as a way to help that person understand why you've been distant? Could that be a way to start moving closer again?

Is there anyone you are angry at that you could try to sit down and have a talk with? Have you made your best effort to work bad feelings out? And even if you have, has enough time passed that it might make sense to try again?

Is there someone you aren't quite ready to talk to, but you could write to them?

Strained connections don't have to be irreparably broken. This is an important time in life to extend a few olive branches and see where closeness can be reforged.

⁓◡⁕

> "I can work to bring healing to relationships that
> have weakened or crumbled."

"I Want My Kids to Love Their Father"

Of course you do. Anyone who starts raising a family dreams of a loving home with close relationships all around. And their sadness is great when they see signs that their family is not headed in that direction.

But, as I wrote about earlier, you can't determine what kind of closeness your children will have with their father. *His relationship with the kids is his responsibility.* Building a connection with children takes a lot of time and effort. It requires patience, understanding, and an ability to see outside of yourself. You have to make them a priority, and put your own needs aside much of the time. And these are not strong points among abusive men.

I encourage you to work on accepting what is beyond your control in this arena. For example, your children are likely to develop resentments toward their father about the way he speaks to you and treats you. They are going to get their feelings hurt when he doesn't make them a priority and doesn't follow through on things he said he would do with them. They are going to feel the sting of his criticisms and judgments, and as a result they will hold certain parts of themselves back from him. These are all natural processes that you can't prevent.

What you can work on is *your* relationships with the children. What happens with his relationships with them is in his hands.

"I need to accept the ups and downs of my kids' feelings about their father, and be there for them."

Physical Affection

Your partner thinks that whatever he likes is what you should like. His preferences or tastes are superior in his eyes.

Physical contact between partners tends to be one of the arenas where he passes judgment. If you like more affection than he does, then you are "clingy" or "dependent" or "oversexed." If, on the other hand, you don't like to be touched all the time, then you are "frigid" or "cold" or "uptight."

So what is the right amount of touching and affection?

Exactly as much as you want.

In other words, there is no "right" amount, just as there is no "right" kind of music, flavor of ice cream, or color of overcoat.

If you are someone who loves to hold hands all day, cuddle up to watch a movie, or give someone a shoulder rub, you have the right to revel in that. And if you get uncomfortable with a lot of touch and need space around yourself, everyone else needs to respect that. What feels good to us in our bodies is up to us and us alone.

Sometimes people in a couple are forced to accept that they aren't compatible, because their desires about the level of affection and sexuality are too different from each other. But that doesn't make either partner bad or wrong; they just turned out not to be a good match in this crucial area.

"I get to choose how much touching
and affection feels right to me."

CLARITY

Naming the Effects of What He Does

Being involved with a destructive partner can take more of a toll than you realize. Especially while you are still living with him, it's hard to observe what's happening to you.

People on the outside may have noticed. Someone who cares about you may have said, "I'm concerned about you—you don't seem like yourself to me." And if they have, you've probably brushed them off, responding, "Oh, I'm doing fine." But are you?

Ask yourself these questions:

Emotionally: Am I upset or angry about him a lot of the time? Am I tense and worried about how he's doing, or how he's going to react to things?

Physically: Am I as healthy as I was when I met him? Is the stress showing up in my body in any way (aches and pains, weight gain, weight loss, lack of energy)? How am I sleeping?

Life Direction: Have I let my dreams and ambitions slip into the background since I've been with him? Does he discourage me from pursuing my own goals, or try to change them into ones that he thinks would be better?

Spiritually: Have I lost my connection to my deep beliefs? Am I reluctant to share my real beliefs with him?

Socially: Am I struggling in my connections with friends? Have I distanced myself from my relatives (perhaps because he said they aren't good for me)? Does he make excuses not to see people, or to keep me from seeing them?

Sexually: Am I feeling attractive? Are my sexual needs being attended to? Is he making me feel bad sexually?

A relationship is supposed to make you feel good. It should make you stronger and more energetic, and help propel you toward your goals. Is your relationship doing the opposite? Do some writing in your journal in response to this question, striving to answer honestly.

✂✀

"I need to look directly at what's going on
and not convince myself that it's okay."

"I Sure Know How to Pick 'Em"

I generally discourage women from saying that they "chose" an abusive partner. When you first got involved with him, he seemed like anything but an abuser; he was excited to be with you, said he thought you were amazing, couldn't get enough of you. All the ugliness and bossiness didn't show its face until later.

But if you are on your third or fourth destructive relationship in a row—or if you've never been in anything *but* a destructive one—it could be time to start looking at the kind of guy you are attracted to. If you want a man who is smooth and charming, and who "takes charge" from the beginning, you are heading into risky waters each time you get involved. Ditto if you are drawn to a man who is aloof and "hard to get." And trouble is coming if you focus on guys who will flood you with flattery and flowers, and who can make everything dizzyingly exciting from the very beginning.

In other words, a lot of the characteristics that women are taught to view as romantic and sexy are actually the warning signs of an abusive or controlling man.

Start looking in a different direction. Look for a guy who wants to get to know you, who seems interested in being friends with you on the way to becoming lovers. Look for a guy who can make decisions together with you, balancing what he wants with what you want. Look above all for *respect*; you want a man who keeps his word, who values your opinions, who supports your friendships. Love without respect leads to disaster.

Does changing the qualities you focus on mean giving up hope of having a sexy, romantic relationship? No, not at all. The passion and excitement can still be there, but in a completely different kind of package, one that is real rather than pretend.

><e>k

> "My new rule is: Be Friends First. That's how I'll find
> out what kind of substance he has."

Sexual Healing—Part 3

Paying attention to healing sexually is one of the most powerful gifts you can give to yourself. Have faith that you can recover from the ways in which you have been sexually harmed. Many women have reported to me that by healing from these rarely mentioned but profound wounds, they have rediscovered their self-love, their self-confidence, and their ability to take charge of their lives.

Where does this healing come from? You can pursue a number of directions, including:

Finding someone—or various people—to whom you can tell the full truth. Breaking the silence regarding sexual mistreatment is crucial to recovery. You may find loved ones in your life who can handle the truth. But you might also pursue a program for sexual assault survivors, a support group devoted to this subject, or an individual therapist who is trained on sexual trauma. (See "Resources.")

Work with a healing guidebook. I highly recommend *Life, Reinvented* by Erin Carpenter and *I Will Survive* by Lori Robinson and Julia Boyd. These resources are profoundly supportive, clarifying, and effective.

Keep searching for ways to make ongoing injury stop. You cannot control your partner's behavior, but you can strive to develop strategies to protect yourself, or to escape your relationship if that's the only way to get the abuse to end. Healing is far more difficult when you are continuing to get reinjured. Use the support of a women's program.

The fact that you have been sexually mistreated does not say anything bad about you; it only speaks badly of the person who committed those violations against you. But staying clear on this point is difficult, which is a big part of why sexual injuries run deep and can take a long time to heal. There is nothing wrong with you. You have the right to heal, and you will find a path to sexual wellness.

"I am getting on the path to sexual healing."

He May Never Get It

One of the most natural and universal human impulses is our desire to get people who have wronged us to recognize what they did and admit that it was wrong. We want to hear a certain soft sound in their voice, see sadness in their eyes, showing that they feel genuinely bad for having harmed us. We want them to understand that we didn't deserve their actions. And then, if it's at all possible, we want them to actually do something to make up for the damage they caused.

Unfortunately, this natural longing for justice can sometimes backfire. When you have a destructive partner, the desperate need you feel to have him see what he has done is, ironically, part of what keeps you trapped. If you end the relationship, then he is never going to admit how badly he treated you, and he's never going to make it up to you. And that reality can feel unbearable.

But the alternative is to stay involved with him, where he will keep harming you more, and the pile of things he needs to face up to will just keep growing. Longing for justice can keep you roped into unhealthy circumstances.

Start letting go of the hope that he will see. Even if he admits one day that he was wrong, he's likely to just take it back in a few weeks or months. See if instead you can focus on: (1) Knowing—really knowing—inside *yourself* how deeply wrong his behavior has been; and (2) Building close relationships with other people who can really get it and express it to you.

Someday this pain will pass, and you'll stop caring what he thinks; hundreds of women have told me that this is what happens. Have faith.

⤙⫯⤚

"I need to know deep inside myself that what he did was wrong. One day that will be enough."

Getting the Help You Need

Many people are eager to help. But they don't necessarily know when they are needed, and they may feel unsure of what they have to contribute. You will need to reach out to them and guide them in how to be a good ally to you.

Begin by taking the leap to ask for help. Speak up about what you need from people; it's unlikely that people are going to be able to guess how they could best make a real difference to you.

We live in an exaggerated "do it yourself" culture, where we can be reluctant to admit to others when we can't handle everything on our own. But *interdependence*, where we all help one another out, is much healthier than exaggerated independence (or exaggerated dependence).

Second, ask directly for what you need. Do you need emotional support and a caring listener? Do you need advice? Or the opposite: Do you need people to stop giving you advice? Do you need a place to stay for a few days, or someone to look after your kids for an evening while you figure some things out? Be as up-front as possible about what would help the most.

Think of receiving help as an aspect of life that you can take charge of, rather than as a passive process where you wait helplessly to see what people will offer you. Many people will be eager to give assistance once they know what to do.

"There's nothing wrong with me for
needing support; helping each other
is a beautiful part of life."

Letting Kids Cry

When you are in a period where life is already stressful, the screech of children's crying can put you over the edge. These are the times when you may find yourself yelling at your son or daughter, "Just cut it out!" or threatening them with "You'd better stop being that way!"

Blowing up at your kids when they're crying sometimes succeeds in gaining you the peace and quiet that you're craving. But it leads to greater problems with that child soon. You and your child will be at each other's throats more and more.

And you can't afford that. With all the stress your partner causes, you and the kids don't want to create more for each other. The solution? Make a 180-degree turnaround in how you respond to tears. You do not have to stop your children from crying; in fact, it will be better for you *and for them* if you let them cry for as long as they need to. Crying is the number one most effective, most natural form of emotional pain relief for kids. *It makes them feel better*, especially if you are kind to them while they cry.

Try it and see. Try just loving your kids while they cry, and hold them if they'll let you. Let them cry for as long as they keep crying; your boy or girl will know when the crying is done. The rest of the day you'll have a more cooperative, happier child. When we fight against tears, we are fighting against nature's path to emotional wellness.

"I don't have to make my kids stop crying;
in fact, I can support them while they cry.
The result will be less stress for all of us."

Spirituality

You have a core where you are a strong, honest, principled person. You have energy and vision. You have beliefs and wishes about how the world should be. Perhaps some of these crucial aspects of you are buried under childhood injuries. Maybe your life has been a struggle for survival, so you haven't had space to explore the deeper aspects of your soul. Your partner may even actively work to take these foundations away from you. *But they dwell within you somewhere, no matter what.*

When I use the word *spirituality*, I don't mean an outlook that's necessarily religious, or that refers to a higher power or to unseen forces—though it certainly could. I am talking about currents that run powerfully inside of *everyone*, whether they consider themselves spiritual or not.

To me, your spirituality involves two central aspects of who you are:

Whatever you hold to be most deeply *beautiful*
   and
Whatever you hold to be most deeply *true*

These two threads will sometimes go together, with great truth also having great beauty. But they don't always; some truths, such as the truth of oppression and abuse, are ugly ones. Truth and beauty are equally important, when they dovetail and when they don't.

Your deepest truths may involve terms such as "God," "Goddess," "sin," or "everything happens for a reason." Or they may involve other terms altogether, such as "nature" and "science," or "rebellion" and "justice," or "creativity" and "growth." Some people's spirituality involves combinations of *all* of these in one belief system.

Open your heart to the deep rumblings within you, and start making a space for your essential truths to take shape. The most satisfying life is the one that is lived in service to our spiritual core.

"My deepest truths are my own.
They are my guiding light."

Naming the Wrongness

The abusive man has an excuse ("I couldn't help it!") or a justification ("I had to do that!") for every bullying act. But those behaviors are never okay. There is no excuse for a man calling a woman disgusting names or attacking her body image; there is no justification for him to make rules for her like a parent; there is no good enough reason for him to pressure her into having sex. It's just plain wrong.

Staying clear on these points is challenging. He spews his excuses all the time, about how hard life is for him and how messed up you are. And he mixes them with even more abuse such as, "It's your own fault if I call you 'fat,' because you're a pig!"—piling injury on top of injury. So you naturally end up confused, struggling with whether his behavior is justified or not.

To keep your head clear, start making a note in your journal each time that your partner treats you badly, writing in your own words not just what his behavior was but *why it was wrong.* You might write things like:

- "Because what he was saying isn't true."
- "Because I have a right to be heard in an argument."

- "Because he doesn't get to punish me when I 'disobey' him."
- "Because he's discrediting my perspective."
- "Because I have the right to choose my own friends and decide how much time I spend with them."
- "Because it's never okay to treat me that way."

If you can keep identifying what is unacceptable about your partner's actions, you will be more able to hang on to your clarity, your self-esteem, and your belief that you have rights.

$\rightarrowtail$

"There's never a good enough
reason for bullying me."

SURVIVING TO THRIVE

"I Was Happier When We Were Broken Up"

A number of women have brought the following puzzle to me: "My partner and I split up for a while, and I was feeling much better while we weren't together. Now I'm back with him and feeling rotten again. So why didn't I just stay away from him?"

One reason is that women who are happy after a breakup tend to feel guilty about that fact, especially if their ex-partner seems hurt and miserable. So you may find yourself thinking, "What right do I have to be doing so well when he's doing so badly?" But he is the cause of his own misery, and your life should not be sacrificed to his. And remember that he wasn't happy when you were together either.

Another dynamic is that people naturally operate on two levels emotionally, one level regarding short-term needs and a deeper level having to do with the long term. So even though you're feeling good (level one), you have longings for a life partner to profoundly accompany you (level two). And the stirrings from that deeper level can lure you back into involvement with him. So you end up giving up your current happiness for an impossible future dream.

The next time you and your partner separate, observe your inner world, seeing what role these dynamics play in your feelings and decisions. Guide yourself onto a new path, toward a lastingly happier life.

✕ ❦

"I can do what is truly best for me."

HEALING

Giving Up Is Sometimes a Good Thing

Part of how people get through experiences of extreme stress is by telling themselves, over and over, "I can handle this, I can handle this." In many ways, this mantra is important and helpful; believing that you can handle things helps you to muster the strength to get through the day, to keep your job, to look after your children. It's important to have a view of yourself as strong, as competent, as resilient, as self-sufficient.

But sometimes it's powerfully liberating to accept that you just can't do it.

Sometimes it's best to stop fighting, and to take in the truth that:

- You can't manage your partner or get him to change how he treats you.

- 325 -

- You can't be the kind of mother you really want to be while at the same time dealing with your partner's abuse and devaluing of you.
- You can't work through your current challenges alone. You can't be the total hero, needing no one else.
- You can't keep yourself emotionally and physically well in the toxic atmosphere that he is creating.

Why is it sometimes good to give up in this way? *Because of what follows.*

When you finally let go of these battles, you accept that it's time to get assistance. It's time to tell other people the truth about what's happening, as embarrassing as that may feel. It's time to feel okay about needing other people's help; we *all* need other people, that's part of what it means to be human. It's time to consider completely new ways of doing things—perhaps including a period of separation from your partner.

Admitting that you can't handle the life that you are living is a profoundly hopeful step, even though it's a painful one; it is the turning point that allows you to start building a new life, one that will work for you.

"Maybe I just can't do this, and that's okay."

How Much Are You Drinking?

Alcohol offers comfort, and in the short term it delivers on its promise. But in the long run, it can create a lot more problems than it solves.

Moderate drinking—a few drinks a week—is no cause for concern. But if you're drinking more than that, it's worth taking a look at what's going on. I've known many women whose stressful relationships have led them to use more and more alcohol over time, and farther down the road they ended up feeling like they'd been sucked into a pit.

So how much is too much?

One way to approach this question is to examine whether your drinking has increased since your relationship began. If it has, ask yourself why. You may come up with answers like "I'm stressed and it calms me" or "It helps me not feel so upset by what's going on." These are signs that your partner is causing you emotional turmoil and you're slipping into using alcohol to relieve the discomfort.

Other signs of drinking too much include:

- You're ending up behind the wheel after you've been drinking.
- You're drinking when you're looking after your kids.
- You end up crying after you've been drinking.
- You've started drinking almost every day, even if it's "just one or two."
- You're getting drunk sometimes.
- You've tried unsuccessfully to cut down.
- Anyone in your life has expressed concern about your alcohol use.

The longer you keep relying on alcohol, the harder it will be to figure out what to do about your relationship. It may be time to cut down, or even to stop altogether for a while.

$\times$ ◦

"I need the clearest head possible to figure out how
to deal with what's going on."

The Impact of Isolation

A few decades ago, researchers carried out a revealing study into human psychology. They put a volunteer test subject in a room of people. The test subject thought that all the people in the room were other volunteers for the study, but actually they were all "confederates," meaning that they actually worked for the researchers. The volunteer was the only actual test subject.

The researchers had all the people sit in a semicircle and then projected two lines, clearly of different lengths, up on a screen in front of them. They went around the circle asking people to say if the lines looked the same length or different lengths. The confederates would all say it wrong—they said the lines were the same length—and when they got to the test subject, the test subject would say it wrong too. The same result happened repeatedly with lots of different test subjects.

Then the researchers modified the experiment so that one of the confederates—only one—would give the correct answer, and when they got around the circle to the test subject, *he or she would say it correctly also*. And here's the most interesting finding of all: They experimented with making the group larger and larger, and it didn't seem to matter how big the group got; if even one of the confederates gave the correct answer, the test subject would do so also.

I share this account to illustrate that our minds struggle when we feel deeply alone. Isolation causes us to have trouble trusting our own perceptions, and we become afraid to say what we really think. We can even lose our grip on what is real, so that the lies we are being told become convincing.

You have not lost your mind. You are just struggling with the effects of isolation. As you find ways to have more social interaction and receive more validation of your perceptions, the clarity of your thinking will come back together.

⁓ ⌒≈

"Finding ways to be in regular contact with people besides him will help me to stay well."

Recognizing When You've Been Triggered

When we are raising children, we are in some ways reliving our own childhoods. As parents, we tend to have experiences almost every day—whether we realize it consciously or not—that remind us of things that happened when we were young. There are happy memories that get brought up, but also painful and confusing ones.

We can do better as parents when we are aware of what is being triggered from our own pasts. Moments when we are flooded with sadness or anger or frustration around our children can be easier to manage if we make the connections.

Certain kinds of circumstances are particularly likely to bring up old emotions. One is when children get "out of control," getting wild and noisy and refusing to do what we tell them. These are moments when we tend to "become our parents," reacting the way they would have to the chaos. Noticing that we are reliving the past can help us not explode at our own children.

Particular stages in life or seasons of the year also act as triggers. I noticed that when my son was ten years old I started to have some powerful memories, because I was that age when my older siblings all left home. Similarly, I observed that when the leaves turned color in the fall each year I would start to worry that my children were feeling sad, because I used to get waves of grief in the autumn when I was a kid, and those old emotions were being triggered. By making these connections, I could make sure that I didn't lay my own issues on my children.

Be aware of the role your past plays in the present, and take care of yourself when old feelings get kicked up. In that way, you can spend high-quality time with your children, instead of getting stuck in dynamics from long ago.

><?>

"Raising children also means being a child again.
This can be great, but it can also be hard."

"The Man Is the Head of the Household"

Does God want your partner to boss you around? There are some religious people who say that their scriptures require women to obey men, especially within a marriage. A woman who is being mistreated by her partner can therefore find herself struggling with some conflict with her deep religious beliefs. Her gut sense—and her emotional pain—are telling her that what the man is doing to her is wrong. On the other hand, she sees it written in scripture that she should submit to her partner's will, and that God intends for him to be the one to make the final decisions in the home.

Adding to the confusion is the fact that her religion may be part of what keeps her feeling strong and believing in her own value. So her faith is feeding her sense that she deserves better, but at the same time seems to be telling her to accept her current lot.

There is no easy answer to these profound inner battles. But the ultimate decision-maker has to be *you*. No human being, not even a clergyperson, has the right to claim that he or she knows exactly what God wants, or even knows exactly what scriptural writing means; to assert that kind of certainty is to claim to *be* God. So listen to your own inner voices and deep intuitions as the last word. What would the God that you believe in want for you? How would your God want a man to treat his partner? And would your God want you to be mistreated in a way that interferes with your ability to give to your children and to the world?

"I will continue to listen most carefully
to the voice deep within me."

Recognizing Double Standards

Does your partner have a different set of rules for himself than for you? Consider whether any of the following are dynamics in your relationship:

- He is flirtatious with other women or checks out their bodies, but then accuses you of being interested in other men or unfaithful to him.
- He bullies you in various ways, then calls you "controlling."

- He gets enraged from time to time (or often), but when you get angry he makes fun of you, calls you crazy, imitates your voice, or tells you that you have an anger problem.
- He spends a lot of money on himself, but then calls you irresponsible if you spend any.
- He does way more than his share of the talking, then tells you that you talk all the time and don't listen.

I could add numerous further examples to this list; the imposing of double standards is one of the most common markers of abuse.

Over the next few weeks, watch for ways that he jumps on you for behaviors that he feels entitled to do himself, or for doing even one-tenth of what he allows himself to do. Looking at your partner's behavior through a lens of double standards can help you understand why your interactions with him get your blood pressure up so much.

✎

"He has no right to one set of standards
for me and a different set for himself."

SURVIVING TO THRIVE

Leaving Successfully

I would never pressure you to leave your relationship. There is way too much that I don't know. You might not have any money to go out on your own right now. You might have to stay to protect your children from him. You may not feel strong enough. There are many reasons why staying might be the right choice for now.

But if you decide to leave, I want you to succeed, so that you can build the life you desire. And staying away after you leave is the hard part. That's the phase when you have to deal with your fears of what he might do. That's when your loneliness comes up, and your sadness. That's when he makes promises and starts manipulating you.

So to succeed in staying away you have to have a *plan*, and it might be best to put it *in writing*. It could take you a few weeks and perhaps a number of months to make your plan, so start today. Here are some of the points to include:

Which friends and relatives are going to be good sources of emotional support for you? When will you tell them that you're leaving your partner? What plans do you need to have in place for them?

How much money do you need? How are you going to get it, and hide it?

How and where can you tell him safely? (Alone at home with him is not a good idea.)

What steps will you take when you start to feel the urge to go back to him? (Write the answer to this one in detail; include phone calls you will make to loved ones, a support group you can attend, a trip away for a few days, and other steps. *Do not keep it a secret from other people that you are thinking of getting back with him;* isolation is disastrous.)

Keep adding to your plan in the weeks ahead, so that by the time you are ready to leave, you have a plan that can succeed.

✂❀

"When I decide to leave, I need to find
a way to make it work and stick to it."

A Different Kind of Walk

Simple is often best. It can be hard to find the time to exercise, or meditate, or go out to see a counselor. And this challenge can feel even greater if your partner interferes with your freedom. So today I'm going to describe a way to use a simple act—taking a walk—as a path toward clarity and healing.

A walk will help you the most if it's at least fifteen minutes long, but if two or three minutes is all you can get away with you can still get important benefits. Focus on three things while you walk:

1. Your breathing. Feel each breath come in and go back out. Make your breathing a little slower and deeper than it would normally be, but don't exaggerate it; keep it comfortable. Cultivate a mental image where with each breath you sense the oxygen spreading out into your entire body. Let your breathing calm you.

2. The motion in your body. Feel the swing in your arms, notice what the air feels like as your arms move back and forth through it. Pay attention to the sensations in your legs, your back, and your butt (which is where walking is really driven from) with each pace. See if you can release muscles that are tight and feel the walking as pleasurable motion.

3. Your sensory experience of the world around you. Notice what you hear, smell, and see. Try to see how many different sounds, colors, and shapes you can become aware of. Don't count them or name them; just open your senses and let the world come into you through them.

If these three things are too much to stay focused on, pick one. Then choose a different one for the next day.

Take this kind of calming, pleasurable walk at least once a week. Try not to think about your partner, your to-do list, or your worries while you walk; just feel the feelings in your body and senses.

"I can make breathing and walking into a
healing meditation, calming my mind
and connecting me to my body."

The Fear of Being Single

"I was so lonely, but now I'm so happy since I've met you" captures the most common theme to form the basis of popular songs, movies, and books. We live steeped in the message that the top goal in life is to be part of a couple. We feel happy for people who are in relationships, and sorry for those who are single.

But we shouldn't. We especially shouldn't when it comes to women. You may be surprised to hear that research has found that single women are, on average, *happier* than women who have partners.

Why do many women do so well single? First, girls typically grow up with less freedom than boys do, because parents are stricter with them. So adult women often crave a life where no one tells them what to do or keeps tabs on them. A partner can come quickly to feel like a parent.

Second, women tend to feel more able than men to get their needs for emotional closeness and physical affection met through their friendships. If your life has an abundance of love and hugs, you may not feel so quick to jump into a relationship that isn't exactly what you want. Even women who do have partners commonly report that their most intimate conversations happen with friends.

Third, women make greater sacrifices than men do to make relationships work. Women tend, for example, to do more than their share of child care and household work, make greater career sacrifices, sleep less, and compromise their wishes more.

The only sensible reason to be in a relationship is because you want to be there, and not because you fear the alternative. If you were single, you would do fine.

✥

> "I can choose to be a couple or to be single, and I'll be fine either way. I don't have to be in a relationship that isn't good for me."

Boundaries

See if you can form an image of yourself as a cozy and attractive cottage, surrounded by a lovely garden. You might think of the cottage as your heart, spirit, and body; this is your core. The garden represents all the different aspects of the outside of who you are—your interests and activities, your passions and irritations.

This all belongs to you. No one has the right to trample your flowers, to stomp around in your cottage with their muddy shoes, to peek in your windows. This is yours alone.

You can, of course, choose to share the garden, the home, or both. The key word is "choose."

So you build a fence around your place to keep others from damaging it, and to make sure you can have the place to yourself when you want to. The fence is nicely crafted—you aren't trying to make people feel warned away—but also good and strong.

The gate in the fence and the door to the house are the most crucial parts of this little estate. They have to be solid and completely under your control, but also well oiled so as to open smoothly when you want them to. The gate lets people into parts of yourself that you care about, and the door to the house takes the additional step of letting people into emotional or physical intimacy with you. If these portals are falling apart, you'll end up letting a lot of people in that you don't really want, with the result that you keep getting hurt in various ways. On the other hand, if the gate or the door is rusted closed, you will end up missing out on companionship and closeness that would have added so much to your life, and that you crave.

Hold this image for a few days. Ask yourself, "Am I letting people in that I would rather keep out? Am I letting people dig up my lovely yard? Am I shutting people out that I'd really like to share my place with, whose company would make it shine even brighter?" Then see if you can do some maintenance work over the next few months, getting it all working just right.

⋊⊙⋉

"I am a sacred home and garden, to be shared only
by those who will treasure me."

The Fear of Raising Bad Kids

Children do better when we are focused on our excitement about the people we want to help them become, and not on our fears about the bad qualities that we feel we must fend off from them. It's important to avoid what I call "defensive parenting," where our energy is going into monitoring our children for signs of badness and then trying to roughly stomp it out of them, like a spark in the grass that could start a forest fire. When children sense that you have great fears of them turning out badly, they start to think they must be bad; otherwise, why would you be so worried? What follows for kids is self-doubt, guilt, and, ironically, undesirable behaviors.

Work, then, to have faith that your children will find their way through to a healthy set of values and attitudes. When they can feel your confidence that they are going to be good, they move more easily in that direction.

I recognize that serious problems have to be dealt with seriously. If you have a child who is bullying others, or who abuses alcohol or drugs, you have to take strong steps. But even then you want to send the message "I'm giving serious consequences here because I know this isn't the type of person you want to be"—which is very different from using a tone that implies, "I'm doing this because you're bad."

Men who abuse women commonly use "defensive parenting" as their style with kids. If this is true of your partner, notice the effects on your kids, and give yourself extra encouragement to parent positively.

❧

"My children are going to be okay."

Picking and Choosing Religious Messages

You may be surprised to hear that most people who participate in a faith community don't actually agree with every single one of its beliefs and stands. They tend to keep their diverging thoughts to themselves, though, in order to avoid receiving disapproval from others in the congregation. Some spiritual leaders are critical or disapproving of members of the congregation who have any doubts or disagreements, which can contribute to keeping people silent about their true thoughts. The result is that each person walks around thinking that he or she is the only one with some different outlooks.

Did you know, for example, that about half of Catholic women are pro-choice? That's a pretty high rate of stepping out of line.

You get to think for yourself about the messages your religion teaches you. This isn't about disconnecting yourself from your faith. Hold on tightly to what sustains you and what fits with your deepest beliefs. Keep loving the people in your faith community and soaking up their love for you. But at the same time reserve your right to leave aside the parts of the belief system that don't make sense to you. An all-loving, all-wise higher power does not want you to turn your thinking over to *anyone* else, not even to your religion's scriptures.

❊

"My spiritual beliefs are the deepest part
of who I am, and I get to shape them in
the way that's right for me."

When Your Partner Cheats on You—Part 1

Oh, how it hurts. Many women have told me that their partner's infidelity has been the single most hurtful thing he has done. Sexuality is a very intimate aspect of life for most women. Sharing bodies opens a unique level of vulnerability. Sexual wounds, whether through abuse or infidelity, are some of the deepest emotional injuries that people carry.

As a society, we make too light of people cheating on their partners. We tend to accept excuses from friends when they reveal their infidelities, and we say that someone "had an affair" as if it were a kind of unfortunate but minor accident. But in reality, people do big-time damage when they cheat on their partners.

It's important to recognize that your partner's infidelity comes from his selfishness and self-centeredness. He may call it all kinds of other things—such as a sexual urge that got out of control—but those aren't the real causes. He may also try to make it your fault, saying that he cheated because he felt starved for the sex and affection he wasn't getting from you. And another common excuse is "Well, I thought we were pretty much split up anyhow," because you had pulled back from him—but no breakup had actually happened.

Finally, ask yourself the question "Did he cheat on me to get me back for standing up to him?" Some abusive men use affairs as a form of retaliation.

꿈

"If he cheats on me, that's on him.
And it says a lot about him."

Making Safety Your Top Priority

If I stood on a street corner taking a survey, asking people what the top things were they wanted to get out of being in a relationship, I would hear elements such as love, passion, companionship, sex, growth, fun, support, laughter, friendship, affection, security, teamwork, and healing.

But none of these goals can come to fruition unless there is also *safety*. You have to be able to trust your partner and know that he will:

- Not harm you physically or sexually, and not even create the impression that he might
- Not violate your boundaries
- Not betray your confidences, not harm you with deep truths you have revealed about yourself
- Not leave you without first making a very serious effort to work problems out
- Not cheat on you
- Not lie to you (including about finances)
- Not harm your children emotionally, physically, or sexually
- Not damage your belongings
- Not verbally tear you down
- Not make it hard for friends or relatives to come by
- Not impede your progress in life

The longer you are involved with an unsafe partner, the less love, growth, and laughter there will be. And when the positive elements do come in, they will increasingly have a hollowness to them that will keep you from feeling satisfied. In the absence of safety, all of the positive stuff is a fleeting illusion.

So it makes no sense to trade safety away for love, or for affection, or for having a partner (in other words, to avoid being single). It will never work for long. Safety has to come first.

✕◯✳

"I won't settle for a relationship that
I don't feel safe in."

Laugh Your Way Well

You have probably heard of studies showing that laughter can play a big role in helping sick people get well; laughter really is the best medicine. But you are less likely to have heard what those studies found out about *why* laughing is so good for people. It turns out that the reason why it's so beneficial to bodies is because of how much it helps souls.

Laughter has a much more profound and positive emotional impact than most people realize. It relieves stress and anxiety, and can help people to overcome fears and phobias. It clears out people's thinking, helping them to solve tricky problems. After a good laugh, we sometimes can snap out of discouragement and be able to take on challenges that we were feeling defeated by previously. In fact, the research indicates that deep and prolonged laughter has many of the same psychological benefits that you get from an intense cry.

Take laughter seriously. (Get it?) Have laughing fits, milking them for all they're worth, when you're with friends. Don't hold back during a funny movie. Get silly with your kids, and let the laughter come out. There is healing power there.

"I can laugh my way to healing and strength."

"I'm as Bad as He Is"

Does abuse justify abuse in return? If you call your partner an "asshole" or a "selfish prick," does that give him the excuse to call you a "stupid bitch" or worse?

No. Abuse does not justify abuse. People are responsible for their own actions, and being in a relationship doesn't make that principle any less applicable.

What rights do you have if someone is abusing you?

- The right to call that person out on what he or she is doing
- The right to tell the person how wrong his or her behavior is and how it makes you feel
- The right to demand that the person change his or her behavior
- The right to demand that the person stop blaming his or her behavior on you
- The right to take some time off from the relationship
- The right to end the relationship
- The right to seek legal protection if the person's abuse is intimidating you. (Keep in mind here that almost any assault toward a woman by her partner will frighten her, however "minor" it may seem; whereas a man is usually not frightened by his female partner's assault, though he may be very annoyed by it.)

Notice what you *don't* see on this list. Nothing on there says you get to hurt the person or threaten to hurt the person. Nothing says you get to degrade the person or intimidate him or her. Nothing says, "An eye for an eye." Simply put, your partner doesn't get to use your behavior, even if he defines it as abusive, as an excuse to abuse you.

✦

"I don't think I'm abusive, but even if I were, that *still* wouldn't make it okay to abuse me."

STAYING CONNECTED

Small Interactions During the Day

Do you ever joke around and laugh with the cashier at the supermarket? Do you find a way to get a conversation going with the person behind you in a line, even if it's just about the weather? Do you smile at a stranger you're passing and ask how that person is doing?

In the modern world, a typical day contains many quick interactions in our busy lives. It's easy to get in the habit of being businesslike, or looking at the ground and not even greeting people. We miss a lot of opportunities to share a friendly word or have a little fun with someone.

And if your primary relationship is causing you distress, you may harden toward the world, locked into your unhappiness; in fact, you may feel eager to get away from people and be alone because you're hurting so much inside.

But there is more sustenance to be drawn out of these brief exchanges than you may realize. If you joke a little with someone, they often will smile and make some real eye contact. If you see a stranger near you who looks upset and you ask, "How are you doing?" you'll be surprised how often the person actually shares with you what he or she is struggling with, despite not knowing you at all.

Friendships can even begin from these simple moments; I made a lifelong friend while waiting in a long line when I was a teenager. I have another friend who met his wife by enjoying exchanges with her while she was waiting on his table at a restaurant.

So smile a little through your distress and see what connections you can make. Break the habit of looking down, and instead try to meet people's eyes. Find moments of fondness during the day, ones that you might have considered meaningless before.

"I can open my heart to connection
with anyone whose path I cross."

Teaching Children to Think for Themselves

As parents we naturally want our children to share our values, our spiritual beliefs, and our political preferences. We consider it our responsibility to shape their outlook, so it can be upsetting if we find that they are rejecting our religious teachings or are leaning toward the opposite end of the political spectrum from us.

But don't panic. It isn't your job to control your kids' opinions, and trying to do so can derail your relationships with them. You'll end up arguing instead of spending good time together, and they will start to avoid telling you what they really think. Remember that eventually they are going to grow up; you aren't going to be able to always be there, acting like a goalie who keeps bad thoughts from entering their heads. In the long run, it is the ability to think clearly and independently that will best protect them from unhealthy attitudes.

Your best role, then, is to explore their thinking rather than try to correct it. Ask them questions and express interest in the different outlooks that they are exploring. Help them think through different points of view. Guide them toward logical and critical thinking.

Let's take an example: Suppose one of your children declares that she's in favor of the legalization of marijuana. You're not happy to hear this, but instead of shooting her down you ask her to explain her outlook, showing an interest in the points that she makes. Then, after drawing her out, you lightheartedly present counterarguments. For example, you could say, "Well, many people argue that marijuana is a way for people to avoid their problems. What are your thoughts about that?" Make it into an interesting debate, and keep your sense of humor.

The result will be that your child actually does some *thinking* about the other side of the question, and learns to weigh the issues, whereas if you preach at them they'll just tune you out. You'll end up with much safer kids in the long run because they'll learn not to let peers, partners, or the media control their thinking.

✦

"It's more important for me to really engage with my children's opinions than to correct them."

Feeling Like a Liar

Just recently, a woman that I've counseled was spotted by her partner hanging out with a male friend on an evening when she had said she was going to her book club. She explained to me that being dishonest was the only way she could have a social life since her partner didn't permit her to go out. But now he's calling all their mutual friends, telling them what a liar she is and accusing her of having an affair. She feels humiliated, caught like a naughty little child.

Lying isn't always wrong. Specifically, it's justifiable for a woman to lie to her abusive partner when:

- She believes he will hurt her if he knows the truth.
- She has to lie to protect her basic freedoms, such as her right to have friends or keep her own money.
- She is attempting to protect her privacy, such as when she lies to him about what her own thoughts are so that she can keep some privacy in her own mind.
- She is trying to keep her children from being harmed by him emotionally or physically, and so has to cover for them.
- She is planning her escape from the relationship.

At the same time, your sense of integrity is important to you. So don't lie to other people (unless they might pass information back to your partner), and do your best to conduct yourself in an open and honest way wherever it is safe for you to do so. If you let him turn you into someone who really is a liar, you're going to sink emotionally; you need your pride and dignity.

*"Lying to keep myself safe doesn't make me a liar.
I am a person of integrity."*

When Your Partner Cheats on You—Part 2

Finding out about an affair can be a shattering experience. It's tempting, in the midst of that pain, to find soothing ways to explain the affair away—that he was drunk, for example, or that he got seduced. But be careful. His cheating is connected to his overall behavior pattern. It's part of the same problem. The affair is just the latest example of his mean or manipulative actions.

Explaining it away can set you up for continued years of being devalued, including further affairs.

Seek out love and support from other people about what this has been like for you. Don't let him become the person you look to for soothing; that will only further harm your dignity and diminish your power.

*"This is a time for me to draw strength
from my support system and from my
inner self, not from him."*

Preparing Early for a Possible Custody Battle

If you are not ready yet to take the leap to leave your controlling partner, it may feel way early to start preparing for a possible fight over custody of your children. But abusive men are much more likely than other guys to put you through custody litigation, because they want control and they want payback. So I strongly recommend that you start preparing yourself in a number of ways now, just in case.

Here are a few steps to take:

1. Get familiar with the laws in your state, and with the typical practices of the family court in your county.

For example, in most states, if you and your partner were never married it is harder for him to take custody from you. In some states judges push joint custody very hard, which is not good for women who are leaving an abusive partner. Some courts understand the ways in which abusive men use children as weapons, while others refuse to look at that issue.

But do your research carefully. You probably want to avoid looking these things up on a shared computer; use a friend's computer or go to the library.

2. Get legal advice.

Pay for a one-hour consultation with a reputable lawyer in your area to learn something about where you stand. (Again, do this before you decide to actually leave.) See if you can get a referral to a lawyer from a woman who personally had a good experience with one in a similar situation, or from a program for abused women. Many lawyers who are good overall divorce lawyers are not knowledgeable about how to help women protect their children from abusers.

3. Build good relationships with adults who are in your children's lives.

Schoolteachers, sports coaches, therapists, scouting leaders, and other respected adults in your community who know your children well may be important witnesses and references at custody time. Make sure that these people can see that you are a responsible and caring mother, and that your children value their time with you.

"He has given me some nasty surprises before.
Just in case, I am going to get ready
regarding child custody."

Healing After He Has Had an Affair—Part 1

Infidelity can leave you mistrustful, rejected, and stinging in pain for a long time. No one has the right to minimize to you how hurtful a thing he has done—least of all your partner.

The most tempting way to ease the pain is also the most self-sabotaging: working to get him to reassure you that he loves you and that the affair was a mistake that meant nothing to him. Don't go down this path. Looking to him will further erode your dignity, increase your partner's power over you, and make you more vulnerable.

Instead, take a significant time away from seeing him (and insist that he stay somewhere else for now). During that time, take care of yourself in the following ways:

- Spend time with friends or relatives you are close to, and open up to them about how hurt you feel.
- Write extensively in your journal about what this has all been like for you (this is important to do).
- Find places where you can be alone to cry, scream, rage, and pound cushions. Let it all out.
- Reflect seriously on the question of whether your relationship needs to end. Spend some time envisioning life without him, even if the thought is a painful one.
- Take long walks alone or with a friend or a pet. (If you don't have a dog, borrow someone else's for a couple of hours. Dog owners are always looking for more exercise for their pets, and the companionship will do wonders for you.)

Work hard to maintain clarity about the fact that this is 100 percent his issue, and you did not cause it. He is responsible for his own choices.

Be gentle and kind with yourself, and proceed on the assumption that this wound can heal fully but that it will take time, attention, and compassion. Don't let your healing depend on what your partner does or does not do; keep it in your own hands.

~

"I will heal from what he has done, and
I won't try to do it through him."

Keeping Yourself Sane

There are days when you just can't fight your partner.

Some days his tongue is a sword that's cutting you to pieces, and you finally feel too torn down to struggle with him anymore.

Some days he seems to have a comeback ready for anything that you say, so trying to get him to hear you or understand you is like hitting your head against the wall.

Some days he's a tinderbox, and you can tell that if you dare stand up for yourself he's going to make you pay a really high price.

Some days he's acting out right in front of the children, and you feel like you have to take it because otherwise they'll be caught in the middle of a bad scene.

Some days he's scary.

But giving in completely is dangerous to your spiritual survival. So even if you have to give in on the outside, keep a place *inside* you where he doesn't win.

On the outside, you might have to do the following:

- Be quiet even though you have every right to say more
- Say that you're sorry even though you've done nothing wrong and he's the one who should be apologizing
- Cast your eyes down and look defeated
- Tell him he's right
- Clean up a mess that he made and that he should be the one to clean up

But on your inside, invisible to him, keep telling yourself:

- "I'm only behaving as though I'm giving in because I have to."
- "He's wrong, and what he's doing is wrong."
- "I'm pretending I'm sorry, but I'm not, because I did nothing wrong."
- "He can bully me, but down deep I'll never give in."

Maintaining this secret fortress is essential to keeping yourself sane and well.

>-◝≮

"I'm not defeated even if he forces
me to look like I am."

Having a Hard Time with People Treating You Well

The past lives inside of us. Old feelings, and especially old injuries, can surge up inside of us in the midst of present-day interactions. And since these triggered emotions don't carry big signs that say "OLD FEEL-INGS," we can have a hard time telling whether we're reacting to the present or to the past.

To add an additional wrinkle, *good* experiences in the present can actually trigger memories of old *bad* experiences. In particular, when someone we care about is kind and loving toward us, we can get flooded with old feelings about times when people were mean or rejecting—the opposite of what is happening now. The wounds that get reawakened can lead us to go through some of the following reactions (mostly inside of ourselves, though sometimes we may say them aloud):

"You're saying you love me now, but as soon as I let myself really care about you, you're going to leave me." (Because important people dropped out of our lives before.)

"You're just trying to set me up to take power over me and run my life." (Because people we trusted used the appearance of love to bring us under their control.)

"You're just being nice to me because you feel sorry for me." (Because we've been so torn down in the past that we can't imagine anyone would really love us for who we are.)

"Any minute now you're going to start to find all kinds of fault in me and put me down, so I'm going to shield myself emotionally by finding things wrong with you first" (Because we've been picked apart by people we cared about.)

As you strive to have close connections with friends and relatives, or with a new dating partner after your destructive relationship ends, be aware of what is going on in the stormy seas of your emotions. Remember to check in with yourself from time to time about whether you are reacting to old stuff. We are all going to get triggered emotionally sometimes, but we don't have to let those old wounds run our current lives. You can sort out what's old and what's new, and make your current relationships work.

"Old feelings are just that: feelings. I don't have to be pushed around by them."

Respecting Children's Boundaries

Little children can seem like stuffed animals. They are so fun to cuddle, squeeze, and kiss, just the perfect toys. Except they aren't toys, they're people. And like all human beings, they have the right to the space around them and to control of their own bodies.

Adults seem to be largely unaware that children have rights, and that those include the right to have their boundaries respected. You can be a huge help to your kids by doing the following:

- Respect children's right to not be touched (including hugs or kisses) when they don't want to be
- Do not require children to touch others when they don't wish to (such as not requiring them to give hugs or kisses to relatives or to sit in someone's lap when they don't want to)
- Respect their right to privacy in the bath and toilet and when changing clothes, and their right to be behind a locked door when doing those things
- Respect their right to *emotional* boundaries, including the right to not talk about things they want to keep to themselves (encouraging them to open up is okay, but requiring them to is not)

- Do not tell children what they think or feel; respect their right to define their own thoughts and feelings

By honoring these rights in your children, you help them to feel safer in the world. You will also be teaching them to expect others to respect their boundaries, which will make it easier for them to defend themselves and to cry out for help when adults or other kids attempt to take advantage of them.

And there's an additional, crucial reason to raise them this way: Angry and controlling men often do not respect children's boundaries, and sometimes even attempt to humiliate or intimidate children for asserting their boundaries. The better you treat them, the more likely they are to see how wrong his behavior is and to report it quickly to you if they feel invaded by him.

✕?✕

"I am going to respect my children's boundaries
and do everything in my power to ensure
that other people do too."

EACH NEW DAY

Is Your Faith Working for You?

At my weekend retreats for women who have ended abusive relationships, I meet many people whose religious or spiritual faith has been a wellspring of strength and courage. Their belief in a higher truth has propelled them past the man's claim that his word was The Truth. Their faith communities have offered them love, validation, and sometimes financial support and places to stay. They walk accompanied by a higher power that breaks their isolation and gives them hope, helping them feel that they are flowing into a positive plan that exists for their lives. They find that they can travel or move to a different part of the country and quickly find new people to connect with and a new community to belong to.

At the same time, I've met a similar number of women whose religions have contributed to keeping them trapped. Some of them struggle with dogmatic training they've digested with messages such as:

"It's wrong to divorce a man no matter how badly you've been treated."

"A woman's suffering is a challenge that God wants her to endure and come to terms with."

"The man is the head of the household and therefore he has the ultimate say in a conflict."

"A wife should be focused on meeting her husband's needs and understanding his troubles."

Take a look at the impact your spiritual community and beliefs are having on your ability to protect your rights. If your faith is making you stronger, lean into it even more heavily. But if it is undercutting you, look for ways to distance yourself or even consider trying out some other churches to find a place that might be a greater source of sustenance to you.

"My spiritual beliefs and my faith community should support me in living with dignity and rights."

When Your Partner Cheats on You—Part 3

I could distill large portions of what I have written in my books down to just two sentences:

Your partner is 100 percent responsible for his own actions.

You don't make him behave badly.

There is no time when it is more important to apply this principle than when your partner cheats on you. He may come up with all kinds of reasons why it's your fault, partly or entirely:

You weren't being affectionate or sexual enough with him.

It didn't seem like you really wanted to be in a relationship with him anyhow.

You're too critical of him; you always find things wrong with him (meaning that you call him out on how he treats you).

You have wounded his self-esteem or his manhood somehow (usually, again, because you stood up to his abuse and control).

You suspect him too much of cheating on you, so he decided to just go ahead and do it. (Yup, I've really heard this excuse from abusive men.)

What he's attempting to do is turn the whole thing around backwards, so that *his* infidelity becomes something that *you* have to answer for. He'd like you to have to be the one to prove that you really love him, and he'd like you to have to work extra hard to keep him happy so that he doesn't stray again. In other words, he can use his affair to gain deeper control over you, playing on how wounded you feel by what he did.

This is a crucial time to set things back the right way. If he cheated, the burden is all on him. He's the one who has to prove that he is a good partner; he's the one who has to work harder; he's the one who has to focus less on his own needs and more on yours. Make it clear that for the next couple of years you'll be looking to see whether he is someone worthy of staying with.

And if he doesn't think it's fair that his infidelity should place him on a very long probation, then he's telling you everything you need to know about his outlook on relationships and responsibility.

><️>⚶

"He's not going to get away with turning this around to use against *me*."

Staying for the Kids

Caring parents are always trying to figure out how to put their children's needs first. This effort shouldn't mean that our needs disappear, however; we are parents, but we are also human beings who need love, sleep, friendship, and solitude. The balancing act can get tricky.

Nowhere does this struggle appear more starkly than it does for the woman who is being torn down by her partner. She needs so urgently to escape the toxic environment that is poisoning her soul, but she doesn't want her children to pay the price for her partner's abusiveness.

Here are a few points to reflect upon in this struggle:

1. The best thing for children is to have a mother who is really well. Study after study has found that your happiness, energy, and safety are what benefits your kids the most. So if you're in a situation that is profoundly unhealthy for you, that isn't helping them.
2. Kids actually do better being raised by a single mom than they do in a two-parent family where the man abuses their mother.
3. Unfortunately, some abusive men use their manipulative skills to get the children to blame their mother for the breakup.
4. You may be concerned that if you leave your partner he'll go for custody of the kids or he'll mess with their minds during his visitation with them. And you know how important it is for the children to have you in their daily lives and know that they can count on you.

With all of these pros and cons to think about, there are obviously no easy answers. But the fact that you are thinking so hard about what's best for your children is in itself a great gift to them. You will find the best way to move forward.

"My kids need me to be there for them, but they
also need me to take care of myself."

Healing After He Has Had an Affair—Part 2

You forgive him. He promises he won't do it again. You feel deeply wounded, but you also want to understand him. And you have a powerful craving for an outcome where he still loves you, and where the affair didn't really mean much to him—anything that will lessen those feelings of rejection and humiliation. So you and he decide together that what he did was an aberration.

Now what happens?

The reality is that your relationship with him is no longer the same. He has just added power to his side of the equation, whether that was his intention or not, because now you have to worry about whether he's going to stray again. You'll tend to get nervous anytime he's unhappy about how your relationship is going, which can make it harder for you to stand up to him. You're likely to start working harder, catering to him more, making sure to keep him with you. You end up in a one-down position.

So I would like to see you give some serious consideration to the following solution: Tell him that because of the affair, you need some time apart from him, a month or two of living in separate places and not seeing him at all. It's not a breakup; in fact, I would tell him that if he sleeps with anyone during the separation, your relationship is over.

A separation like this is important to restoring your dignity after an affair, *and your dignity is crucial*. It's also important to send him the message that he won't be able to cheat on you, make an apology, and have life go on as if it didn't happen. He needs to experience a serious consequence, and he needs to see that it's now up to him to prove that he's worthy of you, not the other way around. If you don't take this step, you are likely to find yourself in a relationship that is permanently altered for the worse, and where you will never feel your feet quite firmly under you again.

> "I am not going to be left feeling lower than him. If he can't take serious steps to restore my dignity, we're not going forward."

Reminding Yourself How Intelligent You Are

Think back for a moment over the past two months. How many things has your partner said or done in that period that have made you feel smart? Now how many things has he said or done that have made you feel stupid, uninformed, or unthinking?

Even if these two questions come out 50–50—and I bet they don't—those are pretty bad proportions; 95–5 or 100–0 would be a lot more like it. Even when partners disagree, they shouldn't be making each other feel stupid or ignorant.

So with your partner giving you such a negative and inaccurate reflection of how your mind works, it can get hard to remember the truth. What are some ways you might help yourself do that?

Begin by taking a few minutes today to do these two pieces of writing in your journal.

1. Describe something you did before you met your partner that demonstrates intelligence, good judgment, or quick thinking. It might

be a decision you made, an emergency you handled, a paper or test in school, an accomplishment in your work.

2. Describe something you have done since being with him that shows the same qualities.

Next, make some notes to yourself about any positive comments anyone has given you about your mind. Include observations you've heard of any creative abilities you have in art, music, theater, dance, or writing (these all involve intelligence, though we don't always think of them that way). Also write down other ways that people showed that they thought you were smart even if they didn't say so in words; an example might be a person who hired you for a job that required responsibility or good reasoning ability.

Read back over these points in your journal from time to time. And try at least once a week to add a description of something you have done, recently or not, that shows that your mind functions well. These truths will help keep his distortions at bay.

"I can create my own reflections of who I am,
and use them to remind myself."

STAYING CONNECTED

Looking at Faults Through a Different Lens

First let's take a look at faults through the wrong lens: the one your partner looks through. He sees people's faults—especially yours—as incredibly frustrating and stupid. He takes the attitude that people are just choosing to be "that way," and that it's ridiculous that they don't just "do things right." He doesn't want to hear any excuses about what might make someone handle any aspect of life in less than a perfect way. And he acts as if these faults are affronts against *him* specifically; he acts offended that people have issues.

None of this applies to his faults, of course. His view of his own issues—to the extent that he's even willing to admit they exist—is that they require patience and understanding because of what he has come through in life, or because his current challenges are so large. But you're not likely to see him cut other people the same slack, especially not you.

Although you can't make him change his outlook, you can keep his from becoming yours. Remind yourself as you look at your children, at other people, and at yourself, to keep these points in mind:

- By and large, people are doing the best they can. People rarely make mistakes on purpose.
- There are often reasons that we don't know about for the irritating things people do.
- We make mistakes ourselves all the time, and we need to remember that fact when we are bothered by things that other people do.
- Children need at least as much room to make mistakes as adults do; in fact, we should show them extra patience and understanding. They are trying to get it right.

Make an effort not to judge people harshly. Decide to be someone who judges in people's favor whenever possible, reserving criticism for when they are really out of line. Be patient and forgiving toward yourself, which will help you be the same toward others.

*"I don't have to judge people harshly just
because he does. I want to be more
forgiving of others and of myself."*

School and Homework

Kids need to be physically active most of the time, and outdoors whenever possible. But schools have set up a learning environment where kids are sitting at desks or tables for several hours in a row, which makes no sense for their development and is unhealthful for their bodies. This is the reason they are "bouncing off the walls"—they are being held captive. Wouldn't it be great if they could learn by being directly involved in the world?

While you can't instantly change the education system, you can be a tremendous help to your kids just by understanding that schools are not designed well to meet their physical needs. When your kids come home frustrated, upset, or restless, consider these feelings natural and predictable reactions to having spent the day sitting in a classroom. They are desperate for physical activity and motion, though they may not realize it. Validate their feelings and support them by being loving and affectionate with them, and allowing them to decompress.

Some parents believe that responsibilities should always come before play, so they require their children to do homework or chores when they first arrive home from school. I don't recommend it. School is so restrictive that kids need their afternoons to belong mostly to them.

They need to be active, so you may have to pull the computer or game controller out of their hands and send them out the door. Adequate exercise and motion are crucial to their mental and physical health (as study after study has found).

Of course your kids will have homework that they'll need to complete later on. Support and help your children to get these assignments completed efficiently so they become a learning tool rather than just another burdensome task.

x◦〉k

"My kids' reactions to school and homework are natural. I can be there for them about it all."

EACH NEW DAY

Meditating

Learning to meditate is easy, and the benefits are many. Meditation helps us to quiet our minds and improve our focus. It has positive physiological effects, giving rest to our overworked hearts and nervous systems. It can bring steadiness to volatile emotions and help us find ways out of stuck places in our lives.

To start learning to meditate, just find a quiet place, indoors or out, to sit comfortably. You can have your eyes open or closed, whichever helps you to feel calmest. Pay attention to your breathing, and try not to think about anything else; just mentally watch your breaths go in and out. When you find your thoughts starting up—which they certainly will do—gently return to feeling your breathing and let the thoughts drift off. Meditate for anywhere from five minutes to twenty, depending on how much time you have.

When you finish, come back into the world gradually, as if you were waking up. Take a moment to stretch out a little bit, and start moving slowly; don't jump full-speed yet back into your day. Later in the day you might make some notes in your journal about how it felt to meditate.

⟊⟊⟊

"Meditating can help me calm and center myself."

CLARITY

When He Takes Apologies Back

Listen to Abby's story:

> "Darryl cheated on me a year ago, and I was devastated. He kept saying that I had caused it by being cold to him and refusing him sex, and that a man 'has to get it somewhere else eventually if he's not getting it at home.' So for months we were living together but not really a couple, barely speaking to each other. Then one day he finally apologized. He said he knew that having the affair was wrong and that he had really hurt me. And he looked like he felt bad for real. After that things were much better between us for a few months, though I was on edge of course. Well, a few weeks ago he erupted at me, saying he was sick of me not trusting him, and that I was making way too big a deal about one little affair that was so short, and when the hell was I going to get over it? I feel crushed."

What I pointed out to Abby was that Darryl had just retracted his original apology. His new statements and behaviors had rendered the earlier apology completely meaningless; that was why she felt so terrible. He'll still insist, "Hey, I said I was sorry," but he's wrong to claim that, because his new statements have erased the previous apology.

One of the (endless) battles of life with a selfish or self-centered partner is trying to get him to own unfair and destructive things he has done. If you succeed in persuading him to say that he's sorry, your hopes rise a little, and if his apology sounds sincere, your hopes rise more. After a while you even start to trust him a little, and then one day it all comes crashing down.

Start to notice how none of his apologies stick for more than a few months (at best). And notice how much emotional energy this roller-coaster ride is draining out of you.

>◦⟨⟩◦<

"When he takes an apology back it's
worse than if he'd never apologized
in the first place."

Do Abuser Programs Work?

Do programs for abusive men lead to change? The answer is that, when they are run well, they work as well as we can expect them to in the short time they are given. A typical length for a batterer program is twenty-six weeks, and in some states even shorter. We are talking, then, about undoing twenty or thirty or forty years of destructive socialization that has made an abusive man who he is, all in six months! The expectation is far-fetched.

Look at substance abuse recovery by comparison. If a man (or a woman) who had been drinking or drugging heavily for many years claimed to have licked the addiction through *once a week counseling* for a grand total of *six months*, substance abuse experts would laugh the person out of the room. The common outlook in the recovery field is that you need to go to three or four meetings per week for a year just to get a good *start* on dealing with your issues, and you have to really work the program between meetings.

Why would it to be easier for a man to overcome a problem with violence or bullying toward women than to deal with a drinking problem? The only abusive men who change are the ones who work on their problem seriously for years, and who take full responsibility for getting to their meetings, paying for them, and doing diligent work on their issues between meetings. In other words, the question isn't really whether the program works; it's whether he works the program.

"I've seen plenty of his quick fixes. He needs
to maintain a complete transformation
in how much he respects me."

HEALING

Is Therapy the Answer?

Our society's answer to everything that troubles people has become "You should go to therapy." But is talking with a psychotherapist succeeding at making people feel better? The outcome research is mixed; it shows therapy having modest benefits on average, with many clients not finding it particularly helpful.

Under what circumstances does therapy work for a woman who has had, or still has, an abusive partner? First, the therapist has to get what controlling and degrading men are like. The sessions become counterproductive when the counselor starts to make the abuse partly your fault, or makes excuses for your partner's behavior. It also doesn't help if you get analyzed about "why are you in a relationship like this"; the reality is that any woman can find herself involved with a man who turns out to be a bully.

Second, the therapist has to respect you and support your right to make your own decisions. If you are under pressure within the therapy to stay with your partner, or to leave him, or to continue in therapy when you want to quit, that's inappropriate. It's important that the counseling not start to have control dynamics like your relationship.

Third, you have to feel that your therapist cares about you and is happy to see you, and you need to feel good being with him or her. If you find the counselor too businesslike or analytical, you'll end up feeling even more starved for love and kindness.

In short, it can take some hunting to find a therapist who is a good match for you.

Don't think of therapy as the only option. It is one approach among many healing paths that I've mentioned earlier in this book. The best place to begin is usually at a program for abused women.

"I will make therapy work for me or find
a different path to healing."

Listening to What You Know About Yourself

Healing is stimulated by developing a kind and supportive relationship with yourself. From that base, you can reach to have that same quality of relationship with your children, and then with other people you have contact with during your day. This is how you create the context in which deep recovery can happen.

You yourself are the closest and most accessible person to you. Turn your attention toward ways that you can be a loving, thoughtful friend to yourself.

Here is one way you might begin:

> **Stop believing anything he tells you about**
> **who you are, what you're like,**
> **what you need to do differently, and**
> **what your faults supposedly are.**

Someone who saw you clearly would never treat you the way he does; in other words, his behavior toward you is proof that he doesn't really know you. So all of his put-downs have nothing to do with the truth about you.

When I say to stop believing him, I don't mean that you should argue with him about the devaluing things he says about you. I get it that often it's better, for your own peace and safety, to be quiet so that he'll feel triumphant and leave you alone. But in the privacy of your own mind, where he can't hear what you are saying, keep reminding yourself that he is distorting and twisting everything, and he is so very wrong in his view of who you are. And keep telling yourself, like a mantra, the truth about your own goodness.

*"I am a smart and capable woman.
I know the truth about me."*

People Want to Help

We live in a society where people have a hard time asking each other for help. As a culture, we value self-reliance and the separate existence of each human being. Many people believe we shouldn't need anyone, that we should be capable of doing things all by ourselves.

Being able to count on yourself is, of course, a great thing. You don't want to be a helpless person who needs everything done for you, and who can't take responsibility for your own life.

But at the same time, people *do* need each other.

In order to heal from abuse, you have to believe that you deserve help, and find ways to reach out for a hand. There are so many people out there who are eager and able to help—though sometimes it can be difficult to figure out who they are and where they are. Help is on the way. Don't give up on looking for people who will believe you, support you, and assist you.

*"There are a lot of good people in
the world who want to help. I am not as
alone as he makes me feel."*

Talking to Kids About Healthy Relationships

One of the main hopes parents have for their children is that they will grow up to have healthy long-term relationships. Yet, oddly, we almost never say anything to kids about how to do this. We show them how to brush their teeth and comb their hair, train them in math and sports, and teach them right from wrong. So why aren't we telling them what a healthy relationship is all about?

By the time children are about twelve years old, it's time for you to start talking to them about dating and partnership. They particularly need to hear these key points:

- It's great to choose someone whom you find attractive, but you also need to like and respect the person's personal qualities.
- Two partners in a relationship are equals, and they have equal say over decisions. Neither partner has the right to rule or have the last word. Mutual respect is key.
- Jealousy is not a sign of love.
- In a good relationship, partners spend high-quality time together, but also spend time apart pursuing their separate friendships and interests.
- Sexuality is not about one person "getting some" from the other. It is a mutual, shared experience that should only happen when both partners are ready, and it needs to make both partners feel good or it's not okay.
- Good partners don't control each other, and they raise their complaints or grievances without putting each other down or making the other person feel afraid.

If you haven't had this conversation with your preteen or teenage children, have it soon. It's extra important for you because of the need to counter the unhealthy example your partner sets for how to behave in a relationship.

And if, when you talk with your children, they point out that your own relationship doesn't follow these rules, be honest with them about it. You and your kids can analyze together the problems in your partner's behavior (or in your own). In this way, they can learn to choose how they want their relationships to go, rather than unconsciously following the model that your partner's treatment of you sets for them.

"Children can be prepared for healthy
relationships the same way we teach
them about other aspects of life."

A Humane Philosophy of Living

What people *do* sends a much stronger message than what they *say* about how to live. Read through the following list of negative attitudes and reflect on whether your partner's behavior is sending these messages:

"Whoever speaks the loudest, the most insultingly, and with the most certainty is the one who is right."

"Criticizing people is the best thing to do when you're unhappy. If it's not their fault, blame them anyhow. And if it is their fault, make sure they feel really rotten about it."

"Success is a competition. If you're doing really well in life, that diminishes my success."

"Being too kind or loving shows weakness."

"Love and respect are conditional. I'll show you lots of love and affection as long as you stay on my good side, but when I feel like you're not on my side enough, you're dirt."

"What matters most is that I get my way. Anyone who stands up to me is going to pay for it."

On this next list, on the other hand, is a humane set of values, much more in keeping with what I bet yours are:

"Love is unconditional. Even when we're frustrated or mad at each other, we still find ways to show our love and respect."

"We are focused on encouraging each other. We each want everyone to do well. When one person succeeds, that is a success for all of us."

"We each have wonderful strengths and gifts. There's no need to compare."

"We have each other's back. We're watching out for each other."

"Love and sensitivity are a sign of strength, not of weakness. And that includes having a good cry when we need one, both males and females."

Notice ways in which his philosophies are starting to rule in your home and life, and work hard—undercover if you need to—to replace them with humane, healthy, and happy ones.

*"I have an important and valid vision for
how to live, and I can share that vision
with adults and kids around me."*

The Many Ways to Make an Apology Meaningless

It doesn't matter how heartfelt an apology your partner makes to you if later he takes it back. And he doesn't have to come out and say, "I don't feel sorry anymore about what I did" or "I didn't really mean it when I apologized." He can retract an apology in any of the following ways:

- Saying later that you shouldn't be so upset about what he did and that you should be over it by now (and it's even worse if he says this in an angry, impatient, or judgmental tone)
- Saying later that he felt pressured into making an apology "because you wouldn't leave me alone about it" or similar words
- Repeating the behavior that he apologized for, and then acting like that shouldn't bother you
- Blaming you now for what he did in the incident that he had apologized for (for example, if he goes back to saying that you drove him into cheating on you, or if he says that you are the cause of his legal problems because you "had him arrested" for abusing you)
- Saying "I'm constantly having to apologize to you!" as if somehow it's your fault that he keeps treating you so badly

There are good reasons why his apologies don't affect you much anymore, and why you trust him less and less over time. He keeps knocking all the meaning out of his apologies, and then pitying himself when he sees that saying "sorry" has stopped working.

"Why should his apologies mean anything to me anymore?"

SURVIVING TO THRIVE

The Slow Build of Harm

I have heard the effects of living with an abusive partner compared to (get ready for this) a frog being boiled alive. They say that if you threw a frog into hot water, it would jump back out immediately, alive and with only minor injuries. If, on the other hand, you put the frog into water at room temperature and then very gradually warmed it up, the frog would adapt to each incremental addition of heat, and wouldn't perceive the danger until it was too late and it had cooked.

The point of this comparison is that emotional harm can creep up on you gradually. As a result, it's hard to even tell that your partner's behavior is what is causing your difficulties. It just seems like life is getting harder, or like you aren't the same person you used to be, but you aren't sure why.

Some women don't realize how badly they've been affected until the relationship ends, and they discover what normal life is like; suddenly they aren't tense and worried all the time, they aren't afraid to talk to people, they aren't constantly apologizing. Women have said to me, "It was like I could suddenly breathe again, and I hadn't even noticed I was gasping for air."

Remember the person you were before this relationship started. Was she a happier person? Did she have more friends and social relationships? Was she calmer? Did she feel better about herself? Did she have ambitions and dreams? Was she in better health?

"This is not who I really am.
But I'm still in here, deep down."

Women's Support Groups—Part 1

There is no activity in the world that I hear more positive things about from women than attending a support group at a women's program. The group shows women that they are not alone. By exchanging their stories, women discover how similar the tactics and excuses are that different controlling men use. Participants regain faith in their own sanity.

I have talked to many women who have made close friends, and sometimes a best friend, through a support group. Going to group puts you in an atmosphere where, perhaps for the only time all week, you don't have to pretend or keep secrets (like at work), you don't have to smile when you're sad (like with friends), you don't have to work hard to keep someone from punishing you (like with your partner). You can just be yourself and be real.

Call a hotline as soon as you can (right now, perhaps?) and find out when and where a support group for abused women meets. (See "Resources.") Going to group will be one of the biggest favors you've ever done for yourself.

✂ ❧

"I deserve the support of a group of women
who get what I'm dealing with."

"Should I Leave or Stay?" May Be the Wrong Question

You may spend a lot of mental time struggling with the question of whether to keep investing months and years in a relationship that causes you so much pain. To get your thoughts out of this rut, try focusing on this question instead: "What do I need to do to help myself grow as a person?"

Try the following exercise: Take your journal or a piece of paper. Write in big letters the word "FRIENDSHIPS." Then next to that put down two goals for yourself related to the people you care about, such as "I want to hang out with Megan because I haven't seen her in a while" or "I need to get together with my brother and talk through the tensions that have been brewing between us."

Then write the word "HEALTH." Follow it with two related goals, such as what you want to do for exercise, a doctor visit you need to schedule, or stress-reduction exercises you want to work on.

Follow the same pattern for the following terms:

WORK LIFE / CAREER / EDUCATION

SPIRITUALITY

EMOTIONAL WELLNESS AND HEALING

CONTRIBUTING TO THE WORLD

PARENTING (if you have kids)

When you're finished, you'll have seven categories, and two goals for growth written in each of them.

Look back at this sheet a week from now. See which goals you've succeeded in doing and which ones you haven't. Then, with no self-blame, figure out how to get moving on the ones that are still waiting, and try for another week. Do this for a total of three weeks.

During these three weeks, try to think about your relationship as little as possible. Then, when the weeks are up, look back over your goals one more time, and ask yourself the crucial question: "Which aspects of my life are helping me grow and which ones aren't? And is my relationship *promoting* my growth or *sabotaging* it?"

⚬⚬

"'Should I stay or should I go?' isn't really
the question. The question is what helps
me grow and what doesn't."

STAYING CONNECTED

If Your Faith Community Turns on You

Sometimes reality gets turned on its head, so that wrong becomes right and decency becomes cruelty. I have, sadly, known women who experienced this kind of inversion within their church, temple, or mosque.

The twisting of reality begins when the woman takes the leap to tell people that her partner rips her to shreds verbally, or that he pushes her around physically, or that he degrades her sexually.

To her shock, some people react as if the source of the ugliness were in *her* instead of the abusive man. She starts to get whispered about, people stop smiling and stop reaching out to her, and she feels the atmosphere around her turn to disapproval and rejection. And instead of supporting her, the community *rallies around the abuser*, viewing him as the victim of a vicious, falsely accusing woman. I hope this never happens to you. But if it does, it becomes deeply important for you to battle against isolation; when a whole community turns on you, you can feel as if you're suddenly living on the moon. Reach out for help (see "Resources"). Try not to internalize the message that you are bad; you've done nothing wrong. Your spiritual community should be there for you, and they are the ones who are behaving badly.

Fortunately there are spiritual communities that come through for abused women. I hope you are able to find one soon. In the meantime, draw on resources and keep yourself connected.

✕✲

"Abuse is the opposite of spirituality."

GUIDING CHILDREN

Steering Your Daughters Away from Abusive Boyfriends

You can raise girls who will know what it takes to stay away from destructive men. Knowledge is power, as are self-esteem and self-respect.

The first and most important step is to teach girls that being in a relationship when they grow up, including being married, is an *option*. This is not what most girls learn; their families and their society tend to tell them, loud and clear, "You *must* have a man as soon as possible, and you must eventually choose one to spend your life with."

Well, if she must, then her only choice is to get with the best man she can find, right? And if the best one isn't that great, well, that's the way it goes, right?

Oops.

Until a girl has reached at least age twelve, don't ask her about her interest in boys and don't make romantic or joking comments about her friendships with boys. Why? Because you want her to learn that close, respectful relationships with males are normal and do not have to involve a sexual or romantic aspect. The more she gets used to respect from males in her life in general, the more she will expect it from partners.

Second, treat your daughter with respect yourself, and require her siblings to do the same. She'll get used to it, and then she won't want to live without it.

Third, when she is a preteen, explain to her about controlling or abusive partners versus respectful, equal, supportive ones. Review with her the warning signs a girl should watch for, which you can find in chapter 5 of *Why Does He Do That?*

Last, help your daughter understand the concept of *mutuality*. The example that your partner sets teaches her, unfortunately, that a relationship is about what the woman should do for the man. You want her, instead, to feel that each partner has an equal responsibility to be generous and supportive toward the other, and that love is a two-way street. Encourage her to expect nothing less.

✥

"I can help my daughter navigate these waters;
all girls should get that guidance."

The Technology Trap

There are so many places to try to escape to nowadays. You can stare into your laptop. You can keep checking your phone messages. You can spend the whole day on Facebook. You can get on Twitter and keep yourself occupied every second. You can watch YouTube videos.

Meanwhile, you're sinking deeper emotionally. Technology is actually no escape at all. The more you are involved with these little devices, the more ways your partner has to control you. Facebook should be called Open Book, because it makes your life so visible. He can use it to keep an eye not just on you but on your friends and relatives as well. He can use your phone as a leash for you, where you have to keep checking in with him constantly so that he can know what you're doing and thinking every second.

Pouring your attention into electronics can appear to take your mind off of your tensions and wounds, but on a deeper level your anxiety just grows. Studies have shown that the more involved with technology people get, the more scattered, depressed, and emotionally hungry they become. So lift your eyes away from that screen and look around at the world. The answers are out here, not in there.

꿈ꦩ

"I don't need to be afraid to be a participant in the world. I can set things right in my life."

Will He Change If He Stops Drinking?

If your partner exhibits most of his worst behavior toward you when he's been drinking or drugging, you can get the impression that his addiction is the cause of his abusiveness. Does it make sense, then, to focus on persuading him to get sober and start attending AA?

Unfortunately, abusive men don't make lasting changes in their relationship behavior when they get off of a substance. If your partner stops drinking he may handle his work life better, and he may improve some of his other relationships, but the problems in how he treats you will mostly stay the same, and can sometimes even get worse. When he first stops drinking he's likely to be kinder for a while, which can get your hopes up. But in a few months his abusiveness will reassert itself.

The only way he can overcome his abusiveness is to deal with his abusiveness. If he deals with his pain from his childhood, or if his health improves, or if he breaks out of an addiction, those steps will help him, but they won't help you. The only way he'll become a good partner is when he actually confronts and changes his abusive and entitled attitudes.

"Drinking and drugging are no excuse
for how he acts."

"Is There Any Way Out of Here?"

I have talked to hundreds—yes, *hundreds*—of women who have gotten out of destructive relationships. And almost all of them tell me that they went through deeply dark times, times when they couldn't imagine that a better life was possible. If you have days, or weeks, when you feel that you are trapped forever in this toxic environment, I can assure you that countless other women have gone through similar periods yet have found a way out. Don't give up.

What made it possible for these women to take their lives back? Here are, in order, the top factors they report to me:

1. The support of a program for abused women. Women tell me over and over again that what made the greatest difference to them was calling an abuse hotline multiple times, meeting several times with an advocate, and attending a weekly support group for abused women. These services are free; they are open to you even if your partner has never used outright physical or sexual violence; and you don't have to leave your partner. In fact, you don't even have to be planning to leave him. (These services should also be fully open to you if your abusive partner is another woman.)

2. Their children's love. When you realize that your children love you, that can help you to realize how wrong your partner is about how bad and unlovable you supposedly are.

3. The love of friends and relatives. Anyone in your life who treats you as a valuable person helps to put you on the path to freedom, by helping you to believe in yourself. Value people who value you, and try to stay away from people who don't.

4. Having a way to survive. Hide money under a mattress. Get a degree or a certificate that opens up job possibilities to you. Learn how to budget and manage money. (See the "Resources" section at Lundy Bancroft.com, under "Economic Empowerment.")
5. Believing that they deserved better. Don't stop seeing yourself as a worthy person.

A better life will come to you if you keep working toward it. You will have days of feeling hopeless—everyone has them—but don't let that hopelessness take over. Fight until you win.

✒

"I will find a way, no matter what."

HEALING

Women's Support Groups—Part 2

Most people in the United States live less than an hour's drive from the nearest support group for abused women. Sometimes public transportation is an option, especially if you live in an urban area. Some of the programs offer child care while women attend the group. And they're all free and confidential.

So why don't more women go to groups? What gets in the way? Let's look at some of the myths about support groups:

"Those groups are for women whose husbands totally beat them up." Actually, more than half of the women in a typical group are most concerned with what their partners are doing to their minds.

Some of them have experienced no physical abuse at all, only verbal abuse and control.

"I'm not ready to leave him yet, and I may never be." Support groups are not about leaving abusive partners; they are about support. Most women in groups are still involved with the man and have not made up their minds what to do.

"The women at the abuse program are anti-male." Let me guess where you heard this from: Your partner perhaps? Being against abuse has nothing to do with being against men. I have met a couple of thousand women over the past ten years who work in abused women's programs, and I haven't found a man-hater yet.

"Those women just complain; they don't do anything about their situations." When women speak aloud about abuse, that is not a waste of time; it's a crucial part of the journey to freedom. Perhaps part of what you are feeling is self-judgment; in other words, you feel impatient with yourself for the problems you haven't been able to solve. Work on forgiving other women for being stuck at the same time as you forgive yourself, and sit down to talk together.

"I don't want to listen to all those horrible stories." Actually, you'll find it helps you a lot to learn about other women's lives. You'll see how strong women are, how they find ways to stand up for themselves, how they move toward freedom.

✳

"I look forward to the companionship
and inspiration of other women who have
dealt with abusive partners."

"I'm Not So Great Myself"

One of the greatest traps when it comes to unhealthy relationships is the one where you try to figure out whether you are a good enough person to deserve better. This challenge can be deepened if you grew up with parents or siblings who tore you down and made you feel worthless.

What sort of woman deserves to be treated well? Only an honest one? Only a sober one? Only a faithful one who never even makes eyes at anyone other than her partner? Only one who is never selfish or short-tempered?

And is anybody left once we've used the list above?

The reality is that almost everyone has told a lie at some point or other; women with volatile partners often feel they have no choice but to lie in order to protect their own safety. Most people have had some time when they overindulged in a substance. Most people have felt some sexual attractions outside of their relationship. Everyone has days when they are crabby or self-involved or rude.

If there are problems in your behavior, your partner has the right to respectfully call you out on those, the same as anyone else. But he has no right to use your behavior as an excuse for his, or to abuse you for not being perfect.

✠

> "Everyone has a right to be treated well, not just
> perfect people (who don't actually exist)."

If Your Background Is Toxic

Some women find that being involved with a controlling or abusive partner leads them to some realizations about the family they grew up in. Here are some of the comments I've heard:

"I didn't even realize there was anything wrong with how he treated me, because that's how I'd been treated my whole life."

"Now I see that my father tore my mother down all the time just the way my partner does to me. I always thought it was kind of her own fault, but now I get what was going on."

"My family took his side against me, believe it or not. I guess the truth is they're a lot like him."

"With him I never know where I stand, and I always feel like my head is getting messed with in some way or other. And I'm starting to see that a lot of my relatives are the same way."

Fortunately, a lot of women with destructive partners don't come from this kind of background at all; those women can often count on support and assistance from their families. But perhaps you don't have a supportive family behind you. Perhaps you're having to come to terms with the fact that patterns of cruelty, or manipulation, or mind-twisting were a big part of the atmosphere you were reared in. Does this mean your fate is predetermined, that this kind of life is the one you are doomed to endure for good?

Absolutely not. Every day there are women who are finding their way to rise above the double whammy of a toxic background and a toxic partner. It may be a long road, but it leads to deep growth and transformation. You can learn to distinguish healthy living from destructive patterns. Over time you will be able to build a new life for yourself, surrounded by kindness and by the human values that you want to have as your foundation.

✤

"My background is not a mark on me; I will
keep on rising until I'm up and out."

The Fear of Raising Soft Boys

Boys do not need us to toughen them up. The pressure that parents feel to do so is based on myths.

The confusing point is that boys do have an easier time in many ways if they can be fairly tough. (So do girls, for that matter.) So why shouldn't parents focus on toughening up their children?

First, boys get far too many messages about toughness already. They are swamped with them from video games, action movies, action figures, bodybuilding magazines, their friends, their sports coaches, older boys, and countless other sources. (I am a former boy and an athlete myself, so I know what I'm talking about.)

Second, boys are mistakenly taught to equate toughness with being unfeeling and unafraid. They learn never to cry, never to back down from a fight, never to admit fear. These attitudes actually have nothing to do with true strength; there are men who are very courageous, and who can endure a lot, who also cry freely and who open up about their fears. Tough and sensitive can go right together.

Third, real strength and fake strength are very distinct. Many men move through life with their chests stuck way out in front of them, holding their faces impassive, and intimidating others, while actually being scared to death inside. You don't want to teach your boys to put on a "tough guise" while suffering in private.

And, last but not least, some boys just don't want to be tough, especially physically. No amount of pressuring or shaming those boys is going to change their style, though it will certainly succeed in destroying their self-esteem. If you have a boy who just isn't inclined in that direction, the sooner you accept that quality in him, the happier you and he will be.

Know that a boy who is comfortable in his own skin will grow up to be a great man. You can play a significant role in making that happen.

〜❦〜

"Sensitivity in my boys is a strength."

EACH NEW DAY

How Not to Pick the Wrong Guys

The story is always the same. It might be a movie, a music video, an ad, a romance novel. We can hardly go a day without absorbing some version of it: Woman meets a man, falls deeply in love, and never needs anything other than him again. Her friends, her career, her children— none of it matters now that she's got him.

And what is the man in the story like? He's decisive, a take-charge kind of guy who controls the situation. Because of that he is instantly sexy and sexual. He is charming and suave. He ignores her resistance and pushes past it, his mind made up. He doesn't ask her what she wants, because he knows exactly what she needs. He has no need to get to know her first as a friend, because he is all about romance. And while it is made known that he has been bad to women in the past, he has realized that was wrong and he's giving all that up for his new leading lady.

Come to earth out of storyland as fast as you can, because this guy has abuse and control written all over him. He is exhibiting a huge collection of the exact warning signs that I teach women to watch out for. He's controlling, he doesn't respect women's boundaries, he is putting on an image, and he has a history of mistreating partners.

Look for these red flags so that if you leave your partner you won't find yourself with another man just like him. Females shouldn't throw themselves at the feet of the wrong guys, or any guy for that matter. Wouldn't it be better if the woman stayed upright?

✤

"I can unhook myself from social messages
about what kind of guy I should go for."

CLARITY

Trying to Be Attractive Only for Him

Some men have a powerful ability to extinguish the sexual energy of a relationship. Then they blame the woman for it.

The man's jealousy and possessiveness are often the root of the problem. He wants you to be sexy and attractive, but only for him. So he criticizes you if you go out in public looking good. ("What are you going out dressed like that for? You got the hots for some guy?") Perhaps he starts to call you degrading names for making yourself alluring. The result is that you feel like you'd better not dress up around him.

But later he turns it all around and says that you never make yourself sexy anymore. You can't win, because he wants other people to be impressed by how attractive you are, but he doesn't want them to look at you. He doesn't want you to dress up, but he wants you to be dressy when he sees you. He doesn't want you to desire sex if he's not in the mood, but he wants you to always be in the mood. The reason you can't make any sense out of all this is that it makes no sense.

For you to feel sexual, you have to feel appealing to him. (In other words, in order to feel attract*ed* you have to feel attract*ive*.) And to feel appealing to him, you have to feel attractive in general—in other words, attractive to other people also. There is simply no way to be attractive to him alone. So when a man wants a woman's sexuality to exist only for him, he is ensuring that it will fade away.

And that's his fault, not hers.

"My sexuality is mine; it doesn't belong to him.
He's lucky that I choose to share it with him."

Frantic Thoughts

Your thoughts may be running at breakneck speed: "What do I need to get done today? What is bothering him? I have to make the kids' dentist appointments. How come he quickly switches what screen he is on whenever I go into the room? How can I get him not to call me ten times a day?"

Some of this franticness is just the mad pace of modern life. But it also comes from living with an angry and controlling man. The ups and downs of his behavior leave you trying to guess what is going to happen next, trying to analyze his moods, trying to keep him from exploding.

Today I'd like you just to notice what your thoughts do. Don't try to change them or slow them down. Just observe them. Ask yourself: How much of the day do I spend thinking anxiously about him? How much time does that leave for thinking about myself, or about my kids? How much of the day am I worrying about his moods? How much of my mental energy is going into trying to prove that I'm not the bad things that he says I am?

Try not to analyze it all too much. Just notice what goes on in your mind.

"Today I am watching my thoughts go by, without judgment. I'm noticing how many are really mine— for me and about me—and how many have been taken over by tension about him."

HEALING

Power

Some days you may feel like a bottle bobbing in ocean waves. Sunny calm days come during certain periods and you float contentedly. But before long another tempest is coming through, the spray and the breakers are pounding you, the sea has turned scary and cold. You are a small point in the world, and forces that are huge and random are governing your life.

And perhaps today has been one of the stormy ones.

You do not have to be a bottle in the waves forever. The reality is that you have more power than you know. You can find where the sources of power dwell inside of you and tap into them. Those veins of will and energy exist inside of each person.

Form an image of the deepest parts of yourself. Perhaps you see paths through a forest, or tunnels under the ground, or rivers of light. Seek a spot where there is fire, where there are wild and fierce animals, where there is a surge like a volcano erupting. Close your eyes for a few minutes and feel your power gathering and rising.

"I am going to find the way to let
my power surge and soar."

More Thoughts About Him Calling You "Controlling"

Today let's look at some more points about those times when your partner turns the tables on you, saying that you are the controlling one:

You have the right to have complaints and bring grievances. One thing you'll notice about living with a controlling man is that no way to raise a complaint seems to be the right way, no matter how careful you are in how you say it. Meanwhile, when he has a complaint about you, he doesn't hesitate to lace it with put-downs.

You have the right to have personal preferences. There is a difference between *asking* for things to be done in a certain way (in a relationship or in a home) and *bullying people* into doing things that way. When you have some requests or preferences about how things are done, he is likely to call that "controlling," even if you aren't nasty about it.

You have the right to have standards about how you are treated. In any relationship, you get to declare what your "red lights" are—meaning the kinds of treatment that are simply not acceptable to you. If your partner decides that your standards are too restrictive to him, he can choose to end the relationship, but he *can't* choose to run the red lights. People's boundaries have to be respected.

Payback is the key issue. When someone gets you back for resisting his control, that is when true control begins. The person who uses payback is the one with the control issue.

"He's calling me controlling so that he won't
have to look at how he treats me."

STAYING CONNECTED

Resolving Conflicts with Other People

It's impossible to make a relationship with an abusive man go better by changing how you interact with him; his issues don't have anything to do with you. However, you can improve your relationships with *other people* by improving your skills at working through conflicts; here is where you will get the greatest rewards from your personal growth.

Try applying the following principles, and see the difference it makes in your close connections.

1. When a loved one is upset with you, ask questions before responding. The better you can understand what the person is feeling and how he or she views things, the more constructively you will be able to move forward. Fight the temptation to launch immediately into defending yourself or counterattacking, since it will make the other person feel not heard and will escalate the conflict.

2. Remember that you are a good person. Your loved one isn't saying you are terrible (or shouldn't be, anyhow); he or she is just upset with you. People get aggravated with each other; it's normal.

3. Own what you can. Take a look at your actions and see if you made a mistake you could sincerely apologize for. If so, the sooner you stop defending yourself and begin taking responsibility the better. Nothing helps to calm a conflict like an honest apology. But at the same time . . .

4. Don't apologize just to make peace. You don't want to sell yourself short by taking responsibility for something that you don't believe is yours. You can always say that you are sorry the person feels hurt, but don't say you're sorry for what you did unless you really are.

As in so many aspects of life, strive for balance; don't take on more responsibility than you should for other people's anger or upset, but don't fail to examine your own actions either.

"I can work through tensions
with people I care about."

Talking to Kids About Sex

Many parents feel that once they have explained the facts of life to their children—a conversation that can feel awkward—they are over a hurdle and can be done with the sex talk. Some parents take their girls to the doctor to put them on birth control or buy a box of condoms and let their kids know where they can find it, but they may avoid talking about the important issues that need to be explored.

Yes, your teenagers need to know how to avoid pregnancy and sexually transmitted diseases. But they need just as badly to not be emotionally injured through sexuality, and not to do harm to others. So, after safety, the most crucial topic is *consent*. Explore in detail what consent looks like. Explain that if someone gives in to sexual contact following a campaign of pressure by the other person, that's not consent. Similarly, consent is not possible when someone is impaired by alcohol or drugs.

And anything that is not consensual is *sexual assault*, even if it doesn't fit their image of an assault.

Talk with teenagers about positive sexuality as well; about sex that is mutual and respectful. (I don't mean that you should speak in detail, which would just make your kids die of embarrassment.) One of the best ways to help kids know when they have been used or disrespected sexually is to make sure they have some idea of what sex looks like when it's right.

Even if you want to encourage your kids to consider sexual abstinence, the above conversations still need to happen, for two reasons: (1) They will be in a sexual relationship someday, and they need to start preparing mentally for that now, and (2) that "someday" may arrive sooner than you would like. It's safest for them if you are prepared for that reality.

"I want to be sure my kids are sexually respectful and sexually respected."

When It Just Couldn't Be Him

Today I'm writing for women whose partners are held in high esteem in their communities, who are the kind of guy that other people look up to and wish they could be like. He may have even gotten himself into a respected position such as clergyman, police officer, head of the Rotary Club or a similar service organization, admired businessperson, college professor, or elected representative.

Who wants to believe that a man could rise so high in public, while in private he calls his partner vile names and humiliates her in front of her children, degrades her sexually, or slams her up against the wall?

Nobody, unfortunately.

Over the years I have spoken with many women who face the loneliness and distress of being torn apart by a man who is a pillar of the community. When she dares reveal what he is doing to her, she often finds that people are angry at her instead of him, assuming that she must be making it all up.

Thousands of women across the country are living with this same hidden abuse by "great men." You will eventually be able to find people who will believe you, and even to talk to women who have lived through similar circumstances. What is happening is real. You are not crazy. The fact that he can fool everybody is no reflection on you.

"I don't care how admired he is;
that doesn't make what he's doing right."

Pornography

I believe in positive human sexuality. Sex is a natural and pleasurable part of life as long as both partners feel safe and respected. There is nothing shameful about naked bodies. So why am I so concerned about pornography and its effects?

Pornography is a school of sexuality; in fact, it's the main place Americans get their information about sex (to the tune of $10 billion per year). And what is it teaching us?

- "Love and respect are irrelevant to sex, which is just a body function."
- "Women exist for men's sexual use, without needs or feelings of their own."
- "Women should like whatever practices men want to engage in, no matter how demeaning or depersonalizing."
- "The more women look like little girls or teenagers, the sexier they are; in other words, men should desire sex with underage females."

My concern is that pornography promotes a *kind* of sexuality that is exploitative, has violent undertones, and glorifies offending against children. A huge percentage of women have told researchers that they have been pressured by partners into participation in unwanted sexual practices that the man saw in pornography.

In short, pornography is the opposite of a sexually liberating force.

You may not share my reactions, so let me zero in on the points that I think matter most in practical terms:

1. If you are bothered by your partner's use of pornography, you have every right to be. Your objections do not make you uptight, repressed, frigid, or whatever else he may say. And he should never pressure you to do things he has seen in pornography.
2. If you use pornography yourself, explore carefully whether your participation is voluntary and how it is affecting your self-esteem. If you use it together with your partner, take a careful look at how it's affecting the dynamics of your relationship.

The deepest question is about what fulfills and frees you sexually. Anything that leaves you feeling demeaned or controlled is the antithesis of true sexuality.

"Sex is about pleasure and fulfillment,
not about pressure and degradation."

SURVIVING TO THRIVE

Preparing to Leave a Scary Partner

Does your partner have scary rages? Does he tower over you, screaming and pointing his finger in your face? Has he ever pushed you, hit you, or locked you in rooms? Has he made threats to harm you? Has he ever said that he'll kill you if you ever leave him?

Tragically, a tremendous number of women are trapped in their relationships because their partners are dangerous. If you are in this position, you undoubtedly spend time playing out scenarios in your head of what he'll do if you try to cut things off with him. Perhaps you have even had to consider whether your life would be on the line.

Here are some points to reflect on. First of all, his behavior is *wrong*, even if he isn't scaring you on purpose; he has no right to make you feel like a prisoner.

Second, start planning now for how to leave, even if you aren't sure that you will actually choose to do it. Go to "Resources" at Lundy Bancroft.com, and start working through the steps under "Preparing to Leave a Scary Partner."

Third, try to take in the fact that you are not responsible for him. If you are afraid that he will commit suicide, remember that you are committing spiritual suicide by staying with him. Your life counts as much as his does.

And you will help the world the most, bringing great benefit to those who love you, by doing what is best for you.

✺

"I don't have to be trapped here forever. I can
marshal my resources and find a way out."

The Psychiatric Medication Trap

It is common for doctors to recommend psych meds to a woman who is in emotional distress, even if the problem is that she has an abusive partner. Be careful about taking this path; going on medication can be a slippery slope, with a cascading set of side effects. Make sure you have pursued all other possible solutions first, including improved exercise and diet, attending a support group, and other healing approaches.

If you are suffering from anxiety, difficulty sleeping, trouble focusing, or depression, these are actually some of the most common effects of emotional abuse. Physical or sexual mistreatment can accentuate these symptoms further. It may make much more sense for you to pursue ways to get free from your controlling partner. Begin by working closely with an advocate at a program for abused women. (See "Resources" at Lundy Bancroft.com for more information on finding an advocate, and on alternatives to psych meds.)

"There's nothing wrong with my chemistry;
my problem is I'm being treated horribly."

Understanding Traumatic Attachment

Have you ever heard of the "Stockholm Syndrome"? This expression was coined decades ago when a group of people who were taken hostage became loyal to their captors, and after their release refused to cooperate with law enforcement in capturing the men who had held them.

Why did this happen? Why would people defend their kidnappers?

What researchers have discovered is that abuse and cruelty that are *mixed with kindness* have profound psychological effects. For example, when your partner switches back and forth between times of acting like he hates you and times of being loving and affectionate, you are likely to feel *more* attached to him than you would feel to a man who was consistently good to you! This strong—but unhealthy—bond is known as "traumatic attachment" or "traumatic bonding."

Dozens and dozens of women have asked me over the years, "Why is it so hard for me to leave my partner, when he's been so awful to me? Why do I keep giving him another chance? Why do I still care?" One of the top reasons is that you are suffering the predictable effects of traumatic bonding.

Watch what happens inside you the next time your partner goes through one of his terrible periods and then goes back to being loving or kind toward you. Notice how incredibly close you feel to him when he gets nice, precisely because of how hurt and desperate you were feeling during the bad period. His kindness gains huge power because he is connecting with you right where you feel most wounded by him.

As you increase your awareness of this dynamic, you can make the conscious choice to hold more of yourself in reserve. Don't give your heart to him so openly when he comes back from his cold or mean periods. Observe your own process and you will gain more control over the attachment that you develop.

⚜

"Why should I feel so close to him just because he's
finally being nice to me?"

Helping People Understand

Women who are in abusive relationships often feel like nobody gets it. One of the most common reactions I receive from women to my book *Why Does He Do That?* is "I feel like you're the first person who really grasps what I've been living with."

So what can you do to increase your ability to get through to people?

One way, interestingly, is to get them to talk about *their* experiences. Ask them about times when they have loved someone who had some unhealthy patterns. Have they loved a parent who was abusive or rejecting toward them? Have they ever been close to someone who was alcoholic? Around the holidays do they have to deal with relatives who get them upset?

If they can come up with at least one example—and most people can—ask them how they felt toward the person. Were they prepared to just axe the person from their life? If not, why not? Did they ever feel shocked or betrayed by the person? How do they feel when they think about the person now?

The point is to try to guide people to realize that they have been in similar circumstances at some point in their lives. See if they can remember how hard it is to give up on someone you love. See if they can remember how betrayed they felt, yet they still kept caring for the person.

The truth is that people do know what you are going through, because they've been there in some form or other themselves; they've just forgotten what it was like. See if you can awaken their memories.

✄

"Everyone has been through some form of what I'm
dealing with, whether they remember it or not."

Trying to Cover for Their Father

A man who controls a woman or tears her down ends up causing a lot of emotional distress for her children. The kids hear how he disrespects and insults her, and it hurts their feelings to see their mom being treated like that. When he gets intimidating or scary, they are frightened for her, for each other, and for themselves.

Most abusive men are uneven, at best, in how they treat children, tending to be impatient and self-centered as parents. So the kids are getting hurt by how he treats them directly, on top of what he's doing to Mom.

It's tempting in this context to make excuses to the children for their father:

> "I'm sure he would have shown up if he could have, honey. He must have had a lot of work to do. He'll make another plan with you."

> "Oh, sweetie, he didn't mean to call me that name. He was just very upset."

> "I know it's embarrassing when he acts that way in front of your friends, but it was my fault for forgetting to pay the phone bill— that's what he was angry about."

> "He didn't hit me, darling; I bumped my face on the door."

Break the habit of covering for him; otherwise it will backfire against you later. You want to raise children who trust their own perceptions; if you train them to think they're imagining things, they'll be vulnerable to being preyed upon by other people. Plus he's likely sooner or later to try to convince the children that everything was your fault; if you've made excuses for him along the way, he'll be more able to turn them against you.

It's natural that you want to ease your children's hurt feelings, but it's too risky to do that by misleading them. Instead, love them, hold them, and let them talk and cry out their hurt feelings. And keep showing them, through your own actions, what a good parent does.

"I have to let the children come to
their own conclusions about their dad."

Why the Fear of Homosexuality Matters

You may feel that people's opinions about homosexuality don't affect your life one way or the other. I'm going to encourage you to think differently.

First, a huge proportion of abused women—about half in my experience—get called "lesbian" by the abusive man. He'll hurl that at her to punish her sexually, or because she has a close friendship with a woman that he feels jealous of. Some women tell me that they have distanced themselves from their friendships because of fear of being labeled lesbian in this way.

But his name-calling wouldn't have any impact if the society rejected the idea that being lesbian was bad, would it? It would be like having him yell at you, "You New Yorker!" when you're from Oklahoma, or "You musician!" when you're a jewelry maker.

Second, some of the harshest insults that an abusive man makes about a woman's parenting are based on his fear that the kids will grow up to be gay or lesbian. Does he ever say that you're making your son "a mama's boy"? Does he ever say that your daughter is dressed too "masculine"? Did he freak out when your little boy asked if could try on a dress? (By the way, boys showing interest in "girl" things is common.) Does he make fun of your kids if they are physically affectionate with their same-sex friends?

All these put-downs have their roots in homophobia.

Prejudice and insulting remarks about gay men and lesbians are not an "out there" problem. You can't control your partner's homophobia, but you can work hard to keep it from distorting your own beliefs and running your life.

⸻

"I have a right to close, loving, and affectionate
relationships with my women friends."

CLARITY

Does My Partner Have a Personality Disorder?

A set of mental health problems known as "personality disorders" have come into public awareness in recent years, forming the basis for books, websites, and talk-show discussions. You may have heard people talking about "narcissistic personality disorder" or "borderline personality disorder," for example. You may also have heard someone referred to as a "psychopath" or a "sociopath," a condition known to psychologists as "antisocial personality disorder." (That term makes it sound like the individual doesn't like to go to parties, but it actually refers to someone who goes through life conning, using, and manipulating people with no conscience at all about the damage they do.)

Here are the key characteristics of a man (or woman) with a personality disorder:

- He repeatedly causes harm to other people or to himself through selfishness and explosiveness; or through having exaggerated and hyperdramatic emotional reactions to life's difficulties; or through using people and then discarding them.
- He doesn't believe he has a problem. On the contrary, he believes there's always something wrong with someone else and he is the victim. He may have bouts when he hates himself or considers suicide, but then he returns to his usual habit of blaming everyone else.
- If anyone points out to him that he's got problems, he takes that as further evidence of how unfair the world is and how badly people misunderstand him.
- He is remarkably skillful at twisting anything you say around to turn it back against you, and to make it seem like you're attacking him.
- His behavior comes out toward other people, at least once in a while, not just toward you.

The specific categories of personality disorder are not proving to be that important or helpful, so I don't recommend concerning yourself much with those; the characteristics above are what matters most.

Regrettably, personality disorder shows even lower rates of change than abusiveness does. If you found yourself saying "Yes!" to everything on the list above, you can look in "Resources" at LundyBancroft.com under "Personality Disorders" to learn more about the waters you are navigating.

> "Whatever his problems are, I won't let him make
> me crazy. I'm going to be okay."

"But I Want My Kids to Have a Father"

Do you ever consider the possibility of ending your relationship? If so, you've perhaps felt deterred by not wanting to put your kids through a divorce, and not wanting them to stop having their father in their daily lives.

I recognize that this question leaves you with a lot to think about.

Here are some points to include in the mix. First, he is free to stay as involved as he wants after you split up. As long as he is being a safe parent, no one is going to bar him from extensive time with your kids. You don't take them out of his life by breaking up with him.

Now, you may say, "But I know if he can't be with me he's not going to choose to be around the kids much either." If this is true, it shows how selfish and self-centered he is, and how little deep caring he actually has for the kids. And in that case, they are better off in the long run spending less time with him anyhow.

Which leads me to my second point, which is: How good a role model is he for your children? Is he modeling appropriate adult behavior for them? Is he teaching them to respect women? Is he modeling maturity and accepting responsibility for one's own actions? Remember that kids learn much more from what their parents *do* than from what they say.

And last, take a look at how his behavior and attitudes are affecting *your* relationship with the children. You are their mother, and your connection with them needs to be your highest priority. If being with him is harming your ability to be as good a mother as you are capable of, that concern should be at the top of your list.

"Spending less time around him might
be better for my kids and for their
relationship with me, not worse."

When You Know You Need a Good Cry

Let's look today at those times when you can tell that you need to cry out a bunch of pent-up emotions, but you can't do it. How do you get that cry to come out of you when it's stuck?

There are several techniques to get the dam to break:

- Make a crying date with yourself, actually setting aside time and finding a way to be alone. Tears are more likely to come when you know you won't have to choke them right back off again.
- Collect some of the music that has brought you to tears before. Listening to your favorite sad or touching song can get your crying started, and once the ice breaks, you'll move on to crying about the issues that have been weighing on you.
- Spend some time thinking about memories from long ago. It's usually easier to start crying about sadnesses from far in the past.
- Let your crying take you where it wants to go. Sometimes you will

be sad about an old loss, and suddenly you'll find that instead you're crying about an event from yesterday, or tears about a recent upset may carry you into sobbing about an earlier period in life. Your soul knows which piece it needs to grieve today.

- Photographs can be powerful for evoking emotion. So can certain passages from books, pieces of poetry, or scenes from movies.
- If you have a trusted friend, see if she would sit with you or hold your hand while you cry. You also can imagine her there even if you are actually crying by yourself, to help the tears flow.
- Anger can unlock crying. Yell into a pillow or pound on couch cushions, and keep at it for a long time. Try to feel powerful; the more your rage comes from a place of power, the better it will unleash your tears.

Almost anyone can learn to cry deeply if they train themselves to do so. Learning to cry is a skill, like studying an instrument or developing your athletic abilities, and it requires time and space. The more effort you put in, the deeper the rewards.

"I can have that good cry I've been
needing. It will heal me."

Taking Pride in Being Female

Women are 51 percent of the world's population. They do 70 percent of the world's labor according to the United Nations. They do 100 percent of the pregnancies and deliveries, 100 percent of the breastfeeding. They do more than their share of the loving, nurturing, forgiving, and peace-making. They are crusaders for justice and freedom all over the world. They are brave, soulful, inspiring spirits. They are our mothers, grand-mothers, daughters, sisters.

Either overtly or subtly, the abusive man creates an atmosphere that is negative about femaleness. His behavior, and sometimes his words, send the message that men are smarter, more competent, more logical, more important. He views women—at least women he has relationships with—as hysterical, as needy, as stubborn, as weak; in short, as inferior to men.

(At the same time, he may talk a great line about women's equality, if that's the face he likes to put on for the world.)

For a girl who grows up in a home where Mom's partner devalues her, questions inevitably arise inside her about her own worth as a fe-male. A boy can absorb the message that he is superior to his sisters.

See if there are spots in your spirit where your partner has made you feel like being a woman makes you less. Then work on taking pride in being a woman. Take pride in the history of women as a group. Take pride in the leadership women are currently taking in the world to keep the best of our human potential alive. If you have daughters, take pride in their femaleness and encourage them to do the same.

"I am a woman, and I come from a proud history of
thousands of generations of women."

An Image of Women Together

A few times a year, I lead weekend retreats for women who have ended abusive relationships. I call these workshops "The Life That Awaits You." Over the weekend, between twenty and twenty-five women gather together to:

- Share the hurts they still carry from being mistreated, and get each other's validation about what it was all like
- Heal together through small group exercises, working in pairs, journal writing, games, and music
- Drink in the excitement of the life that stretches ahead of them, now that they are no longer being torn down

For days after each of these retreats I feel the glow around me of all the love, courage, and outrage that pours out of the women during the weekend. Women are beautiful. The human spirit is beautiful. The abuser tries so hard to destroy the woman's spirit—even if he's not aware of his own motivations—but during the retreat women are able to look into one another's eyes and see that the abusers have not succeeded. The women discover that they still have their energy to fight, their belief in themselves, their fierce loyalty to their children. Yes, the men have done harm, but they have not squelched the spirit's flame. When women come together, their spirits rapidly gather warmth and roar back up into a huge fire.

Draw strength from picturing these women together for the weekend. This is the reality of who women are: brilliantly smart, courageous, and loving. This is the reality of who *you* are. They've survived and so can you.

"Other women are behind me, including
women I have never met. We are natural
allies who belong together."

Who Knows What's Best for the Kids?

Parents enter into child-rearing with a mixture of nervousness and excitement. We have our worries: Are our children going to turn out all right? Are we going to be good parents? Are we going to re-create the mistakes our own parents made? But we also have a vision of family life going well, and feel eager to build an atmosphere where children grow and thrive.

My hope for you is that your home is taking a shape close to what you had dreamed of. But I'm also aware that a destructive partner can take over the family tone and shape it to his bad attitudes. At the same time, he'll say the problems come from your faults as a mother.

Work for today to keep clear on this point: Your partner is not a good authority on how to raise children. He may sound like he knows absolutely that his way is right and yours is wrong. But his certainty is just a continuation of his attitude that his judgment is superior to yours. And it isn't. If he knew so much about what's good for kids, he would be treating their mother well; that's the single most important thing a father can do.

Trust your own instincts about how best to help your children along. Focus on bringing your own vision to fruition.

> "I am the expert on my own children.
> My partner's not such a good role model right now,
> so it's up to me."

Stirrings Toward Women

Feelings are feelings. They just happen. We can make choices about which ones we want to act on, but we can't decide not to feel them without a significant cost to our emotional well-being.

I am leading up, then, to a question that a remarkable number of abused women have asked me: "I'm finding that I am getting attracted to women sometimes. What do you think about that?"

I think it's just fine. Here's why:

First of all, the reality from research is that the great majority of people, female or male, have times of feeling attracted to members of their own sex. This has nothing to do with whether you approve of homosexuality or not; you're just as likely to have these feelings either way. But a good number of people choose to act on these feelings, with percentages rising in recent studies; around 8 percent of men and 15 percent of women now define themselves as gay or lesbian.

Second, in order to deal with the effects of your partner's abuse, you have to look for every possible source of inner strength to draw from. In this process, you sometimes discover some new or surprising aspects of who you are. Perhaps on a deeper level you've had some feelings for women for a long time, but it's coming out now because of all the thinking and self-reflection you're doing.

Don't worry for now about whether it's right for you to act on these feelings; you can decide that later. Just focus on loving and honoring all aspects of who you are today, including all the different feelings you have.

ᘹᗖᕱ

"My feelings of attraction toward women or men are
natural and are my own business."

CLARITY

Abuse Is Not Sexy

Being put down and called terrible names doesn't put you in the mood for lovemaking. Neither do rage, threats, or violence. A partner who is rarely loving or affectionate except when he wants sex, and who only cares about his own pleasure, isn't exactly a turn-on either.

In short, a man who is angry and controlling doesn't make himself very appealing.

If you've experienced a decrease in your sex drive—especially in your drive to have sex with *him*—don't be surprised or alarmed. Losing interest in intimacy is a natural reaction to being mistreated, devalued, and degraded, all of which are the opposite of sexy.

On the other hand, you may crave sex more than ever, precisely because he's withholding it and leaving you feeling starved for affection. Or perhaps when he's making love is the only time he acts like he loves you.

He may throw your decreased desire in your face, calling you "frigid" or "lesbian" or accusing you of cheating on him. Or, if your sex drive is strong, he may demean you by saying that you're too sexual or calling you a "nympho."

The problem is not in you. If he wants to have a healthy sexual relationship, he has to stop abusing you, make himself attractive, and be affectionate other times than just when he wants sex. He also has to respect your desire and initiative.

Stay true to your own sexuality. If you can safely resist his bullying, do so. If you have a lot of sexual energy, enjoy that by yourself. Your body belongs to you.

⚘

> "I can remain a sexually healthy person.
> He's not going to ruin that for me."

The Temptation to Get in a New Relationship Right Away

When you break up with an abusive partner, it's hard to be single. His verbal abuse has made you feel unattractive and undesirable, so you feel like no other man will want you. You may be reeling from his cheating or sexual rejection as well. So you may feel the need to find a new man quickly to reassure yourself that someone will have you.

There are other challenges. If your partner was scary, you may get anxious when you are alone at home, especially at night; you crave a new man there to help you feel safe. Ending a relationship is hard economically, since you aren't sharing rent and expenses anymore, so you may be tempted to quickly find a new partner to help pay the bills.

But slow down. The more quickly you get involved in another relationship, the greater the risk that your new partner will be abusive too.

Why? For a couple of reasons. First of all, abusive men sense when a woman is in trouble, and they jump in to play the hero. They like it that you'll feel indebted to them for helping, and that they can play the superior role of the one who is "together" while your life is not.

Second, you need your eyes wide open to recognize the early warning signs of an abusive or controlling man, as I wrote about earlier. If you are too eager to find a man fast, you aren't going to notice the red flags; then later you'll be asking yourself, "How did I not see what he was about?"

You are going to be okay. Don't rush things. Move carefully, give yourself time to heal, and stay wise.

⤝⟩⤞

"I don't need a new partner right away; in fact, I
need some time to myself."

HEALING

"You Don't Want to Be with Him, So Why Do You Care if He's with Someone Else?"

If you have tried to break things off with your partner, you may have been surprised to discover how upset you felt at the thought of him getting involved with a new woman. Friends may have a hard time understanding; if he's so bad, they say, what difference does it make that he's seeing someone?

But your feelings are natural. So much of the wounding in a destructive relationship is about not being loved in the way you deserve and long for. You can remember the early times when he seemed crazy about you and found you attractive, but after that he seemed mostly to find things wrong with you. When you hear that he's seeing another woman, all those hurt feelings roll up into a huge ball, and you think, "Why can he love her but he couldn't love me?"

Now, we know that he isn't going to treat her any different than he treated you. He's being good to her now because they are a new item, same as he did with you. And he might be extra nice to her for a while, just to goad you. But it's not real.

You can't expect your feelings to follow what's logical, though; emotions don't work that way. Having friends say things like, "There are plenty of fish in the sea" is no help at this kind of time.

Hang in there. You'll be feeling better pretty soon; much better, in fact, than you felt when you were with him. Ride out these painful feelings and know that good times are coming.

"It hurts to see him with someone else,
but I'll keep reminding myself that I wouldn't
want to trade places with her."

Enjoying Time Alone

How long has it been since you spent an extended period of time, a few hours or even a whole day, by yourself? If the last time is deep back in history, you may find the idea unappealing. "Why spend hours alone? Won't I just be lonesome?" You might feel that way for the first while, but it will fade, and instead you'll start to enjoy your own company, as if you were spending the day with a dear friend. Alone time is one of the best antidotes for the effects of living with a partner who is hard on you.

Here's how to make the hours nurturing. First, see if you can spend part or all of the time walking in a pretty place. If you don't feel safe walking alone, bring a dog (yours or someone else's). If you spend time at home alone, plan to make it special, by taking a nice bath or listening to your favorite music. Try to stay off the phone and the computer and really be with yourself.

Second, be kind. Make jokes with yourself. Stroke your arms like an affectionate friend might. Think about what you like about yourself. Dream about the future.

Third, spend a good chunk of the time writing in a journal.

And fourth, try to really let your head clear out. Spend long enough alone that your usual daily thought patterns can fade away. Seek peace. Think of this as time spent with a loved one you haven't seen for a long time; in other words, get to know yourself again and catch up.

*

"I'm a great person to spend time with.
I'm going to rediscover myself."

Your Spiritual Community Should Have Your Back

I hear heartwarming stories from women about ways in which their faith communities have rallied around them. Just recently a woman at a workshop I was leading described a whole set of loving and helpful actions that her congregation had taken:

- They took her seriously when she revealed that her husband was abusing her, and they immediately started checking in with her often about how she was doing.
- They asked her if she needed any assistance from the church's emergency fund, and they offered her places to stay with her children if she decided to leave her husband, or if she needed to flee abruptly.
- They made extra efforts to reach out to her children.
- They were unhesitating in expressing to her how wrong the treatment was that he was subjecting her to.

And there were a couple of things that they wisely *didn't* do:

- They didn't confront him about his behavior until she felt ready to have them do so.
- They didn't put her under any pressure to stay with him and "make it work," and they didn't make excuses for his behavior or make it her responsibility to understand his problems.
- At the same time, they didn't pressure her to leave him.

This is how it should be. An abused woman deserves nothing less than this from her support system. Other communities should draw tightly around the woman in the same way—groups of friends, a workplace, a club, a yoga network, or any other social circle she is part of. I hope you receive this level of thoughtful, committed support.

⚜

"I want my people 100 percent behind me,
and I deserve that."

Teaching Children Gender Equality

Kids who grow up in a home where a man abuses their mother absorb what's going on. Children are powerfully intuitively; they sense when situations are unsafe, they feel people's happiness or anger, they are aware when certain adults have power over others. They may not put it into words, but on a deep level they get it.

Your children therefore need some clear leadership from you about the need for males to respect females, in order to counter the negative messages they get from your partner's way of treating you. It's never too early to start talking to kids about respect and equality. Insist that your boys behave appropriately toward girls and women. Don't let them put girls down or say that boys are better. Don't let them exclude girls from their games or events. Teach your girls to expect and demand fair treatment and to notice when they are being spoken down to.

Age three is a good time to start with these messages for boys and girls. And if your kids are already past that age, all the more reason to start right away. Bring gender issues up frequently—at least once every week or two. Weave this awareness into your children's consciousness.

You will be giving them the best defense against the disrespect and superiority that is being modeled for them by your partner.

"Children who learn respect and
equality early stick to it."

Resistance to Oppression

Men have no right to keep women down.

But isn't keeping the woman down what a controlling man's behavior is all about?

Women have *rights*, and those rights don't somehow vanish when you walk into the door of your home. Those rights are with you always, and can't be justifiably taken away from you for any reason. No one gets to control what you can say, what you wear, where you go, what people you are with, or how you spend your money.

So when a man bullies or intimidates his partner, he is behaving oppressively. His behavior is connected to all kinds of other injuries that men do to women, injuries that lead women to have to struggle for justice and equality on many fronts.

Viewing this picture from a slightly different angle, though, we also see that when you stand up for yourself with your partner you are *resisting* oppression. When you demand that he speak to you respectfully, when you threaten to leave him if he doesn't change, when you insist on your right to control your own money, when you tell him to leave you alone, when you demand respect for your mothering, when you seek a protective order or call the police, when you fight back against his domination in any way, you are not only fighting for yourself, but for the rights of all women.

Your partner tries to shame you for your resistance. But keep reaching to be proud of the principles you are standing for, to see yourself as joined to women all over the world who are fighting for what they deserve, demanding what is theirs.

✦

"I am a woman, fighting for myself
and for all women."

The Abuser Crusade

When a man has destructive relationship patterns, the last thing he needs is to discover philosophies that actually back his attitudes up. But the sad reality is that there are websites, books, and even organizations out there that encourage men to be at their worst rather than at their best when it comes to relating to women.

Some of these groups come under the heading of what is known as "men's rights" or "fathers' rights" groups. Their writings spread the message that women are out to control men, humiliate them, and take their money. These groups also promote the idea that women who want to keep primary custody of their children after divorce are evil.

The irony is that we live in a country that has refused to pass an amendment to the constitution to guarantee equal rights for women; yet some men are still out there claiming that women have *too many* rights and that men don't have enough.

Other groups don't use the language of "rights" but promote abusive thinking by talking about the "natural" roles of men and women. They claim, for example, that men are biologically programmed to be the ones making the key decisions, and that women are just naturally the followers of men's leadership.

Human personalities and preferences are not determined by biology. There are women who love to watch football and men who would much rather be dancing. There are women who hold in all their feelings and men who burst into tears freely. No one has the right to tell anyone what they "naturally" are or must be.

If you see your partner coming under the influence of a philosophy that is harming your relationship, take some steps to research it. If he starts to attend workshops or read books that seem to be worsening rather than improving how he treats you, try to use the Internet to make contact with other women who have been hurt by these philosophies. The clearer you can be about what he is getting into, the more you'll be prepared to defend yourself.

"If his new philosophy is making him a worse
partner, I'm not buying into it."

Making Peace with Child Welfare

Few experiences are more stressful in the life of a parent than to have the state's child protective personnel knocking at the door. Fear, embarrassment, and anger are some likely first reactions, with questions running through the parent's mind such as "Are they going to take my children away? Is everyone going to treat me like a child abuser now?"

If the mother has an abusive partner, she has the additional worries of "Is he going to blame me for the fact that child welfare came? How is he going to react?"

If child welfare does get involved with your family, do your best not to take it as a personal reflection of you as a mother. A man who abuses a mother causes her children emotional distress, and that distress sometimes becomes noticeable to school personnel, neighbors, the parents of the children's friends, or other community members. These people may even realize what a hard time your kids are having before you do; the chaos and tension that abusive men cause in a home can make the children's emotional pain hard to notice.

Make it your top goal to keep your relationship with child welfare personnel as non-adversarial as possible. The more hostile your relationship with the workers becomes, the more likely the child welfare system is to become punishing—and sometimes irrationally so—in its responses. Do everything you possibly can to get along with them, even if you have to fake it a little because of how angry you feel.

Your best bet is to figure out what they want from you, and work hard to give it to them. Do they want you to attend certain classes? Do they want your kids to talk to a therapist? Do they want you to meet with a domestic violence advocate? Work hard to follow through on what they are asking of you, even if you don't think you or your kids need the help. The secret to getting your child welfare case closed is to develop a reputation with them as being a mother who is friendly, cooperative, and willing to use services.

> "I'm upset that child welfare is here,
> but they have power, and I need to focus
> on getting along with them."

How Can He Be Involved with Someone New So Soon?

It's a common scenario: A woman breaks up with her controlling partner, and while she's reeling from everything that has happened, she finds out he's already dating another woman. She feels shocked. How can he dive in that fast with someone else?

First of all, he's probably kidding himself. Abusive men are like cats, shaking themselves off quickly, and don't want to admit that the end of a relationship bothers them. Your partner quickly finds a new woman so that he can send you the message "See, you aren't important. I can just replace you. No big deal." But the reality of what he has lost by not being with you is going to catch up with him.

He also may be in that percentage of men who simply can't form a meaningful emotional bond with any woman. For that man, partner relationships are about getting his needs met for sex, easy companionship, and caretaking, not about really connecting heart to heart. Ask yourself, "How often, and for how long, did he ever get close to me in a real way?" If the answer is "hardly at all" or "only for a very short time at the beginning," he belongs in this category. His life is a series of superficial relationships.

Third, he may be focused on trying to get you back. Some women who are escaping mistreatment cave in and get back with the guy precisely because he has started to date someone else. He may have found a girlfriend quickly because he doesn't think you'll be able to handle it. Don't crack. Remember that the more effort he makes to show off that he's got a new girl, the more that proves that he is still focused on you. You'll actually get over him faster than he'll get over you.

"I'm going to focus on my own healing, not on what he's doing or whom he is dating."

A Letter to the World

Here is a huge point that I wish people would understand:

The worse a man has treated a woman, the harder it can be for her to leave him.

This is the opposite of how most people think. The world says, "Why would you stay with someone who has been so terrible to you? There must be something wrong with you."

The reality is that the meaner the man has been, the more damage he has done to the woman's confidence and self-image, the more harm he has done to her friendships, the more he has undermined her support system, the more he has harmed her finances, and the more he has made her feel exhausted, confused, and depressed. And these are precisely the resources she needs to draw from in order to have the strength, courage, and money she needs to end the relationship.

Gradually over time, insidiously and manipulatively, he has sapped her strength, her belief in herself, her clarity of thought. The longer she has been abused, the more she's likely to believe that she couldn't live without her partner, that she would just be too lonely, helpless, and broke. This is the most bitter irony of abuse: The abuser's behavior takes away from the woman exactly what she most needs in order to escape. It isn't something wrong with women that creates the abuse trap; it is the abusers and their allies that create the abuse trap.

You are going to find a way to unravel this harm and take back control of your life. Feel proud of how much strength you have as you work in that direction.

"It's not my fault if I can't find a way out of this situation right away. I'm doing my best and getting stronger."

STAYING CONNECTED

Not Bringing Him into Your Relationships—Part 1

An abusive man has a way of making his presence felt even when he's not there. Women have described to me various ways in which patterns that their partners have set in motion have made it hard for the woman to be close to other people. I want to focus on two dynamics they have described to me.

The first dynamic is:

Your experience with him makes it hard for you to have a voice.

Your partner has silenced you over and over again. One impact of this pattern is that you have found it harder and harder over recent years to speak up for what you want and need. You have perhaps become overly compliant with friends or loved ones, going along with what they are doing or planning and not feeling able to assert yourself.

The result of holding your own desires back so much is that over time you will come to resent people. It will start to feel as though they aren't being sensitive to your needs, or like they are steamrolling over you. But if you aren't speaking up for yourself, they don't have a way to know what you want.

So remind yourself that not everybody is like your abusive partner, out to punish you for having a voice. Work on increasing your ability to assert your needs and stand up for what you want. Practice phrases such as:

"No, I don't really feel like doing that today."

"I'm more in the mood for something else."

"I'd like you to stop what you're doing, that's bothering me."

"Here's what I would like."

"Hang on, I don't think you're getting what I'm saying."

As you become more outspoken, you will not only be benefiting yourself but also your loved ones; it's better for all relationships when people speak up about their needs and desires.

"What I want matters, and I can make my wishes known to people."

Take Pride in Yourself as a Mother

Your children love you and look up to you, because you are their mother.

And your children's love can be an important part of what carries you to freedom.

Dozens of women have told me that their close relationships with their children were what turned life around for them. The abusive man would make the woman feel stupid and inferior and unlovable. But then she would look at her relationships with her children, and she would think, "My children think I'm lovable. They want to be with me. They don't think I'm so bad."

And those thoughts would lead to stirrings of rebellion, reflections such as "Maybe I don't deserve the way he's treating me. Maybe I don't need to be around him to have love in my life. Maybe he doesn't know what he's talking about." Be proud of yourself as a mom. Take pride in the love you show your kids, in the care you give them, in the closeness you are building with them. Notice what they do well, and remember that you are a huge reason why those good things exist in them. Your children's love for you can show you important truths about who you are, and about your own goodness. The best moments between you and your kids are glimpses of reality, outside of the darkness that your partner's negativity brings. That positive image is who you really are.

"I'm a really good mom, and my kids love me."

Respect for Abused Women

We live in a society that places a high value on appearances. People get credit for acting as if everything is fine, and can be looked down upon for letting their pain show. We kid ourselves that we can tell how well people are doing by what kind of smile they put on for the world each day.

If you had a window into people's hearts, revealing what they have endured over the course of their lifetimes, you would uncover a weight of injustices and betrayals. Yes, people are traumatized by floods and earthquakes, but not nearly as often as their hearts are broken by cruelty or violence from other human beings, usually ones they loved—their parents, their partners, their mentors, members of their community.

Many people who hear about an abusive relationship say things to themselves like, "I'd never let someone treat me that way" or "If she stays there, she's part of the problem." At my trainings, I press therapists, police officers, child protective workers, and judges to drop their superior attitude. The irony is that almost everyone has been subjected to some kind of abuse themselves. If they haven't been abused by a partner, then they've been abused by a parent or an adult relative when they were kids, or a tyrannical boss, or a superior officer in the military, or a sports coach, or a dangerous bully. When people block out these kinds of experiences and forget what they were like, they easily slip into being judgmental and impatient with abused women. They need to awaken their own memories of injustice and betrayal, and then offer a kind ear and heart to others.

> "I deserve complete respect from
> my community. What has happened
> to me could happen to anyone."

His Techniques for Reeling You Back In

Our society has a crucial concept exactly backwards. We think that leaving an abusive or controlling man should be easier for a woman to do than leaving a man who has been good to her. The reality is the opposite; it's harder to successfully break out of a destructive relationship.

Part of the challenge is that an abusive man has a range of maneuvers that he uses to make it hard for the woman to go away—and even harder for her to stay away. If you are considering leaving your partner, it's important to make plans for how you will get past the obstacles he'll create. Here are some of the things he may try:

- He may quickly get involved with someone else, knowing that you will have a hard time staying strong in the face of that.
- He may act helpless and like a victim by not eating, not taking care of himself, not going anywhere, and saying he can't live without you.
- He may not let you get space from him. He may call or text multiple times, pressuring you to get together "just to talk," maybe even say-

ing he knows it's over but just wants to be friends. He won't respect boundaries or limits that you've requested and won't drop contact, stop sending messages through friends, and watching you from afar.

- He may be scary or intimidating, stalking you and threatening you (often saying that he's doing these hateful things "because I love you so much").
- He may threaten to file for child custody.
- He may act sweet and different with you, promising to change his ways.

Spend some time with your journal going over each of the above tactics, putting down what strategies you plan to use—including what self-care strategies—to keep him from reeling you back in these ways.

✘

"I will learn to recognize how he hooks me, and prepare myself so he can't."

"How Much Should I Tell Child Welfare?"

As we looked at last week, it's worth preparing yourself mentally for the possibility that you'll get a visit from child welfare someday. Children tend to know more about what is happening between their parents than adults think they do. When Mom is being mistreated by her partner, kids absorb some of the stress of what she is going through, and sometimes that stress becomes visible to other adults in their lives.

When child welfare workers enter the life of an abused woman, she can have trouble sorting out whether they will become her allies or her enemies. If the workers are aware of her partner's abusive or violent behavior, she may worry that they are going to blame her for what he does. And of course, anyone who faces a child welfare investigation can't help thinking about the possibility that they will take the children, although that is rarely the outcome.

I wish I could tell you that the answer is just to be honest with them. But the reality is more complex. Some workers do a great job of supporting an abused woman and helping her figure out what actions she can take to best help her children. But others are less understanding. So get to know the workers and trust your own instincts about how trustworthy they are. My general advice is to tell them a little about your partner's behavior and see what kinds of responses you get. Avoid sharing too much until you get a sense of where the workers are coming from. If you find that the people assigned to your case are caring, respectful, and knowledgeable about abuse, it may well be worth the risk to give them a more complete picture.

The most important thing is to emphasize to the workers that you care about your children and want to help them. Then wait and see whether the workers are serious about helping you.

"These services are here to help me.
While honesty is the best policy, I need to
let my story out a little bit at a time."

Surviving Trauma Together

I often hear the world divided into two groups: "trauma survivors" and everybody else. I don't think this distinction is real. There is so much trauma in the modern world that no one escapes it.

The secret is to stop seeing ourselves as separate and start realizing how together we all are. You are surrounded by people who have been deeply shaken by dark times they have come through; but most of them have never revealed what they've been through. You are not nearly as alone as it may seem. The supposed division between the traumatized and the non-traumatized is an illusion.

Here are the real divisions:

- People who remember they have been traumatized vs. people who have forgotten and blocked the trauma
- People whose trauma was recent vs. people whose trauma was longer ago
- People who can make themselves seem okay in public despite the trauma vs. people who can't hide it
- People who were believed when they told what happened to them vs. people who were treated as liars or exaggerators, or were simply ignored when they told
- People who are currently alone in dealing with the effects of trauma vs. people who are receiving support
- People who have been traumatized by events we all agree are bad (tornadoes, homicides) vs. people who have been traumatized by things that much of the society continues to defend and excuse (violence against women, poverty, war)

In our societies and communities, we need to take steps to heal the divisions among these different kinds of trauma survivors. *The people on the list above are all trauma survivors, and are all of us.* We should be together.

✕◦◗▸

> "Whether I know it or not, I'm surrounded by people who have been through extreme experiences; I am not the only one."

YOUR OWN BEST FRIEND

"I'm Not One of Those Feminists"

Somehow the term "feminist" has gotten negative meanings attached to it. Largely due to negative media portrayals, feminism got associated in people's minds with women who hate men, are angry and hostile, and find something wrong everywhere. That view was convenient for those people who didn't want women to have their rights.

"Feminism" actually just means the belief that women should have equality and respect in every aspect of life. As in most campaigns for equality, much of the emphasis in feminism is on the question of *equal say*, meaning that a woman should have a full voice over all of the decisions that affect her life.

Nowadays women seem to feel under pressure to distance themselves from feminism, apparently out of a fear of being labeled radical. I hear quite a number of sentences that begin, "I'm not a feminist or anything, but . . ."

Believing that women should have equal rights is hardly something to be ashamed of. When a woman gets pressured into backing away from that stand, she loses her natural connection to women (and men) who want better treatment for their sisters all over the world.

Of course the media can shine a spotlight on the few feminists whose behavior or politics come across as irrational, but that's no excuse to discredit the whole group.

This issue is especially important for women who are in an intimate relationship in which they aren't being respected. For you, holding on to a belief in your right to dignity and equality is important to the survival of your spirit. Every time you attempt to stand up for yourself you are fighting for all women, and every time women around the world speak out for their rights they are fighting for you.

"I am proud to speak up for my rights."

Not Bringing Him into Your Relationships—Part 2

Last week we looked at one of the ways that your partner's unhealthy dynamics can creep into your relationships with other people.

Here's another important one:

Your experience with him makes you start to react to people as if they are trying to bully or control you.

The wounds that come from being abused by a partner can lead you to become hyperalert to signs that someone is pulling something on you. Developing wisdom and self-protectiveness is a great thing, of course, but you can have problems in your relationships if you carry that to an unhealthy extreme. Many women have told me that they have gone through a phase where they verbally jumped all over people who hadn't really said or done anything that bad. They realized they were reacting to each person as if he or she were the abusive man.

Work toward a middle course. Develop clear standards for what kind of treatment you will tolerate from people. And do call people out on their behavior or tone when you don't feel respected. But try not to assume that people's intentions are bad, or that they are out to manipulate you; most people mean well most of the time.

The simple version is: Defend yourself more, but don't go on the attack. Strive for approaches to standing up for yourself that don't slam other people. Work to resolve conflicts, not to bring down a hammer. Your dear friends and relatives are not your abusive partner.

"I can stay clear in my head that
other people aren't him."

Heroic Moms

I have great admiration for the quality of mothering that abused women give their children. Being fully present for your kids is so difficult in the midst of being torn down by your partner, and even more so when he disrespects you right in front of them and makes you look bad. He may say you're messing up the kids because of all the things that are supposedly wrong with you; but the reality is your kids *need* you, and your importance to them is greater than ever because he is such a poor role model.

Do your best to shut out your partner's critical voice, and notice what you do well as a mother, day in and day out. You are coming through for your kids in so many ways. Your physical care of them, your affection and cuddling, your encouragement, are crucial to them. Notice all the ways in which you are setting a positive example to counter his influence.

If you have ever had child welfare or the family court involved in your life, you have perhaps been subjected to disapproval and condescension from evaluators and other professionals. Countless women have told me of having social workers and judges treating a mother as though she's the problem, rather than addressing her abusive partner. You deserve admiration for how well you've done under incredibly difficult and complicated circumstances. Social systems should be offering help and support, not criticism and superiority.

Abused women are their children's lifeline. Take pride in what you do.

※

"I am fighting so hard to be there
for my kids, and I'm doing really well
considering what I'm up against."

Take a Break from Advertising

Advertising is heavily aimed at women, because women do most of the shopping. Advertisers have developed skill at making women feel like they aren't good enough and that they need to make purchases to fix their flaws. In a typical day, a woman is exposed to dozens of photo or video images of women who don't look or act anything like real women, to make her feel inadequate.

The more advertising you are exposed to, the more you'll feel that you're fat, have too many wrinkles, have the wrong skin and teeth, don't keep a nice enough house, and have an unending list of other faults to improve. Even though these promotions are making you feel worse about yourself, it's still easy to get hooked on looking at them, because they offer the promise that your shortcomings (which they invented) can be solved. It's a nasty trick.

Do your self-esteem a favor. Cut down dramatically on how much advertising you absorb. Turn off the TV, or at least mute the ads and ignore them. Read a book instead of a magazine, and especially stay away from beauty magazines, catalogues, and websites full of perfect-looking women. Take the mirrors down in your house, leaving up just one or two.

Believe it or not, before advertising entered every home, women used to feel like they were fine the way they were. All different shapes, sizes, and looks were okay. In fact, in much of the world, bigger women, for example, were considered especially attractive. Don't buy into the gimmicks. You are beautiful.

> "I'm fine the way I am. I am going to stop looking
> at images that make me feel flawed."

A Final Look at Who the Abusive One Is

We've taken a couple of looks at how an abusive or controlling man seeks to convince his partner that she's the controlling one. But what if you aren't sure that his behavior is really all that bad? Here's how to know if the problem really is you:

- He's kind to you most of the time, and can treat you reasonably decently even when he's mad or upset with you.
- He takes responsibility for his own actions, rarely or never blaming them on you. And he doesn't get scary.
- He has asked you repeatedly, and in a decent and thoughtful way (not in a stream of put-downs), to change specific behaviors of yours, and you seem to keep returning to doing the things he has asked you not to do, even though his complaints are reasonable.
- He has shown willingness to work on things you want him to work on and has taken real steps regarding those issues (not just making promises).

If all of the above points are true then maybe you do need to look at your treatment of him. Maybe he isn't a controller, and you're the one who needs to change. But otherwise your partner is doing what so many abusive men do, turning things into their opposites to have even more weapons to hammer you with.

Here is the bottom line: You are responsible for *your* behavior, but you are not responsible for *his* behavior. If he says that you are the cause of his bad behavior, then he is the one with the problem, not you.

"I can be in a loving relationship with myself today, and trust my own wisdom and intuition. He is not going to sell me his view of what kind of person I am."

AFTERWORD

Thank you for taking this journey toward healing, clarity, and justice. I hope the past year has led you to a greater understanding of the life and love that you deserve. I hope also that you now feel stronger, sharper, and better supported, so that you can take the necessary steps to create the life you want. You know what you need to do; trust your inner wisdom and move courageously—though not recklessly—to seize the day.

Educational experts say that we have to learn a concept or a skill at least twice before it starts to stick; this is why teachers always want us to have review sessions. So keep this book around, opening it up from time to time to read an entry. If you keep returning to these guideposts, you will help yourself stay on track.

I am wishing you all the best as you enter the next stage in your life. A life of dignity, freedom, and advancement awaits you. You are worth it.

ACKNOWLEDGMENTS

I now have worked for more than twenty-five years in the field of men's abuse toward women. Over that period, I have received so many ideas and insights, so much support and validation, and so much concrete assistance with projects that I could not possibly thank all the people who deserve it. Many of you have already received my thanks in previous books of mine, so I am going to focus here on people to whom I have particularly owed debts during the last two or three years. I'll also take this opportunity to mention some people who got missed along the way.

For their generous assistance, professional support, comments on drafts, and contributions to my education, I want to thank Bettina Aptheker; Susie Smith; Patrice Lenowitz; Sarah Cortes; Ted Bunch; Connie Valentine; Dori Ostermiller; my outstanding agent, Wendy Sherman (who has had my back for over a decade now); and my wonderful editor at Berkley Books, Denise Silvestro.

For their personal friendship and love during this period, my profound gratitude goes to my children Fabienne and Liam, Patrice Lenowitz, Eugenia Carrion Gamarra, Susie Smith, Wil Klass, John Maher, Tim Murphy, Amy Waldman, Carlene Pavlos, Jay Silverman, Katie Koti, my siblings, all my EF! friends, and many, many others.

RESOURCES

National Domestic Violence Hotline for the United States and Canada: 1-800-799-7233

Rape, Abuse, and Incest National Network Hotline: 1-800-656-4673

National Suicide Prevention Lifeline: 1-800-273-8255

For a very extensive list of additional resources on abuse in relationships, including categories regarding assessing your partner's dangerousness, leaving a dangerous partner, safety planning, substance abuse assistance, immigrant women, teens, women of color, child custody litigation, child welfare, economic empowerment and financial planning, sexual assault, sexual abuse, mental health assistance, and many other subjects, go to **LundyBancroft.com**, and click on "**Resources**".